DEFINING MOMENTS

100 INSPIRATIONAL MOMENTS
100 GREAT PLAYERS

DEFINING MOMENTS

100 INSPIRATIONAL MOMENTS
100 GREAT PLAYERS

Mike Leonetti

Red Deer Press

Published by Red Deer Press, A Fitzhenry & Whiteside Company
195 Allstate Parkway, Markham, ON, L3R 4T8
www.reddeerpress.com

Published in the United States by Red Deer Press, A Fitzhenry & Whiteside Company
311 Washington Street, Brighton; Massachusetts, 02135

Cover and text design by Daniel Choi
Cover image courtesy of: Gettyimages
Hockey cards courtesy of: Upper Deck, Fleer, Pro Set, Topps and Hockey Hall of Fame.
NHL, the NHL Shield and the word mark and image of the Stanley Cup are registered trademarks of the National Hockey League. NHL and NHL team marks are the property of the NHL and its teams. © NHL 2011. All Rights Reserved.
Printed and bound in Canada

5 4 3 2 1

We acknowledge with thanks the Canada Council for the Arts, and the Ontario Arts Council for their support of our publishing program. We acknowledge the financial support of the Government of Canada through the Canada Book Fund for our publishing activities.

 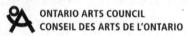

Library and Archives Canada Cataloguing in Publication
Leonetti, Mike, 1958-
    Defining moments : 100 inspirational moments, 100 great players / Mike Leonetti.
Includes bibliographical references.
ISBN 978-0-88995-452-6
    1. Hockey players--Biography. 2. National Hockey League--Biography.
I. Title. II. Title: One hundred inspirational moments, one hundred great players.
GV848.5.A1L453 2011   796.962092'2   C2011-906863-X

Publisher Cataloging-in-Publication Data (U.S)
Leonetti, Mike, 1958-
    Defining moments : 100 inspirational moments, 100 great players / Mike Leonetti.
[374] p. : cm.
Included bibliographical references.
Summary: The game of hockey through profiles of 100 players, highlighting great moments that defined, started, or just plain rejuvenated a career.
ISBN: 978-0-88995-452-6 (pbk.)
1. Hockey players -- Biography. 2. National Hockey League – Biography.
I. One hundred inspirational moments, one hundred great players. II. Title.

796.962092/2 dc23   GV848.5 A1.L4664 2011

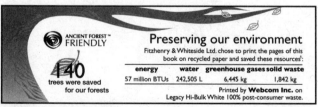

This book is dedicated to all the hockey heroes,
past and present, who inspire us all
with their great moments of achievement.

Contents

INTRODUCTION

Hockey is a game that is loved and admired by millions of people in dozens of countries. This book is a collection of stories for all of us who love the game—from beginners who are just starting to play it to those who continue to admire the great athletes who play the sport for a living. This book is a positive celebration of the game for every fan—from the very passionate ones to those who still like to rent the ice from time to time for some midnight hockey, long after they know the dream of playing in the NHL is over. All that is good in the game of hockey is in the following pages, with each story offering insight into those who have been the most dedicated—determined players who have accomplished something significant at the highest level.

For anyone who might think this is just another hockey book that glorifies the history of the game, it would be wise to look at the contents more closely. This book is chock-a-block full of current National Hockey League players whose fascinating stories are just unfolding. Many great names from the history of the game and a large number of Hall of Fame players are also profiled because their stories are just as interesting. Whether it's a past or current hero, the stories all have a common theme—players who take the responsibility needed to become the highest of achievers. These stories will not only inspire, they will also provide hope and show that character is often the best measure of success.

It should also not be interpreted that all these stories are pure and clean, or that all players have led a perfect life. In fact, the opposite is often true and in some cases, the realities both on and off the ice are actually rather harsh. Hockey players are all very real people and go through trials and tribulations just like everyone else. However, these profiles show that dedication, attention to teamwork, sticking with it or knowing when to make necessary changes are all a part of what successful players do during their playing careers.

The players profiled in this book come from all parts of the world—from Canada, the United States, Sweden, Finland, Slovakia or the former Soviet states—and they all have become great NHL players. They have all experienced victory and sorrow—yet they are usually humble in victory and gracious in defeat. If there is one common trait among them, it is that they all believe they can make it work and, based on their level of accomplishment, who could argue?

Hockey will always be a part of who they are and we as fans will always remember them for their great moments. The more than 100 profiles in this book not only feature special moments in their lives but also a memorable game (in some cases, games) where they made an impact—some among the best remembered in NHL history.

This writer has had the pleasure and privilege of writing many hockey books. However, this one is very special because it is all about achievement—from the player who made it to the Hall of Fame to the journeyman player who had one brief, shining moment in his career.

During the 2010-11 NHL season, the game of hockey was often under the microscope and did not always find favorable public opinion. And many times, it was not easy to stay a fan of this great sport. For this reason and many others, it is my sincere hope that the reader will find these stories compelling, heartening and ultimately, inspiring. They remind us all of how thrilling the game of hockey can be—and what it can teach us about life.

I hope you will agree.

Mike Leonetti
Woodbridge, Ontario

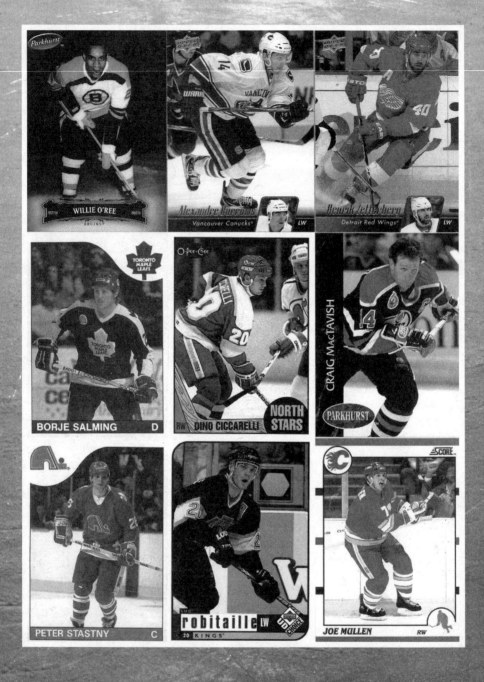

AGAINST ALL ODDS

For some players, the chances of getting to the NHL were so remote it's a wonder they even tried. In some cases, it was where they were born that was the main issue, while for others it was how they grew up. Players that were drafted so low virtually had no chance of making it to the NHL—yet they found a way to get noticed. Injuries or personal problems affected some players to the point where it looked like they could never get to the big league. Despite obstacles, many players went on to remarkable NHL careers. In this chapter, we'll focus on the following players who made it "Against All Odds":

Alex Burrows
Igor Larionov
Stanislas "Stan" Mikita
Borje Salming
Craig MacTavish
Joe Mullen
Henrik Zetterberg
Luc Robitaille
Peter Stastny
Dino Ciccarelli
Tyler Myers
Willie O'Ree
P.K. Subban

ALEX BURROWS

BORN: PINCOURT, QUEBEC

NHL SEASONS: 2005–06 TO PRESENT

DEFINING MOMENT: JANUARY 30, 2010

Alex Burrows is the perfect example of how hard work (on and off the ice) can help overcome long odds. Playing in the lower minor league can seem like a death sentence for many a hockey career, but with determination and good people in your corner, a life of NHL hockey is still a possibility.

Burrows was a decent junior player when he was with the Shawinigan Cataractes of the Quebec Major Junior Hockey League, although he did not play for them until he was 19 years of age. In 2001–02, the 6'1" left winger scored 35 goals and totaled 70 points, then added 20 more points in the playoffs. Needless to say, Burrows was never drafted by an NHL team, but he was invited to the New York Islanders training camp in the fall of '02. He did not impress anyone with his performance and was forced to seek work in the East Coast Hockey League (ECHL), where he earned all of $500 a week playing for the Greenville Grrrowl. He had only 26 points in 53 games, but he stayed in that league for two more seasons, having his best year in 2003–04 with 73 points (29 were goals) in 65 games.

In the off-season, Burrows worked back home in the landscaping business and also played ball hockey (he was an excellent player, winning national and world championships) to stay in shape. His work in the ECHL did not go unnoticed, and the

Manitoba Moose offered him a contract to play in the American Hockey League. In 2004–05, the fast-skating Burrows scored nine goals in 72 games for the Moose, but things were looking up. He caught a large break when his former Manitoba Moose coach Alain Vigneault was made coach of the Vancouver Canucks for the 2005–06 season. Burrows would play in 43 games for the Canucks in 2005–05, scoring seven times. He also got into 33 games for the Moose, notching 12 goals. It was a long, slow process for Burrows, but he was developing—and Vigneault loved Burrows's work ethic.

It also helped that the NHL was looking for less expensive players to fill out the bottom of the roster (that is, players for the third and fourth lines), thus giving the 188-pound Burrows an opportunity he seized with both hands. A 12-goal season in 2007–08 made Burrows more confident that he could play in the NHL. Soon he found himself playing alongside the Sedin twins—Daniel and Henrik—and he scored 28 times in 82 games during the 2008–09 season. Shortly after that, he signed a four-year contract worth $8 million—quite a raise from the $500 a week he was getting just a few short years ago! "I didn't want to rob a bank," Burrows said after signing the contract. "I didn't want to take what I didn't deserve. I feel good about being on this team and feeling I can contribute. I think it's a lot of money. I'm really happy but I can't let it affect me; I just have to keep working and playing hard. I like it here. I've got great teammates here I really care about, great friendships. I like this environment of hockey. I didn't want changes."

The big contract did not hinder Burrows in any way as he upped his goal total to 35 during the 2009–10 season. His best night of that '09–'10 season came on January 30, 2010, when the Vancouver Canucks visited the Toronto Maple Leafs on a Saturday night. It was the kind of night that would help define his career coast to coast. *Hockey Night in Canada* was carrying the game on national television as the Leafs jumped out to a 3-0 lead in the first. Vancouver's starting netminder, Roberto Luongo, was knocked out of the game and it looked like the Leafs were going to coast to an easy victory. Burrows, however, had different ideas.

He first gave the Canucks some life with a short-handed goal in the second by stealing the puck away from an inattentive Leaf, going in on a breakaway, and beating Vesa Toskala with a backhand. He then teamed up with the Sedins for third-period tallies to give the Canucks the lead. Burrows assisted on two goals (one by each twin) and scored on the empty net with 28 seconds to play to seal a 5-3 win for the visitors. It was a four-point game for Burrows, the first of his NHL career. He was a plus three on the night and played 22:22 during the contest. Burrows's efforts were played out under a national spotlight, and suddenly he was not just the guy who played alongside the Sedins.

After the game, coach Vigneault commented on his team's work ethic, but he was most likely referring to his top line. "I do believe there's a lot of character (on the team) and our guys never quit. We just push and work, push and work. And we got it done." It was a perfect description of his hardest-working player—Alex Burrows. Toronto defenseman Francois Beauchemin, a long-time NHL veteran, said of the Canucks top line, "They're getting better every year. And Burrows is a big component to their line. He's got some speed, a good shot and agitates a little bit."

Many may disagree with Beauchemin's "a little bit" comment as Burrows has made it an art form to get under the skin of opponents. Proof of this comes from Burrows's penalty minute total (as high as 179 in 2007–08), but he is hungry to stay in the lineup every night and knows he has to work hard when playing with highly talented players like the Sedins. Even if he has to do all the physical work, Burrows does not mind at all—as long as he can play in the best hockey league in the world. Perhaps the best summarization of Burrows's rise to the NHL ranks comes from the man who first gave him an opportunity. Craig Heisinger was the general manager of the Moose when he gave Burrows his first chance to play in the AHL: "He (Burrows) is the one who has worked so hard to get where he is. He's the one who made the most of his opportunity. We have given lots of players opportunities and some don't make the most of their opportunity."

Just a few years ago, nobody thought that Burrows would beat the odds, but through great determination and perseverance and a good break or two, he has become a very effective NHL player.

Alex Burrows has recorded 218 points (including 111 goals) in 442 career games to date. In the 2011 playoffs, Burrows scored two key overtime goals (one to eliminate Chicago in the seventh game of the opening round and the other in the finals against Boston) as the Canucks made it all the way to Game 7 of the Stanley Cup final.

IGOR LARIONOV
BORN: VOSKRESENSK, USSR (RUSSIA)
NHL SEASONS: 1989–90 TO 2003–04
DEFINING MOMENT: JUNE 8, 2002

Russian-born center Igor Larionov was already 29 years old when he signed his first NHL contract with the Vancouver Canucks in 1989. He was one of the most accomplished players in the history of Soviet hockey, winning two gold medals at the Olympic Games (one in 1984 and one in 1988) and a total of four times at the World Hockey Championships (1982, 1983, 1986, and 1989). He was also instrumental in helping the Soviets win the Canada Cup in 1981.

Sensing that the Soviet Union would one day start releasing players to the NHL, the Canucks spent a late draft choice (214th overall in 1985) on the slick, highly skilled pivot and then hoped to one day get him in their lineup. The chances of the Russians letting go of their players, however, still appeared fairly bleak.

Like many Soviet players, Larionov hated the oppressive Russian hockey system. All control in this system rested with the coaches and those who managed the Soviet sport programs. One coach in particular dominated the Russian national team players—Viktor Tikhonov. He was mostly despised: he was there to win at any cost, even if that meant keeping his players away from their families. In fact, Tikhonov was more than willing to demand that his charges be kept from their families for up to 11 months of the year while making them live in barracks! Few Soviet players had the will or the desire to fight the system or Tikhonov, but Larionov was one of the few. At one point, he was kicked off the national team because it was believed he might defect (much like youngster Alex Mogilny did to join the Buffalo Sabres), but Larionov was later allowed to return. Larionov, however, made it clear he would not play for his coach any longer, and the Russians soon realized they could use the NHL money that was paid to secure releases and also get a piece of the player's contract.

Larionov played for three years in Vancouver, with his best year coming in 1991–92 when he had 65 points (his highest point total in the NHL). He then played one year in Switzerland (which allowed him to be totally free of Soviet control) before rejoining the NHL with the San Jose Sharks. Early in the 1995–96 season, he was traded by the Sharks to the Detroit Red Wings where he excelled in their puck-control system of play. He won two Stanley Cups with the Red Wings (in 1997 and 1998) before trying his hand with the Florida Panthers. The Florida club hoped to reunite Larionov with superstar Pavel Bure, a one-time Soviet teammate, in the hopes of igniting their team. But the Panthers played a terrible dump-and-chase game that was not anywhere near close to Larionov's liking. He was sent back to Detroit, where he helped the Red Wings back to victory in the Stanley Cup finals in 2002.

It was the Red Wings against the Carolina Hurricanes. Game 3 in Carolina was the pivotal contest, which went into overtime. After 115 minutes of extra time, Larionov (who had scored once already) calmly waited for a Hurricane defender who had missed his check to slide past him. Larionov then went in on goal, lifting a blazing backhand drive over goalie Arturs Irbe, just under the cross bar, giving Detroit a 3-2 victory. After the game Larionov said, "I am just every day enjoying my life and enjoying being around these guys. The way this team plays, we played back home when I started my career with the Red Army team. We tried to control the puck, tried to make plays. That's what the game should be. It's enjoyable for the players to play that system and good for the fans." Carolina never recovered and Detroit easily won the Cup in five games, giving Larionov his third NHL championship. It was the last great moment of his playing career—but not his final triumph.

In 2008 Larionov was elected to the Hockey Hall of Fame, one of the very few Russian-born players to be elected to the prestigious shrine. He finished his career with 644 points in 921 NHL games but will probably be best remembered for fighting the Soviet system and coming out on top. As one of the early Russian players to come over to North America, he and his cohorts opened the door for many others to follow and pursue a better life. His election to the Hall of Fame would have not been possible had he not shown the courage to challenge those who ran his life in the former Soviet Union. Against all odds, the superbly talented Larionov proved that you can challenge a system and still be a winner.

Igor Larionov was elected to the Hockey Hall of Fame in 2008.

STANISLAS "STAN" MIKITA
BORN: SOKOLCE, CZECHOSLOVAKIA (SLOVAKIA)
NHL SEASONS: 1958–59 TO 1979–80
DEFINING MOMENT: APRIL 14, 1961

Stanislas Gvoth was born on May 20, 1940 in Sokolce, Czechoslovakia, just after the start of World War II. Gvoth was born in a small village where his parents made the most of what little they had. His father, George, worked in a local factory, while his mother, Emelia, farmed in the fields close to home, helping to provide the family table with food which was in short supply. The Gvoths lived in a one-story building divided into sections to accommodate four families, holding as many as 20 people at one time. When German forces invaded the country, two Nazi soldiers actually lived in the house for sometime, though young Stan had no idea why they were there or what was going on at the time.

Although he lived very modestly, Stan was like any other boy and played sports, including soccer and a form of hockey. He had a pair of makeshift skates (blades attached to boots), which gave him a little idea of what hockey might be like. The Germans were eventually defeated, but the spoils of conflict meant that communist Russia now controlled Czechoslovakia. It is quite likely young Stan would have lived out his life under this repressive regime but for a family relative who had another idea.

Joe Mikita and his wife Anna had moved to Canada years earlier and came back for a visit in 1948 when Stan was eight years old. A childless couple, they longed for children of their own and offered to give Stan, their nephew, a better life in Canada. It was thought that the offer was something of a joke at first, but the Mikitas (especially Joe) were very serious. Stan's parents were naturally reluctant to give away a son, but they also knew Stan would have a chance to live a much better life across the ocean. The notion appealed to the adventurous youngster, even though he knew it would take him away from his real parents. One night, his mother thought he was crying about not being able to go, but she soon discovered he was actually crying because he was hungry. That swayed her, and she gave her permission. Stan fought off the conflicting feelings of leaving his family, and it became especially difficult as he started for Prague, and then a new land. He hung on to a pole at the departure station and would not let go, but eventually the train had to leave and Stan was placed on board. He was headed to Canada and the small town of St. Catharines, Ontario. This is how Stanislas Gvoth became Stan Mikita.

Mikita had a hard time at first, considering he did not know a word of English, but a teacher took a special interest in him and he progressed quickly. He was soon playing hockey like other boys in Canada and found out he was pretty good at it (as he was at other sports like football and baseball). Trying to fit into a new country was not easy and he smarted when others called him a foreigner or "displaced person" (shortened to DP), a term used after the War to describe those displaced from the European theatre. Mikita often sensed resentment and hostility and as a result, became a scrappy, sometimes mouthy young man who always kept a chip on his shoulder. He was also attracted to local gangs and hung with a bad crowd, but his burgeoning hockey talent saved him from a life of crime. Soon he was signed by the Chicago Blackhawks, who just happened to have their junior team, the TeePees, located in St. Catharines. Mikita moved up through all the hockey levels and was considered one of the best junior prospects in all of Canada. In 149 games with the Teepees, Mikita scored 85 goals and totaled 222 points. He was ready for the NHL.

Mikita never spent a day in the minors and was on a Stanley

Cup-winning team in just his second full season—1960–61. Chicago had a young and very talented team led by the likes of Mikita, Bobby Hull, Pierre Pilote, Elmer Vasko, and goalie Glenn Hall. The Blackhawks would meet the Montreal Canadiens in the first round of the playoffs, and it was expected that the five-time defending champions would easily take out the upstart Chicago club. However, the series seemed to turn when the Blackhawks won a long overtime game at home (on a goal set up by Mikita) and ousted the mighty Habs in six games. Chicago's victory meant an all-American series, with Detroit providing the opposition.

Bobby Hull led the Chicago side to a 3-2 win in the first game with two goals. Then it was Mikita's chance to show he belonged, providing a great performance on April 14, 1961. The series was tied 2-2, and the game all tied up at 3-3 going into the third period. Chicago Stadium was raucous; the Blackhawks came out firing to start the final period with Mikita leading the way with two goals on way to a 6-3 victory. His first goal, just 2:51 into the period, came on a Blackhawk power play; his second came on a drive from 30 feet out that Detroit goalie Terry Sawchuk could not handle. "I only played 20 minutes of hockey and so did (the) other guys, except Glenn Hall," Mikita said of his performance in the game. About going back to Detroit for the sixth contest, Mikita was speculative: "That 20 minutes won us a game and moved us 60 minutes away from this town's first Stanley Cup in 23 years. But we won't be as fortunate again."

Although Detroit scored the opening goal, it was all Chicago afterward as the Blackhawks romped to a 5-1 victory. Mikita helped set up the Cup-clinching goal by teammate Ab McDonald in the second, and then took a nasty hit from Red Wings defenseman Howie Young. Mikita had to go to the Chicago bench for a while, but he returned to finish the game. He finished his outstanding playoffs with 11 points (6G, 5A) in 12 games, and had proven to all that he was indeed a legitimate NHL star. It was thought this might be the first championship of many for the superbly talented Chicago team, but it turned out to be the only Cup-winning team Mikita played on—and it took the Blackhawks franchise until the 2010 season to win their next title!

In 1963–64, Mikita won his first Art Ross Trophy for most points in the regular season; he took the same trophy in 1964–65 and again in 1966–67—a year that saw Mikita win two other major awards: the Hart Trophy (MVP) and Lady Byng (most gentlemanly). Mikita repeated this remarkable achievement in the 1967–68 season as well. Hockey's "triple crown" had been won—twice!—by a player who might never have played hockey, let alone in the NHL, had he not beaten all odds in getting to Canada.

Stan Mikita scored 541 goals and recorded 1,467 points in his career, all for the Chicago Blackhawks. He was elected to the Hall of Fame in 1983.

BORJE SALMING
BORN: KIRUNA, SWEDEN
NHL SEASONS: 1973–74 TO 1989–90
DEFINING MOMENT: APRIL 17, 1976

Defenseman Borje Salming would have been perfectly content to play hockey in his native Sweden, even if it meant he would be a part-time professional player (with little money to be made). He was also good enough to play on the top teams in Sweden by the time he turned 20; but for Swedish players of the era, the National

Hockey League seemed so far away that the odds of them even trying to play in North America were very remote. Borje's brother Stig, for instance, had been considered a good player in Sweden, but never got the chance to play in the NHL. There were exceptions, though. The most famous Swede to play in the big league at the time was Ulf Sterner, but he had returned home unable to adjust to the style of the North American game. Yet there was no doubt Salming was a very talented and gifted athlete. Eventually, he caught the eye of the Toronto Maple Leafs who, like most NHL teams, were initially not even aware of him.

Toronto scout Gerry McNamara was in Sweden to look at a goalie when he saw Salming's team play a squad from Barrie, Ontario at Christmas time in 1972. McNamara quickly noticed Salming's smooth but confident style and made note that the 6'1" 193-pound defenseman would not back down against the aggressive Barrie Flyers club. In fact, Salming was tossed out of the game and, while he was in the dressing room, McNamara came to see him. Handing Salming a business card, he asked, "Would you like to come over to Canada and play for the Toronto Maple Leafs?" Not knowing what else to say, Salming replied with a simple "Yes." The Leafs moved quickly to put Salming's name on the negotiation list and by the fall of 1973, he was in Toronto for training camp. Salming's initial two-year contract with the Leafs had him making more money than he could have dreamed about in Sweden.

The NHL in the early Seventies was pretty rough, with one team, the Philadelphia Flyers, implementing a brawling approach to the game. "The Flyers were feared and renowned throughout the NHL," Salming wrote years later. "They didn't have just a couple of ruffians, they had twenty! They played a violent style, fighting at the drop of an insult and they were successful. No team was tougher or more intimidating. The Flyers were the undisputed heavyweight champions of the NHL and they didn't take kindly to rookies from Sweden."

Salming prepared by keeping in top physical condition when he arrived in Toronto, and the lean defenseman refused to be intimidated by anything on or off the ice. His first physical encounter was against the infamous fighter Dave "The Hammer" Schultz of the Flyers. Although Salming did not exactly win what turned out to be a minor scuffle, he had shown the hockey world that this Swede was ready to take on all challenges. It was important for Salming to stand up to the physical abuse because Swedish players had developed a reputation for using their sticks instead of fighting; something highly frowned upon in hockey. It would have been easy for Salming to return home and forget about the NHL— but that was not in his nature.

Salming recorded 39 points in 76 games, and was a team-best plus 38 during that 1973–74 campaign in his rookie year. He would never look back or wonder if he belonged in the league. Soon he was a league all-star (a total of six times over his career) and a resilient force on the blueline for his 16 seasons as a Maple Leaf.

Salming was never more challenged than on the night of his 25th birthday, April 17, 1976, when the Flyers were playing the Leafs in a best-of-seven playoff series. It was a night that defined his character and proved his mettle. The Leafs had dropped the first two games but had won their first game on home ice to get back into the series. During that 5-4 win, Salming suffered a savage beating at the hands of Mel Bridgman when the two got into a fight. Salming's face took the brunt of punches thrown by an unrelenting Bridgman.

Leaf fans had seen Salming take some hard punishment before and hoped he could bounce back. In typical Salming fashion, he did, this time with some really great play. It was the fourth game of the series, and it turned on a goal Salming scored when he took a pass from captain Darryl Sittler, then cut straight through the middle of the ice to go in on Flyers goalie Bernie Parent. "I know Parent always stands up as much as he can, so all I did was shoot up high. It went in on his glove side, up under the crossbar," Salming recounted of his beautiful goal. The Gardens crowd erupted in cheers for a man who had been so brutally destroyed just a game earlier. "I don't think I am a hero. But when it (the crowd erupting in cheers) happens in the game, you just can't think about anything else. It just feels real nice." The Leafs won the game 4-3 and pulled even with the Flyers in the series, but that's as far as they would get.

Although the Leafs were a good team through the early years of Salming's NHL career, they were not able to get very far in the playoffs. However, Salming's consistent play made him a Toronto favorite and his success in the NHL opened the doors to many other Swedes and European players. Salming had beaten the odds to become an NHL star. He did it by showing he could play with skill, finesse, and determination.

Borje Salming holds the Maple Leafs team record for most points by a Toronto defenseman (768) and most assists (620). He was elected to the Hall of Fame in 1992.

CRAIG MACTAVISH
BORN: LONDON, ONTARIO
NHL SEASONS: 1979–80 TO 1996–97
DEFINING MOMENT: MAY 15, 1990

Center Craig MacTavish was a long shot to make the National Hockey League. The 6'1", 195-pound forward did not play major junior hockey, but instead tried division two NCAA hockey at the

University of Massachusetts at Lowell. While he produced good numbers there (133 points in 52 games), he was not exactly considered a prime NHL prospect. The Boston Bruins were located closest to the school and gambled on the smart but plodding skater, selecting him with the 153rd pick overall in the 1978 NHL draft. MacTavish turned professional at age 21, splitting his first year between the Bruins (28 points in 46 games) and the American Hockey League. The next two seasons saw him play more in the minors than in the NHL, but he performed well in the AHL (130 points in 159 games played over three seasons) and that got him a full-time job in Boston for the 1982–83 campaign.

By his second full season in Boston, MacTavish had become a 20-goal scorer and it looked like he was going to be an effective member of the Bruins for the foreseeable future. However, on the night of January 25, 1984, MacTavish made the mistake of getting behind the wheel of his car after having consumed too much alcohol. He slammed his vehicle into a 1976 Ford Pinto driven by 26-year old Kim Radley. Radley was severely injured in the crash and, four days later, was pronounced dead in hospital. MacTavish pleaded guilty to vehicular manslaughter and faced one year in prison as a result. He also had to settle a civil law suit brought forward by the Radley family. He missed the entire 1984–85 season and faced a very uncertain future after his release from prison. Luckily for repentant MacTavish, the Bruins released him from his contract, which allowed him to get away from the local notoriety of the horrific accident. Bruins general manager Harry Sinden showed great compassion to MacTavish by letting him become a free agent and giving him the opportunity to start over again. However, the hockey player was realistic about his situation. "It's not over and it's not behind me," MacTavish stated. "So many things remind me of what happened in my terrible mistake, in my fatal mistake. There are going to be hecklers. But really, it's not something they're going to bring up that I'm not thinking about."

MacTavish signed with the Edmonton Oilers and played his first season with them in 1985–86. Despite missing an entire season, he had a good year with 23 goals (his career best mark) and 47 points in 74 games. The timing of his move could not have been better, for MacTavish was with the Oilers for their Stanley Cup wins in 1987 and 1988. He was usually good for about 20 goals a year and although he did not produce high numbers in the playoffs, he often held the important role of trying to shut down the opposition's best lines. MacTavish was also a top penalty killer. He could create some offence when the opportunity arose, and he rarely missed a game.

In the 1990 playoffs the Oilers faced, ironically enough, the Boston Bruins—MacTavish's old team—in the finals. The opening game was scheduled for Beantown the night of May 15, 1990. If there were any mixed emotions from MacTavish, he hid them rather well and went about the task of defeating his former club. Edmonton had a 2-0 lead going into the third period, but Bruins superstar defenseman Ray Bourque scored two goals to send the contest into overtime. The first two overtime periods did not produce a winner and it looked like the third extra session was also going to end with no scoring. Then MacTavish dug deep and started the play that led to the winning goal. This was the defining moment that marked his post-tragedy career.

He took the puck just past center ice and broke in over the Bruins blueline with Jari Kurri. He passed the puck to Kurri and went to the front of the Bruins net. Kurri moved the disk back to the little-used Petr Klima, who was trailing behind on the rush. Klima did not hesitate and fired a wrist shot as soon as the puck hit his stick. The hard, accurate drive eluded Boston goalie Andy Moog, and the Oilers had the victory at 15:13 of the third overtime period. "Those were two exhausted hockey clubs," Edmonton coach John Muckler said afterward. "Thank God Petr put it away." The Bruins never recovered from the devastating loss (they had taken 52 shots at Bill Ranford in the Edmonton net) and lost the cup to the Oilers in five games.

MacTavish became so respected in Edmonton that he was named team captain for two seasons before he was traded to the New York Rangers. MacTavish won another Cup with New York in 1994 (he took the last faceoff in the Rangers end to close out the seventh game), and he also played for Philadelphia and St. Louis before retiring. He returned to Edmonton to coach the team for a number of years, highlighted by a trip to the Stanley Cup finals in 2006.

Considering the odds of MacTavish doing anything significant in the aftermath of his serious accident, his achievements as a player and coach are truly remarkable. One of the ways MacTavish tried to heal the wounds of what he had done was to stay in contact with the parents of the woman he had killed in the accident. While there is never any real closure to what happened, MacTavish found a positive way to deal with the aftermath of a tragedy, which helped to make him a very productive hockey player once again.

Craig MacTavish recorded 480 points in 1,093 career games. He also posted a 301-252-103 record as coach of the Edmonton Oilers. MacTavish was also the last NHL player to play without a helmet.

JOE MULLEN
BORN: NEW YORK CITY, NEW YORK
NHL SEASONS: 1981–82 TO 1996–97
DEFINING MOMENT: 1989 STANLEY CUP FINALS

The odds against Joe Mullen becoming an NHL player were enormous. He was born on February 26, 1957, to a family with seven children. They lived on West 49th Street in the lower West Side of Manhattan, in an area known as Hell's Kitchen. The Mullen family lived five stories up in a three-bedroom apartment in a building that housed drug dealers and other questionable characters associated with gangs. The father, Thomas Mullen, was a maintenance worker at Madison Square Garden, but that did not mean young Joe and his brothers got to see many New York Ranger games. The Mullen brothers actually began playing hockey on rollerblades, using empty parking lots and basketball courts as their ice surface. Joe and his brothers used sports as a way to stay out of trouble. Neighbors realized they were not bad kids and kept an eye on them as they made their way around the mean streets of New York. On occasion, the brothers and their friends would ride a bus to New Jersey to play hockey on ice—but that did not happen very often.

As luck would have it, Rangers general manager Emile Francis was walking outside the old Madison Square Garden and happened upon a group of boys who were getting ready to play a game of hockey. Francis followed them, thinking they may have found some ice surface, but then he realized that these boys with hockey sticks and Ranger sweatshirts were going to play on rollerblades. When he returned to his office, Francis approached the president of the Rangers, Bill Jennings, and told him what he had seen. He suggested the Rangers start a New York league for young-sters who wanted to take up hockey. It was agreed to quickly, and the New York Junior Hockey League was born with games played in Madison Square Garden on Wednesday and Sunday afternoon before Rangers games. The initial investment of $100,000 was to pay off not only for the Rangers but also for the entire National Hockey League.

Joe Mullen was 14 when he played for the start-up league's New York 14th Precinct in 1971–72, and he scored 13 goals in 30 games. The next three seasons saw him play for a team called the New York Westsiders and he scored 14, 71, and 110 goals—incredible totals, though the competition might not have been the best compared to junior hockey in Canada. However, Mullen and his brothers did get the attention of U.S. colleges who had hockey programs. Joe and three of his brothers (including Brian, who would also go on to play in the NHL) gained scholarships at Boston College. Joe played there for four seasons, scoring 110 goals in 111 total games played. Mullen was not very big (5'9" and 180 pounds), but he was fast on his skates and had a good shot. He was undrafted by the NHL, but the St. Louis Blues signed him as a free agent in 1979. Mullen spent three seasons in the minors (scoring 120 goals) be-fore getting promoted to the big team during the 1981–82 season. In only his third NHL season, Mullen scored 41 goals and notched another 40 markers in 1984–85. Soon his contract requirements made him too rich for the Blues, so they dealt him to Calgary.

If Mullen had exceeded all expectations in St. Louis, he was even better as a Flame, scoring 47, 40, and 51 goals in his first three years in Alberta. In 1988–89, Mullen not only scored 51 times, he also had a career best 110 points and made the NHL's first all-star team. The Flames were the best team in the league that year and faced the second-best team, the Montreal Canadiens, in the Stanley Cup finals. It was Mullen's turn to shine when he needed to the most.

The Canadiens had a 2-1 lead in games as the teams battled in the fourth contest at the Montreal Forum the night of May 21, 1989. There was no way the Flames could go down three games to one, and they took a 2-0 lead in the second period with Mullen scoring the second Calgary goal. Montreal crept close in the final stanza but Mullen's empty net goal sealed the 4-2 win. "I think we have to play with a lot of desperation," Mullen said. "That was what we really needed to do. We showed a lot of character. We have a lot of talented players on this team— a lot of leadership, too. We showed tonight that we had a lot of guys ready to take the bull by the horns."

Two nights later in Calgary, the Flames took control of the series with a 3-2 win. They started off with a goal at the 28-second mark by Joel Otto, and then Mullen added another at 8:15 of the first. The teams exchanged goals to give the Flames a 3-1 lead and they protected their lead until the final buzzer. The Flames would later clinch their first Stanley Cup in team history when they beat Montreal 4-2 back at the Forum (becoming the only visiting team to win the Cup in the venerable arena). It was Mullen who assisted on an empty net goal by Doug Gilmour to seal the game.

Considering where Mullen had come from, it was remarkable that he was parading the Stanley Cup around the Montreal Forum—one of hockey's greatest shrines. His life story was more like a Disney movie at that moment, and his contribution to the Flames victory was a testament not only to his talent but also to his desire to excel in hockey and in life. As shown by Mullen, who had risen from the most unlikely circumstances to become a great professional player and a Stanley Cup champion, hockey dreams can come true—even out of the mean streets of Hell's Kitchen.

Joe Mullen won two more Stanley Cups with the Pittsburgh Penguins and was elected to the Hall of Fame in 2000.

HENRIK ZETTERBERG
BORN: NJURUNDA, SWEDEN
NHL SEASONS: 2002–03 TO PRESENT
DEFINING MOMENT: 2008 PLAYOFFS

Young boys are often influenced by what activities their dads expose them to. When Henrik Zetterberg was a kid growing up in a town north of Stockholm, Sweden, his father, Goran (an appliance store owner), put a pair of skates on his two-year-old son and then watched the youngster make his way across a frozen body of water. The elder Zetterberg had been something of a hockey player in his youth, and he wanted to share his passion for the game with his son.

Henrik was soon playing hockey as much as he could, with his father giving him tips on how to play the game properly. He learned his lessons well and as he hit his teen years, Zetterberg was playing with boys of all ages for a variety of teams. He was always one of the smaller boys (though he grew up to be 5'11" and a sturdy 176 pounds), which forced him to learn to survive by emphasizing skill over brawn.

The Detroit Red Wings have been excellent over the years at unearthing gems late in the NHL Entry Draft, and selecting Zetterberg 210th overall in 1999 was another late coup for the scouting staff. However, even Detroit's ever-alert bird dogs would have to admit they did not expect Zetterberg to become an NHL star—if they did, he surely would have been taken much higher than 210 in the draft! Of the few players selected after Zetterberg who made it to the NHL, none have even come close to having the impact the slick Swede has had on the Detroit club.

The Red Wings were in no hurry to get Zetterberg over to North America, so they let him further develop his skills in Sweden. He would score just 15 to 20 goals a season for Timra IK, but he impressed enough people to be selected for the Swedish Olympic team for the 2002 Games. He enjoyed the experience (especially a 5–2 win over Canada in the preliminary round) and felt that he was now ready to play in the NHL.

Zetterberg joined the Red Wings for his first training camp in September 2002 and was quickly tested by the veteran players and coaches. The defending Stanley Cup champions wanted to see if he was worthy of making their roster. He passed one test by taking all the physical punishment thrown at him and got to play in 79 games as a rookie in 2002–03. He scored 22 goals and added 22 assists—he was indeed ready for the NHL. Zetterberg's goal total dropped to 15 the next season, but he did have six more assists than in the previous year. He spent the lockout year playing in Sweden (recording 50 points in 50 games), and made loud noises about not returning to the NHL if he did not get the contract he wanted from the Red Wings.

Detroit general manager Ken Holland handled the situation very adroitly, and soon Zetterberg was back in the fold for the 2005–06 season. He blossomed as a goal scorer with a team-best 39 goals and a career high 85 points. The Red Wings had the best record in the NHL with 58 wins and 124 points, and Zetterberg dazzled with his great stickhandling and picture goals. He was very prominent on the power play (17 goals with the extra man) and on the penalty-killing unit, because he showed a devotion to playing an all-around game (he was a plus 29 for the season). The new style of NHL has suited Zetterberg perfectly, and he has produced solid numbers each season.

There is nothing like winning the Stanley Cup, the Conn Smythe Trophy, and scoring the Cup-clinching goal to convince everyone that you're one of the best players in the NHL. In the 2008 play-offs, that's exactly what Zetterberg did, silencing critics who did not believe he was a top playoff performer. Not only did he lead Detroit with 27 points (14G, 13A) in the playoffs, he was at his absolute best in defensive situations. On one 5-on-3 penalty kill, he stopped a sure goal by Pittsburgh's Sidney Crosby to preserve a Red Wing victory in the finals. One of the best players in the regular season (a career high 92 points based on 43 goals and 49 assists), Zetterberg showed that teams with great two-way players have the best chance to win the championship.

When the Stanley Cup finals opened on May 24, 2008, it was Zetterberg who led the way for the Red Wings with one goal in the opening game, a 4-0 defeat of the Pittsburgh Penguins. Two nights later, he had an assist in the second game, a 3-0 home ice win for Detroit. But Zetterberg saved his best for the night of June 4, 2008, when he scored one goal (the Cup winner) and added one assist to lead his team to a 3-2 win over the heartbroken Penguins. Zetterberg took six shots on goal in the last game of the series and played an exhausting 23:20 during the tight contest. NHL commissioner Gary Bettman presented the Conn Smythe Trophy to a smiling Zetterberg, who lifted the prestigious trophy over his head.

"It's been unbelievable," Zetterberg said of his MVP status and his first NHL championship. "When we lost in Joe Louis (Detroit's home arena, the sight of Pittsburgh's triple overtime win in the fifth game of the series), it was devastating. We found a way to battle back. It's a great feeling (to win the Smythe Trophy). There are some great names on it." Not only had Zetterberg won the Smythe, he was widely recognized for having held his own against Sidney Crosby of the Penguins, never an easy task. One year later, the Penguins gained their revenge by beating Detroit in seven games, but Zetterberg was still very prominent for the Red Wings with 23 points in 24 playoff games.

Zetterberg was considered to be a long shot to make the NHL

and it was at first assumed he would be a third or fourth line player after earning his dues in the minors. His determination helped him beat the odds and become one the best players in hockey. He may lead Detroit to more Cups before his career is over.

In addition to leading the Red Wings in points with 27 during the 2008 playoffs, Henrik Zetterberg was a plus 16, scored four power-play goals, two short-handed markers, and four of his goals were game winners.

LUC ROBITAILLE
BORN: MONTREAL, QUEBEC
NHL SEASONS: 1986–87 TO 2005–06
DEFINING MOMENT: 1992–93 SEASON & PLAYOFFS

When you get selected 171st overall in the ninth round of the Entry Draft, the chances of becoming an NHL player are fairly remote. That is exactly the position left winger Luc Robitaille found himself in when the Los Angeles Kings chose him late in the 1984 draft. The 6'1", 215-pound Robitaille had enjoyed a successful junior career playing for the Hull Olympiques (he scored 32 goals and recorded 85 points in his draft-eligible season) of the QMJHL, but the scouts were skeptical about whether he could produce at the NHL level. The slick winger would finish his junior career with 155 goals and 424 points in 197 career games—but could he find a home on the Kings roster at the tender age of 20? The good news for Robitaille was that the Kings had finished with the second-worst record in the entire NHL in 1985–86, with a lowly 54 points. There had to be some job openings to start the 1986–87 season.

It turned out Robitaille would never play a game in the minors. He made the Kings right after his first training camp and scored 45 goals and totaled 84 points in 79 games played. His outstanding performance as a rookie earned him the Calder Trophy and set him on course for a very productive career. Over the next five seasons, Robitaille never scored less than 44 goals in any year and recorded over 100 points in three of those same seasons. The Kings were known for their offense, highlighted by Robitaille's magic touch around the opposition net. Most players could only dream of Robitaille's deft touch, and he was certainly willing to go wherever necessary to score his goals. He was not a great skater—which is part of the reason he was drafted so low—but the man they nicknamed "Lucky" played his own game to great effectiveness.

Robitaille was at his absolute best during the 1992–93 season, which started with him being named captain while teammate Wayne Gretzky recovered from a back injury. The designation was temporary, but the ultra-competitive Robitaille took it upon himself to have the defining year of his life.

In the first 39 games of the '92–'93 season, Robitaille scored 30 goals and recorded 56 points—and that was without Gretzky in the lineup! On April 15, 1993, the Kings lost to the Vancouver Canucks by a score of 8-6, but Robitaille scored his 63rd goal of the season and added three assists in the wide-open contest. The four points gave him 125 on the season and set a new NHL mark for left wingers which is yet to be broken. He was named the Kings' most valuable player for the '92–'93 season, but he still had more to give in the playoffs. Los Angeles had never appeared in a Stanley Cup final, but after they acquired Gretzky in the infamous 1988 trade, their chances of getting there became very real—yet they still had not accomplished the feat. That changed during the incredible 1993 post-season.

The Kings were underdogs in each series they played but found different ways to knock off Calgary, Vancouver, and Toronto in the first three rounds to make it to the finals for the first time ever. All three Canadian teams were better than the Kings during the regular season, but timely goals and some nice bounces got them into the final against the Montreal Canadiens. Robitaille had recorded 17 points to this point in the playoffs but he saved his best and most defining moments for the opening game of the finals in Montreal.

It was June 1, 1993. Robitaille was a strong presence in front of the Montreal net from the opening faceoff. He scored the first goal in the first period of the game when he kicked a puck to his stick to beat Patrick Roy with a backhand drive that bounced in off the netminder. "You can try that 20 times and most of the time it will hit (the goaltender) and stay out," Robitaille said later. "This time it went in." It was the kind of marker only the most gifted goal scorer gets. He took seven shots on net in the second period and finally beat Roy again with less than three minutes to play in the period. It gave the Kings a 2-1 lead and was the most important goal of the game as the Kings coasted to a 4-1 win. "That was a big goal," Gretzky said. "We didn't want to go through the period (in which the Kings took 20 shots on goal) without scoring."

The sharp-shooting Kings left winger was inspired by playing in his hometown and recalled that he was just eight years old when he first went to the Montreal Forum. Prior to the game, Robitaille saw Canadiens legend Henri Richard in the building and wanted to make a good impression on one of his childhood heroes. "I don't know what I am going to do tonight, but I don't want him to think I can't play. There are lots of legends here. This will always be a special place for me," Robitaille recounted about his special day. Unfortunately for him and the Kings, the ghosts from Canadiens past rose up and helped lead the Habs over the Kings in five games.

Robitaille would go on to play for the Rangers, Penguins, and Red Wings (where he won a Stanley Cup in 2002) before returning to Los Angeles to finish the last two years of his illustrious career. It was his third stint as a King. It is interesting to note that only 13 players selected after Robitaille in the '84 draft ever made it to the NHL and, of those, only one was a significant player (Gary Suter). Despite being ranked so low, Robitaille beat the very long odds to become one of the best players in NHL history.

Luc Robitaille recorded 668 career goals and was elected to the Hall of Fame in 2009.

PETER STASTNY
BORN: BRATISLAVA, CZECHOSLOVAKIA (SLOVAKIA)
NHL SEASONS: 1980–81 TO 1994–95
DEFINING MOMENT: FEBRUARY 22, 1981

Peter Stastny knew what he wanted to do, but he also knew that his plan was filled with incredible danger for him and members of his family. Living under an oppressive regime in his native Czecho-slovakia was not something he wanted to do for the rest of his life. Most people in the country would have to learn to live and suffer under and within the communist government. But Stastny and his two brothers (Anton and Marian) were hockey players on the Czech national team, whose travels exposed the brothers to many places in the western world. They would all agree that their future was in going to North America to play professional hockey.

The decision to defect could be made with some ease given their status as hockey players, but the execution of a defection plan was anything but assured. "You realized as you matured that you had no future in this country as a person after your hockey career was over. My values were completely different than the values of the regime. Some people were above the law; they could do just about anything. I could not be indifferent to this. I stood up and pointed the finger. It happened that we were threatened that they would take the game (of hockey) from us," Stastny said years later.

He was aware that NHL teams were very interested in his services (he had impressed many as a 19-year-old at the world championships). Once his status as a hockey player was threatened, the decision to leave was made fairly quickly. With the help of the Quebec Nordiques, Peter and Anton Stastny made their getaway (Marian had to stay behind because he had a wife and children). The escape was made during the summer of 1980 in Innsbruck, Austria, while playing in a tournament. The brothers were able to get away without being detected as the Nordique officials had all the paperwork and travel arrangements ready. As worried as the brothers were about leaving Marian behind, Peter realized that he had made the best decision for his future—both in the short and in the long term.

Although the defection was not well received in Czechoslovakia, the Stastny brothers opened the door for other players in that country to come to North America. In many ways Peter and Anton were trailblazers, and their contributions to hockey should be remembered for the very real dangers they were willing to face. It was through their courage that other Czech stars made it to the NHL—players like Ivan Hlinka, Milan Novy, Vaclav Nedomansky, and Jiri Bubla. These players inspired another generation of players like Jaromir Jagr, Dominik Hasek, Marian Hossa, Patrik Elias, and Marian Gaborik.

Peter Stastny soon proved he was worth all the work the Nordiques had done to get him in a Quebec uniform. The 24-year old Stastny played alongside his brother and scored his first NHL goal against Hall of Fame netminder Tony Esposito. On February 20, 1980, both Peter and Anton each notched a hat trick in a 9-3 whipping of the Vancouver Canucks. However, if there was one game that truly defined the brothers in their initial NHL season, it was the very next game against the Washington Capitals on February 22, 1980—a contest that revealed more about the talent level of the brothers than ever before.

Peter opened the scoring for the visitors before the game was five minutes old. Anton added one marker before the first frame was completed, giving Quebec a 2-1 lead. Peter scored twice more in the second period and added two assists while Anton scored one more as well. In the final stanza, Peter scored his fourth of the night at 19:05 to give him an eight-point evening (4G, 4A). Incredibly, Anton matched that total (3G, 5A), while scoring his third goal of the game as well. The Nordiques won the wild affair by an 11-7 count. It is interesting to note that all the scoring came against two quality NHL goalies: Mike Palmateer and Wayne Stephenson— both established, veteran netminders. It was a record-setting performance (most points in one road game) by the brothers who still share the NHL record.

Capitals veteran winger Jean Pronovost could only look on in awe as the Stastny brothers put on a real show. "They are good," Pronovost said after the game. "You can't let them freewheel like they did tonight." Nordiques coach Michel Bergeron said of the stellar performance, "A month ago I gave a rest to the Stastny brothers and I changed my lines around to give us more offensive power. The Stastnys are playing well right now, skating really good. I enjoy seeing that." Scoring his 29th goal of the season, Peter Stastny gave credit to his brother for the outburst. "Anton set me up all night. He could have shot but he decided to pass to me. All good teams watch and pass, always trying to find someone open." The

16 total points the Stastnys recorded versus the Capitals were the most two brothers put up in one night since Max and Doug Bentley of Chicago racked up 13 points against the New York Rangers on January 28, 1943.

Peter Stastny would go on to win the Calder Trophy as the NHL's best rookie in '80–'81 with a 109-point performance, which included 39 goals. He would record 100 or more points in seven of his eight seasons in the league. He was thrilled when Marian joined the Nordiques for the 1981–82 season, giving the Quebec team a threesome of high-scoring brothers. Quebec was in contention for many years, but the team was never able to get to the Stanley Cup finals. Later in his career, Peter played for the New Jersey Devils and the St. Louis Blues, finishing with 450 goals and 1,239 points in 977 career games. Peter Stastny not only beat the odds to get to the NHL, he excelled so much he was awarded the highest honor a player can achieve—induction into the Hall of Fame!

Peter Stastny scored 46 or more goals four times in his NHL career. He was elected to the Hall of Fame in 1998.

DINO CICCARELLI
BORN: SARNIA, ONTARIO
NHL SEASONS: 1980–81 TO 1998–99
DEFINING MOMENT: JANUARY 8, 1994

No matter how talented a young hockey player might be, when he's on the small side and has a medical history that includes a broken leg, the scouts tend to scatter and stay away. Such was the fate of right winger Dino Ciccarelli, who was a very good junior hockey player. As a 15-year-old, he played in hometown Sarnia, Ontario, for a team called the Bees, where he scored 45 goals and 88 points in just 45 games. He then joined the London Knights of the Ontario Hockey League and scored 39 times as a rookie in 1976–77. The following year saw him score 72 times and earn a spot on the OHL's second all-star team. However, disaster struck the next year when he slid into the boards and badly broke his right leg. Getting that leg back into condition was a long and grueling process for the youngster, who seriously thought about quitting and heading back to Sarnia. The hard work eventually paid off, though (he scored 50 goals for the Knights in 1979–80), but the NHL wanted nothing to do with the 5'10" winger who was considered both too small and too damaged. Twice, he was passed over at the NHL draft, with not one team willing to gamble on him. Finally the Minnesota North Stars gave him a shot and signed him in September 1979.

"No NHL team wanted to take a chance on this skinny kid with a bad leg. I wasn't even selected in the Entry Draft. After getting passed by every team, I was just happy to sign a free-agent contract with the Minnesota North Stars," Ciccarelli recalled later. He was sent to the American Hockey League to see if he could handle the pro game. He immediately eliminated any doubts by scoring 32 goals in 48 games for the Oklahoma City Stars. His performance got him called up to Minnesota for the rest of the 1980–81 season, where he added 18 goals in 32 contests. His first goal came against future Hall of Famer Billy Smith of the New York Islanders, which made all his efforts to recover from his leg injury very worthwhile. Ciccarelli also had a great post-season in '81, setting a record for rookies with 14 goals in just 19 games. One of his playoff goals ended the Calgary Flames hope of making it to the finals. Instead, the North Stars won the game 5-3 and got to tangle with the Islanders for the Stanley Cup (they lost the title in five games). Even though the North Stars were beaten in the finals, Ciccarelli had shown he could score at the highest level of hockey. He would never play in the minors again.

In just his second year in the NHL, Ciccarelli would record 106 points (55 were goals), developing a style of play that was gritty, determined, and in the face of every NHL goaltender. He stayed with the North Stars for nearly nine full seasons before he was traded to the Washington Capitals in March 1989 in a major four-player swap. While he put up good numbers with the Capitals, Ciccarelli found himself on the move again—this time to the Detroit Red Wings. It was while he was with Detroit that Ciccarelli achieved a defining milestone only a few players can even dream about—he scored his 500th goal.

On the night of January 8, 1994, the Red Wings were visiting the Los Angeles Kings; Ciccarelli was sitting on 499 career goals. He had missed scoring a goal the night before in San Jose, but that allowed his father to be in attendance in Los Angeles this night. He would hit the post three times, but in the third period he scored his milestone by knocking a shot past Kelly Hrudey in the Kings net. The assists went to Vyacheslav Kozlov and Sergei Fedorov, two of many Russian players on the Red Wings club. The goal was really an insurance marker, giving the Wings a 5-3 lead in a game that would end 6-3. But no matter.

"When it finally happened, I was relieved," Ciccarelli recalled years later. "It was great my dad was able to be there when it happened. When you look at the history of hockey and how few players have reached the 500-goal mark, it really is a special achievement." With his 500th goal, Ciccarelli became just the second player to hit this milestone while wearing a Red Wings uniform—the first being the incomparable Gordie Howe!

Ciccarelli made it back to the Stanley Cup finals only once more before his career ended, with the Red Wings in 1995. However, the New Jersey Devils would defeat Detroit in four straight to take their first championship. In 1996, Ciccarelli was traded to Tampa Bay, where he scored 36 goals in 1996–97—his last good year. He also played for the Florida Panthers, scoring his last eleven goals for that team. "I always considered myself a goal scorer first. I felt that I could help a team in a lot of ways, but it was no secret that scoring goals was what I did best," Ciccarelli said as he recapped his entire career perfectly.

He finished his great goal-scoring career with 608 markers—an astounding number, considering many believed Ciccarelli would not beat the odds to score even one NHL goal!

Dino Ciccarelli was elected to the Hall of Fame in 2010.

TYLER MYERS
BORN: HOUSTON, TEXAS
NHL SEASONS: 2009–10 TO PRESENT
DEFINING MOMENT: NOVEMBER 15, 2010

Anyone who looks up the record of defenseman Tyler Myers will be struck by a couple of facts. The first is that his birthplace is shown as Houston, Texas—a place more associated with football than hockey. He grew up near Houston, where his father Paul worked in the oil business. When Tyler was six, he attended an American Hockey League game involving the Houston Aeros with his father. The very next morning, Tyler's father went out and bought his son some hockey equipment. There was little interest in Houston for hockey, but he managed to find a league where he could get into some games. Tyler also became a Dallas Stars fan and remembers watching them win the Stanley Cup in 1999. He immediately loved the game of hockey—but how could he develop as a player in Houston? The odds of young Tyler becoming a hockey player in the heart of Texas were fairly remote, if nonexistent. However, when he turned 10, his father was transferred to Calgary—a move that changed his entire life. He was now able to develop his athletic skills in a hockey environment. "You get to Calgary and there are 13 teams in just one community. It's a big difference with the atmosphere for hockey (compared to Houston)," Myers later recalled. If he had stayed south of the border, it is likely he would have gravitated toward basketball or football.

His parents had a rule that grades must be high in order to play sports, so it was a good thing that Myers was a top student. He attended the famous Notre Dame school in Saskatchewan when he was 15, but would play his major junior hockey in British Columbia for the Kelowna Rockets of the Western Hockey League. At first Myers played internationally for the United States, but when he acquired Canadian citizenship, he decided he would rather play for Team Canada. In 2009, he played for the Canadian side at the World Junior tournament in Ottawa and was a big reason why his adopted nation won the gold medal.

The other noticeable item on Myers's playing record is his size—6'8" and 220 pounds (second in height only to Zdeno Chara of the Boston Bruins). Hockey scouts had Myers rated as high as the fourth overall prospect for the 2008 NHL Entry Draft, but a knee injury and concerns about his mobility and offensive capabilities dropped him down to 12th overall, where the Buffalo Sabres moved up to take him. The Sabres felt they had a real gem on their hands, but they were not sure when he would be ready to play in the NHL.

Myers got a bit of a break when fellow Kelowna defenseman Luke Schenn (selected fifth overall in 2008) made the Toronto Maple Leafs, leaving the best defenseman role on the Rockets to Myers. Kelowna had a great year in 2008–09 and won the WHL title in the playoffs. Myers posted a junior career best nine goals and 42 points, and was great in the post-season with 20 points in 22 play-off games, earning him MVP status. It seemed to some observers that Myers was a different and more dominating player after coming back from the World Junior tournament. Canadian coach Pat Quinn, a former NHL defenseman, had a great impact on Myers, and this got him ready to play in the big league.

Team management in Kelowna hoped that Myers would return for one more year of junior in 2009–10, but they realized the chances of that happening were remote. The Sabres liked what they saw of the young blueliner and were willing to keep him for at least nine games (a 10th appearance meant the first year of his NHL contract would kick in) before deciding to keep him for the entire season. Myers quickly showed he belonged, recording his first point on October 8 versus Phoenix and then notching his first goal on October 16 against the New York Islanders (a game that saw him record an assist as well). A few games later he scored a goal in a shootout to beat Tampa Bay. His impressive early performance eliminated any doubt about him returning to Kelowna. In fact, he had one of the best rookie seasons a defenseman could ever hope for, with 11 goals and 48 points while playing in all 82 games.

Having a large body usually means that some time has to pass before a player grows accustomed to his frame, but Myers seems to have adjusted just fine. The most noticeable trait Myers possesses is his smooth skating stride while carrying the puck. He can handle the point on the power play with ease, and his shot is more powerful than first projected. Buffalo coach Lindy Ruff used Myers in every situation possible, and he responded well to each challenge. Young defensemen are not supposed to be this good, but Myers registered a plus-13 rating despite all the ice time he was given.

The 2010–11 season started off with more of the same for Myers. He had two game-winning goals in October and three assists against New Jersey on Remembrance Day. On November 15, 2010, the highly touted Vancouver Canucks came to Buffalo to tangle with the Sabres. The game went into overtime and the man who settled the issue with another game-wining goal was none other than Myers. Canucks defenseman Dan Hamhuis lost the puck to Myers right in the slot in the Vancouver end. Myers pounced on the loose disk and drove one past goalie Cory Schneider. It was a hard-fought hockey game that was decided with just 23 seconds to play. "It just goes to show that we battle right to the end...We showed good character...we didn't just fall apart (after giving up the lead). We kept going and pushed right to the end," Myers said of his team.

The 2008 draft was loaded with highly sought-after defensemen, with four selected ahead of Myers (Drew Doughty, second; Zach Bogosian, third; Alex Pietrangelo, fourth, and Luke Schenn, fifth), but the Buffalo Sabres might be the team that got the best all-round player. Who would have believed it possible of a kid born in the football hotbed of Texas!

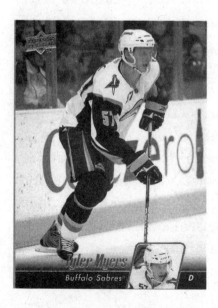

Tyler Myers was named winner of the Calder Trophy as best rookie in the NHL for the 2009–10 season.

WILLIE O'REE
BORN: FREDRICTON, NEW BRUNSWICK
NHL SEASONS: 1957–58 TO 1960–61
DEFINING MOMENT: JANUARY 1, 1961

Willie O'Ree was born in FredrictonFredericton, New Brunswick in 1935. His family was only one of two black families in this area of the Maritimes. O'Ree was the youngest of 13 children and his love for hockey began early in life. Like many youngsters in Canada, a backyard rink was a big part of his life, with other outdoor rinks providing him a chance to play and develop his skills. Although there were no black hockey players to look up to in the NHL as when O'Ree was growing up, he did get a chance to meet Jackie Robinson, the first black to play major league baseball. The 13-year- old O'Ree told Robinson he would play in the NHL one day. And like Robinson, he would break defy all odds to realize his dream.

From the ages of 16 to 18, O'Ree played hockey locally in FredrictonFredericton, but when he turned 19, the fast-skating, 5'10", 175-pound left winger went to play junior hockey in Quebec. During the 1954–55 season, O'Ree had 44 points in 43 games for the Quebec Frontenacs of the QJHL. The next year saw him play in Ontario for the Kitchener Canucks, where he had 58 points (including 30 goals) in 41 games. The NHL seemed to be closer than ever, but a serious eye injury late in the '55–'56 season almost ended O'Ree's dream. He lost most of the vision in his right eye when a puck that struck his retina had shatteringshattered it beyond repair. After some time off, O'Ree returned to the ice and found he still could play the game without being afraid. A call from Quebec Aces coach and general manager Punch Imlach brought him to a try out for the senior league club. O'Ree took advantage of the opportunity and made the team. O'Ree told only two people (his sister and a trusted teammate) about the damage to his eye while letting everyone else assume he had recovered from his injury. He scored 22 goals in 1956–57 for the Aces, a team that would win the QSHL championship.

For the most part, O'Ree was in the minor leagues for the rest of his career (which lasted until 1978–79 when he was 43 years old), but his NHL rights were held by the Boston Bruins. Faced with some injuries before a weekend home-and-home series against Montreal, the Bruins summoned O'Ree up for a Saturday- night game at the Forum the night of January 18, 1958. The 22-year-old became the first black player to suit up for a National Hockey League team. "Sure, I was nervous, but it was the greatest thrill of my life," O'Ree said after Boston beat the first place Canadiens 3-0. "It was much better as the game went on. I had a really good chance to score in the third when (teammate) Jerry Toppazzini gave me a pass in close," O'Ree continued. "I thought I had (Montreal goalie Jacques) Plante good but (Canadiens defenseman) Tom Johnson hooked me." O'Ree concluded by saying, "Maybe I can do better in Boston but it's a day I'll never forget as long as I live." O'Ree played in only two contests during that barrier-breaking season, but three years later, in 1960–61, he was back for 43 games with the Bruins.

Throughout his long minor league career O'Ree would score 20 or more goals with relative ease and on five occasions, he scored 30 or more times (38 was his highest goal total for a single season). It was during his 43-game stint with Boston in '60-'61 that O'Ree scored his first NHL goal. It came on New Year's night 1961 as the Bruins hosted the Montreal Canadiens. With Boston leading 2-1, O'Ree got away from the Habs defensemen and bore in on goalie Charlie Hodge before beating the netminder with a low shot on the glove side for his first NHL goal at 10:07 of the third period. The 13,909 fans at the Boston Garden gave O'Ree a rousing ovation for two minutes in recognition of the first goal scored by a black player in the history of the NHL. It turned out to be the game winner, since Montreal scored to make it a 3-2 game. O'Ree finished with four goals and a respectable 14 points and earned $9,000 as an NHL player.

The Bruins shipped O'Ree's playing rights to Montreal after they had found out about his eye injury, and that took away any chance of his staying in the NHL, since the Habs were too deep in talent. O'Ree never made as much as $20,000 a year playing in the minors but he accumulated some impressive point totals in the various pro leagues he played in—especially in the Western Hockey League where he racked up 639 points in 785 career games played over 13 seasons. No other black player would play in the NHL until Mike Marson did so for the Washington Capitals in the 1973–74 season.

Like Robinson in baseball, O'Ree encountered racist taunts wherever he played, but he never let words bother him. He only responded physically when he was fouled with an elbow, spear, or cross-check, and that was to let the opposition know he was not going to be pushed around. O'Ree's contribution to the game of hockey was much more appreciated years after his playing days were over. O'Ree has helped the NHL in various capacities over recent years for a variety of programs designed to encourage youth. He loves it most when he gets to work with youngsters of diversity—who are starting out playing the game much the way he did years ago— so they won't have to break the same odds that he did so many years ago.

Willie O'Ree was awarded the Lester Patrick Trophy in 2000 for his contributions to hockey in the United States.

P.K. SUBBAN
BORN: TORONTO, ONTARIO
NHL SEASONS: 2009-10 TO PRESENT
DEFINING MOMENT: JANUARY 18, 2011

When Karl Subban came to Canada from his native country of Jamaica, he did not arrive in one of the bigger Canadian cities. Instead he landed in northern Ontario, specifically the city of Sudbury, Ontario. It was there that Karl learned of his new country's love of hockey, and since all those around him loved the Montreal Canadiens, he had to follow along. Karl would marry a woman from Montserrat and have five children (three boys, two girls) with her. The family lived in Toronto, where Karl became an elementary school principal. The oldest boy was named Pernell Karl (or P.K.) and he was on skates by the time he was two and a half years of age. He was playing house league hockey by the time he was four, and at 16, he was drafted into the OHL by the Belleville Bulls. At first, Karl was not quite sure how to put on all the equipment required for hockey, but a family friend helped out and Karl could see a special something about P.K. and his love of hockey.

"I really believe kids must have dreams. P.K. had a dream, a goal to play in the NHL. It was our job as parents to make sure we did everything to support it. We were realistic but what came out of it taught him the value of hard work. How to focus on his goal and how to deal with the good times and how to deal with the bad times," Karl said of his son. "It doesn't matter (what) your background (is), it doesn't matter (what) your race (is). It doesn't matter (what) you(r) religion (is). You have a dream and you work to fulfill it," the father says. It is easy to believe he has the attention of all the kids at his school (located in a neighbourhood that faces many challenges), since his son is proof you can succeed.

P.K. has never lacked for confidence, and while that has landed him in some trouble from time to time, he is a young man who knows where he is going and is not afraid to make a mistake or two on the ice. It did not seem to bother the burly (6', 203-pound) defenseman that Belleville had drafted him in the sixth round. He told coach George Burnett that he would make the Bulls. Subban did just that with five goals and 12 points in 52 games in 2005-06 when he was 16 years old. He notched 56 and 46 points respectively over the next two seasons and that got the Canadiens to take him 43rd overall in the 2007 Entry Draft. Burnett noted that Subban played his best hockey when it mattered most and that put the brash blueliner in good stead with his team. In his final year of junior, Subban racked up 76 points, which included 62 assists.

Subban needed some seasoning and was sent to the Hamilton Bulldogs of the American Hockey League, but he never changed his game one bit. In 2009-10 he had 53 points in 73 games and got into a couple of regular season games with the Habs, recording two assists. He was called up for the playoffs when key injuries struck the Montreal defensive corps, and he quickly impressed by chipping in eight points in 14 post-season games for a Canadiens team that went into the third round of the playoffs.

Bigger things were expected of Subban for the 2010-11 season and the self-assured defenseman did not let his team down. One of his best nights came on January 18, 2011, when the Canadiens hosted the Calgary Flames. In his typical flashy style, Subban scored the overtime winner in a 5-4 Montreal victory. Subban's marker had saved the Habs from some great embarrassment after they blew a four-goal lead. "I scored a goal, I did a celebration (dragging his leg along the ice). I wish I had just put my stick up but that's something I've always dreamed of—scoring the winner in overtime. It was a great moment but the important thing is that we got two points." Subban's high wrist-shot not only earned him the game-winning goal, it also got him the first star nomination for the evening (which saw Subban adding one assist on a goal by teammate Mike Cammalleri).

Showing signs of maturing, Subban credited defensive partner Hal Gill for settling him down during the game against Calgary. "I owe him a lot of credit because after they tied it 4-4, I was pretty upset. I felt it was my fault. I jumped on the ice too early and there was a 'too many men' call. It was (a) series of events. He (Gill) came over to me and maybe if he (didn't), I (would have made) another mistake and the game (would have gone) the other way. He kept me focused and told me to forget about it." In his first full NHL season, Subban recorded 38 points in 77 games played. That total is bound to improve as Subban picks up more experience and learns to pick his spots to jump into the attack more carefully.

Subban has made some enemies on other teams with his over flowing confidence (and a few teammates have been critical as well), but he has never felt his race was an issue. It would be easy for him to dismiss criticisms as racially based, but he has never taken that road. The fact is P.K. Subban is a very hard worker and it is his work ethic that will overcome everything to make him an NHL star. He summarizes his approach very well. "I want to be known as a guy who is going to battle as hard as he can every night and (as someone who is) not going to make it easy on the forwards playing against him, he's going to make it tough for them and he's a guy who can be a game-changer. He's going to help his team win and contribute."

Only Hall of Fame defenseman Guy Lapointe scored more goals (15) as rookie for the Habs than P.K. Subban, who had 14 goals in 2010-11 for the Montreal Canadiens.

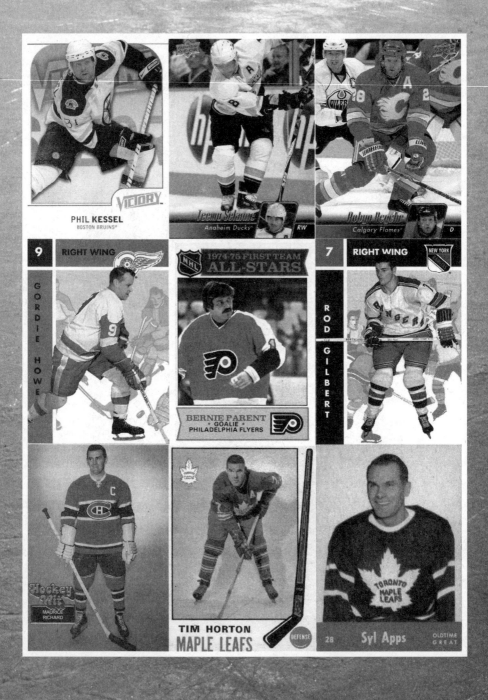

PHIL KESSEL
BOSTON BRUINS

Teemu Selanne
Anaheim Ducks — RW

Robyn Regehr
Calgary Flames — D

9 — RIGHT WING

GORDIE HOWE

NHL
1974-75 FIRST TEAM
ALL-STARS

BERNIE PARENT
• GOALIE •
PHILADELPHIA FLYERS

7 — RIGHT WING — NEW YORK

ROD GILBERT

Hockey
MAURICE RICHARD

TIM HORTON
MAPLE LEAFS — DEFENSE

28 — Syl Apps — OLD TIME GREAT

COMEBACK

Some players suffer such devastating injuries or illnesses that it seems their careers are surely over. Others appear too brittle or past their primes to be effective anymore. Some players are eliminated because they haven't found their comfort levels. On occasion, an entire team can be dismissed. However, just when it seems to be hopeless, some players and teams find a way to bounce back and do something special. In this chapter, we'll focus on those who were left for last and had to find a way to make a "Comeback."

Phil Kessel
1942 Maple Leafs
Tim Horton ✓
Bernie Parent
Gordie Howe
Maurice Richard
Rod Gilbert
Ted Green
Howie Meeker
Teemu Selanne
Robyn Regehr
Patrice Bergeron

PHIL KESSEL

BORN: MADISON, WISCONSIN

NHL SEASONS: 2006–07 TO PRESENT

DEFINING MOMENT: OCTOBER 18, 2008

Cancer is a dreaded disease that strikes across all sections of society. When a young person is diagnosed, it stings all the more. It was in December 2006 that Phil Kessel received the dreaded news. He was just 19 years old and on the verge of an NHL career.

Kessel is a tremendous skater who also happens to be a very skilled hockey player. It's these attributes that have put him under the spotlight since he was 15. During 2002, he nearly led his bantam team to a U.S. national championship, and by 2005, he had led the American team to a gold medal in the under-18 World Hockey Championships. He was named the MVP of that tournament by leading all scorers (16 points, including 9 goals in just 6 games), and was soon being compared to the likes of Sidney Crosby. Dubbed "Phil the Thrill," Kessel went on to play one year with the University of Minnesota (18 goals and 51 points in 39 games), but his performance declined somewhat when he played for the U.S. world junior championship team and scored just one goal. He became draft eligible in 2006 and was selected fifth overall by the Boston Bruins. He now had something to prove.

In the 2006–07 season, Kessel played in 70 games (scoring 11 goals and 29 points). His performance was considered pretty remarkable because of his battle with cancer. Incredibly, he missed just 11 games before he was back in action. His defensive skills were lacking somewhat, but his great speed created many chances at the other end of the ice.

Kessel has never lacked for confidence and has shown a willingness to learn new skills that will make him a better player. He came back the next season to score 19 goals in 82 games (he did not miss a single contest), but found himself benched when the playoffs started. Kessel missed the first three games of the series against Montreal but was put back in for the fifth game. He scored a goal in that game and then added two more in the next contest. If there was any message being sent to Kessel by the Boston coaches, he had certainly received it loud and clear. Although the Bruins lost the series in seven games, Kessel's return from that dreaded disease was easily the story of the playoffs.

Kessel came to the Bruins training camp for the 2008–09 season with a clean bill of health and a desire to be a difference maker. There was no longer any doubt about his status in the Boston line-up because he was put on a line with Marc Savard and left winger Milan Lucic, a trio that can play the game in any fashion. Kessel continued to develop his great offensive skills and made many a defender look silly throughout the '08–'09 campaign. He simply blew by any defenseman who showed the slightest hesitation, or whipped a puck through a defender's legs before the goalie had a chance to react.

Throughout the '08–'09 season, Kessel showed that he was both physically and mentally able to perform at the high level expected of him. One shining example occurred on October 18, 2008, in a game against the Ottawa Senators in which Kessel scored twice and added one assist in a 4-2 Boston victory. Kessel's first goal came off a pass from Savard, which he one-timed into the Ottawa net. His second tally came off a scramble in front of the Senators net when he managed to pick up a loose puck and fire it home. A couple of months later, Kessel had a similar game against Toronto in which he scored twice and added one assist. His second goal, a high rising shot in the slot that went over the shoulder of Toronto goalie Curtis Joseph, was the 100th of his young career. The Bruins were one of the NHL's best teams in '08–'09 and Kessel was a big part of it, finishing the year with 33 goals despite missing five games with mononucleosis. He also had an 18-point game streak between November 13 and December 21, 2008, recording 14 goals and 14 assists over that timeframe.

"I'm shooting more to score than I did in the past two years," Kessel said during the '08–'09 season. "I'm firing the puck harder, getting back to how I used to think the game... Third year in the league, I guess you learn more about yourself. Life changes quick. That's what I've learned the most. Any given day, any second, life can change," he concluded as he snapped his fingers. Kessel has battled through very serious sickness and has also dealt with incredibly high expectation levels. Each time, he has come back stronger and more determined to succeed. His attitude will serve him well and ensure a long career in the NHL.

Phil Kessel was traded to the Toronto Maple Leafs prior to the 2009–10 season and scored 30 goals in 70 games that year. In 2010–11, Kessel scored 32 goals and totaled 64 points, nearly helping the Leafs get back to the playoffs. He has dealt well with playing in the Toronto pressure cooker and is expected to continue to be the goal-scoring sniper the Maple Leafs have lacked for many years.

TORONTO MAPLE LEAFS
1942 STANLEY CUP PLAYOFFS
DEFINING MOMENT: APRIL 18, 1942

Although World War II was raging, the National Hockey League decided to continue operating with a 48-game regular-season schedule for the 1941–42 season. One of the major events of the War took place early in the hockey season when Pearl Harbor was bombed, forcing the United States into the war. Canada had been at war for two years already, with many NHL players encouraged to enlist in the Canadian Armed Services. It was a time when people needed diversions from war, and with hockey the national pastime, there was no stopping the NHL from completing the regular season and playoffs. By the time the playoffs were over, the Toronto Maple Leafs had provided one of the greatest comebacks in sports history—one that has never been matched since.

The NHL featured seven teams in the '41–'42 season—the original six, plus the Brooklyn Americans. Six of the teams made the playoffs. The New York Rangers finished in first place with 60 points (and 29 wins), followed by the Maple Leafs who had 57 (with 27 victories). In a strange system set up by the league, the first- and second-place teams played each other in an opening round best-of-seven, with the winner gaining a spot in the Stanley Cup finals. The other four teams played a best-of-three series until a victor emerged. The Leafs took the Rangers in six games, while the fifth-place Detroit Red Wings emerged as their opponents for the Cup. The Red Wings were generally considered a mediocre club (posting a 19-25-4 record during the season) that managed to get hot at the right time. The Leafs, on the other hand, included league all-stars such as Syl Apps, Gordie Drillon, Wilfred "Bucko" McDonald, and goalie Walter "Turk" Broda. The Leafs were supposed to win the series rather easily, but the Red Wings had other ideas. Detroit had a game plan to stifle the Leafs attack (especially Drillon's) even while showcasing a strong team defense—and for a while, it worked perfectly.

The series opened in Toronto. Detroit came away with a 3-2 win as Don Grosso and Sid Abel notched Red Wing goals. Just before the series started, Detroit general manager and coach Jack Adams said, "We may not have the greatest hockey club in the world but we're loaded with fighting heart and if there's anything that wins championships it's just that." No one was taking Adams too seriously, but when the Red Wings won the second game by a 4-3 count (with Grosso scoring twice more), they suddenly had everyone's attention. The stunned Leafs had lost two games at home, and many of their stars had done nothing. They also lost the first game in Detroit in rather convincing style by a 5-2 score (with Red Wing defenseman Eddie Bush scoring one goal and assisting on the four others). The Leafs now faced a three-games-to-none series deficit. It looked like the Toronto side was done, with the next game scheduled for the Olympia in Detroit.

Mostly everyone had written the Leafs off, with newspapers being harsh in their commentary. The *Toronto Star* reported that Toronto was "a beaten team, mentally, after the last contest (the third game of the series) and coach Hap Day has the seemingly hopeless task of attempting to rally them." But Day had a plan, and he did not hesitate to take extraordinary measures to complete it. First, he benched the team's leading goal scorer, Drillon. He then took defenseman MacDonald out of the lineup. In their place, he inserted industrious forward Don Metz, while Ernie Dickens was added to the blueline brigade. Toronto also added 18-year-old forward Gaye Stewart to its roster, hoping that some youth might revitalize its fortunes. Day told his team, "Don't worry about those (games) behind you and those a few days ahead. The big one is the one coming up which is tonight." If the Leafs needed any more inspiration, a young 14-year-old girl named Doris Klein wrote an impassioned letter to her Toronto hockey heroes, imploring them not to give up and that she would pray for them. Day is said to have read the letter to his team, who responded with a "we'll win this game for her" vow.

At first, it looked like the Leafs were doomed with the red-hot Red Wings scoring the first two goals of the game early in the second period. The Leafs tied the game before the middle frame was over and then outscored Detroit 2-1 (including a key goal by captain Apps) in the period to win the game 4-3. Detroit was very upset with the officials after the game, and a wild brawl ensued between Detroit players, their coach, and referee Mel Harwood. Adams was seen throwing punches at Harwood and some disgruntled Detroit fans attempted to help him. It took rink attendants and the police to restore order. Harwood needed a security escort to get out of the Olympia in one piece. The Red Wings coach was suspended for the rest of the series and the rattled Detroit team came back to Toronto for the fifth game. The Leafs romped to a 9-3 win and then won once again in Detroit, a 3-0 victory behind a great performance by Broda.

The seventh game was played at Maple Leaf Gardens on Saturday night, April 18, 1942, with the entire country enthralled with the Toronto comeback that served as a relief from the horrible headlines of war. The largest crowd ever to see a game in Canada (16,218, with more fans in standing room) jammed the Gardens, only to see Detroit take a 1-0 lead in the second period. But the Leafs had overcome too much adversity to give up now. Dave "Sweeney" Schriner tied the game in the third, and then little Pete Langelle scored the winner for the Leafs with a little over 11 minutes to play. Schriner added another Toronto goal by beating Detroit goalie Johnny Mowers late in the game for a 3-1 final score.

The magnificent Maple Leafs effort completed the greatest comeback of all time.

Only two other teams (the 1975 New York Islanders and the 2010 Philadelphia Flyers) have ever come back from being down three games to none in a best-of-seven playoff series, but none have repeated what the 1942 Leafs accomplished in a Stanley Cup finals series.

TIM HORTON
BORN: COCHRANE, ONTARIO
NHL SEASONS: 1949–50 TO 1973–74
DEFINING MOMENT: 1962 STANLEY CUP FINALS

When the Toronto Maple Leafs recruited Tim Horton and assigned him to their junior development team at St. Michael's College, they had great expectations for the sturdy defenseman. Powerfully built at 5'10" and 185 pounds, Horton was one of the strongest recruits the Leafs had under their control. The Leafs were looking to rebuild their team in the early Fifties after the great years of the Forties. After a two-year stint at St. Mike's, Horton was sent to the Leafs main farm team in Pittsburgh to learn the pro game. He played three full seasons for the Hornets and was finally promoted to the Leafs for good starting in the 1952–53 season. He quickly established himself as a hard-hitting defenseman who was not afraid to carry the puck. Horton also had a low, hard shot, which he unleashed from the point. The hard-rock defender also showed an ability to set up goals from his position on the blueline. After his second season, Horton was named to the NHL's second all-star team. He and other young Leaf recruits looked to get Toronto back to contention—but there were obstacles to overcome.

Late in the 1954–55 season, Horton suffered very serious injuries that nearly ended his career. During a game against the New York Rangers on March 12, 1955, Bill Gadsby hit the Leaf defender with a devastating bodycheck. The Ranger blueliner caught Horton with his head down as he was carrying the puck up the ice at full speed. It was, by all accounts, a clean check, but Horton's leg buckled underneath him, snapping it right above the ankle. The ghastly sound was heard all through Maple Leaf Gardens. Gadsby's devastating check also broke Horton's jaw. The Leaf ended up in hospital for an entire month and his jaw was wired shut. His leg was in a full cast until July, and when the cast came off, Horton's leg looked terrible. As determined as Horton was to return, even he had doubts he could make it all the way back. But soon, he was working to get his leg into proper condition (it took as much as two years to make a complete recovery), making it into half the games of the 1955–56 season. It is interesting to note that Leafs management cut Horton's salary while he recovered and they nearly traded him away as well (Montreal and Boston were reportedly interested).

The Leafs were not a very good team in the mid-to-late Fifties as their rebuilding plan sputtered. Four different coaches were tried, but with little success. Horton was not the favorite of one coach, Billy Reay, who tried to curtail his puck-rushing style. But when George "Punch" Imlach became the bench boss early in the 1958–59 season, one of the first things he did was tell Horton to play *his* game. "I like to carry the puck, have a good look before I pass it. Imlach instructed me to do so. Now I am looking forward to every shift on the ice instead of worrying about the possibility of making mistakes."

The Leafs made a remarkable run to a playoff spot to end the '58–'59 season (secured by winning the last game of the season) and would become contenders for the next 10 years. Toronto made it to the Cup finals in '59 and '60, but lost both times. Their next chance at the championship came after the 1961–62 season, and Horton was determined to make sure the Leafs were going to win their first Cup since 1951.

Toronto got past a pesky New York Rangers club in six games during the '62 semi-finals and then faced defending champions Blackhawks in the finals. The Leafs took the first two games at home, but the Hawks quickly evened the series. Horton then took over the fifth game, setting up three Leaf goals, with Toronto storming back to win 8-4. The Leafs were now one game away from the Cup.

It was a raucous crowd that greeted the Leafs and Blackhawks at the Chicago Stadium the night of April 22, 1962. But the game went 0-0 into the third. Toronto had outplayed the home team by a good margin, but could not score. Then Bobby Hull intercepted an errant Leaf pass and put one past goalie Don Simmons to give the Blackhawks a 1-0 lead. The crowd went wild, littering the ice with all sorts of debris. This break gave the Leafs a chance to recover. Toronto then quickly tied the score, which was followed by a Chicago minor penalty. Horton then took the puck up the ice and made two sharp passes before Dick Duff scored the winner. It was Horton's 16th point (3G, 13A) of the playoffs—a remarkable total for a defenseman in that era. The Leafs held on to a 2-1 lead and Horton's 11-year wait for a championship was finally over.

Horton would go on to win three more Stanley Cups with the Leafs—a very impressive record for a player who came back from near career-ending injuries to become one of the best defensemen of all time.

Tim Horton wore glasses off the ice and, until he started using

contact lens, had to rely on his excellent hockey instincts to get by on the ice. He was elected to the Hockey Hall of Fame in 1977.

BERNIE PARENT
BORN: MONTREAL, QUEBEC
NHL SEASONS: 1965–66 TO 1978–79
DEFINING MOMENT: MAY 19, 1974

Most hockey fans remember goaltender Bernie Parent as a Philadelphia Flyer, but he really began his NHL career with the Boston Bruins. Parent had been a very good goalie for the Niagara Falls Flyers junior team, a club sponsored by the Bruins in the days of the Original Six. The Flyers had won the coveted Memorial Cup in 1965, backstopped by the 5'10", 180-pound Parent who took them all the way to the Canadian junior championship with a total of 16 wins in the playoffs. At the young age of 20, Parent was thrust into the NHL with a very poor Boston team that would win just 21 games in the regular season (with Parent posting an 11-20-3 record). The next season saw the Bruins turn to another young goalie in Gerry Cheevers. That move forced Parent to play part of the 1966–67 season in the minors with Oklahoma City. As the NHL expanded to 12 teams for the 1967–68 campaign, the Bruins decided to hold on to Cheevers and veteran Eddie Johnston, leaving Parent available in the expansion draft. He was snapped up by the Philadelphia Flyers.

Parent immediately fell in love with his new city and team, posting a 16-17-5 record in his first year there (Philadelphia finished in first place in the West Division in their initial year). For the next three and a half seasons, Parent and Doug Favell shared netminding duties, but the team was not really improving, especially in the playoffs. So management decided to help out star center Bobby Clarke by acquiring Rick MacLeish to anchor the second line. However, the Flyers were forced to deal Parent to the Toronto Maple Leafs to complete the deal. Though shocked and hurt, Parent initially liked playing pro hockey in Canada. But when a contract could not be worked out with the Leafs, he chose a less conventional route to get more money—the WHL. Toronto foolishly let Parent get away for a few dollars more and lost one the best young prospects in all of hockey.

Parent signed on with the World Hockey Association for the 1972–73 season. The contract was worth $120,000 a year—a good amount of money for the times. He played in the Philadelphia Blazers, which put him back in his favorite city. But the team had trouble finding fans. It was soon out of money and eventually stopped paying Parent, even though he had won 33 games during the season. Parent, therefore, walked out on his team during the playoffs (after appearing in one post-season contest) and declared himself a free agent for the following year.

Parent's career had come to a crossroads and he was hopeful the Flyers might want him back despite his now-besmirched reputation in "the City of Brotherly Love." At the time, Parent was very concerned about his future, but the Flyers were actually quite pleased at the thought of having him back. A deal was completed with the Leafs to get his NHL rights, and he was soon back in the orange-and-black uniform he so admired.

In the first game of the season, Parent posted a 2-0 shutout at home against his former Toronto mates. He wouldn't look back and would go on to win a league-best 47 games while also grabbing a share of the Vezina Trophy (with Tony Esposito of Chicago).

Parent's comeback would truly be complete if he and the Flyers could do something significant in the playoffs.

The Flyers knocked off the Atlanta Flames in the opening round and just got past the New York Rangers in a grueling seven-game series in the next round. That sent the Flyers to their first appearance in the Stanley Cup finals—although it meant facing Bobby Orr and the Boston Bruins. A late goal by Orr won the Bruins the first game, but an overtime marker by Clarke evened the series. Philadelphia won the next two at home before Orr's brilliance in the fifth game forced the series back to Philadelphia on May 19, 1974. Parent would take center stage.

The Bruins stormed out of the gate, applying pressure early with 16 shots on net, but Parent was equal to the task, turning back every attempt. He made his most spectacular save against Boston's Gregg Sheppard in the Bruins early assault. The Flyers scored late in the first period on a goal (ironically enough) by MacLeish and then hung on to the slim lead the rest of the way. Boston's last good chance came from winger Ken Hodge, but Parent turned it away with his pad and stick. In all, Parent had a tremendous game, stopping 30 Bruin shots to earn the shutout and clinch the Cup for Philadelphia.

"A year ago at this time I was between leagues. I didn't know where I was or where I was going...this is the greatest," Parent said as he was awarded the Conn Smythe Trophy as the best playoff performer. "This is a team thing all the way. The Smythe Trophy, the Vezina should be for the whole team not just for me," Parent stated in a tribute to his teammates.

To prove it was no fluke, Parent won another Cup in 1975, taking both the Vezina and the Conn Smythe trophies once again. Not a bad comeback for someone who was not sure he would play in the NHL again!

Bernie Parent was elected to the Hall of Fame in 1984.

GORDIE HOWE
BORN: FLORAL, SASKATCHEWAN
NHL SEASONS: 1946–47 TO 1979–80
DEFINING MOMENT: APRIL 14, 1955

On the night of March 28, 1950, the Detroit Red Wings were hosting the Toronto Maple Leafs in the first game of their semi-final series. The Leafs were three-time defending Stanley Cup champions and were up 3-0 in the contest. Toronto captain Ted Kennedy started a rush up the ice and Detroit right winger Gordie Howe came hard at the Leaf center. Kennedy noticed Howe at the last second and was able to swerve to avoid the hit. Howe was unable to stop and crashed into the boards with a hard, sickening thud. Blood appeared on the ice and the crowd at the Detroit Olympia fell silent. A stretcher was called for, and Howe was removed by the Detroit trainers. After a quick stop in the Detroit dressing room, the Red Wings team doctor had Howe rushed to the hospital.

Dr. Frederic Schreiber, a renowned brain surgeon, was called upon to attend to Howe. Noting that there was increased swelling on Howe's brain, Schreiber performed surgery at 1 a.m. The procedure lasted 90 minutes. The doctor was able to drain some fluid from Howe's brain while muscle tissue absorbed more of the unwanted liquid. The entire Detroit team was up all night awaiting word on their teammate's condition, and many radio stations (including those in Detroit and others all across Canada) stayed on longer than normal to give updates on Howe's condition. Fortunately, the operation was deemed successful as pressure on Howe's brain subsided and his condition, while still very serious, was reduced from critical. The next day, the Red Wings provided an official update on Howe's status: he was recovering very nicely and while he could not return to the playoffs (the Red Wings would go on to win the Stanley Cup in '50), he should be good to start the next year, the 1950–51 season.

Howe was just becoming a dominating player when he suffered these life-threatening injuries and, not unjustly, many wondered if he would ever be the same player. In fact, he wasn't—he was even better: Howe would lead the NHL in goals and points for the next three consecutive seasons to help the Red Wings become the NHL's best team.

Howe played a powerful, physical game where he dominated with his size, toughness, and nice scoring touch around the net. In 1952–53, he scored a career-high 49 goals and the 1953–54 season saw him notch his fourth straight Art Ross Trophy with 81 points, including a league-best 48 assists. While Howe had enjoyed good playoffs previously (with Detroit taking the Cup in '52 and '54), his greatest post-season contribution came in the 1955 playoffs.

In '54–'55, the Red Wings won 47 out of 70 games, recording 95 points during the regular season and finishing in first place. They easily swept aside the Maple Leafs in the first round of the playoffs in four games. However, another meeting with arch-rival Montreal in the finals proved to be much more difficult, even though Canadiens superstar Maurice Richard was unable to play due to a long suspension imposed by the NHL. The series opened in Detroit, and the Red Wings established the upper hand with two-straight wins. Montreal was hardly out of it though, and won the next two at home. Detroit returned home to take the all-important fifth game with a decisive 5-1 victory, led by Howe's superb three-goal effort. Montreal would not quit and won the next game at home by a 6-3 count, setting up a Game 7 showdown in Detroit on April 14, 1955.

Detroit was solid at home, not having lost at the Olympia since December 19 of that season. It was a tight game until Detroit's

Alex Delvecchio scored the opener at 7:12 of the second period before 15,541 excited fans. The game-winning goal was scored by none other than Howe, who notched his 20th point (nine of them goals) of the playoffs, and in so doing, set an NHL record (now surpassed) for most points in the post-season. Howe re-directed Marcel Pronovost's shot past Montreal netminder Jacques Plante to make the score 2-0 with only 11 seconds to play in the second stanza. Detroit made it 3-0 before Montreal finally got one back, but it was too little and too late for the Montreal side as the Red Wings took their second consecutive championship with the 3-1 win.

Years later Howe reflected on the 1954–55 season and playoffs. "It was our seventh straight first place finish, a feat not duplicated before or since—and something that I will always be proud of—but it would be our last for some time (until the 1964–65 season). Next to the '52 Cup—which I consider my first because I was injured in '50—that '55 Cup is one of my best memories because I scored the (Stanley Cup) winner."

It was a record-setting performance from a player who, five years earlier, had nearly lost his life on the ice! Winning the championship made Howe's comeback from the brink of death a complete triumph.

Gordie Howe was elected to the Hall of Fame in 1972.

MAURICE "ROCKET" RICHARD
BORN: MONTREAL, QUEBEC
NHL SEASONS: 1942–43 TO 1959–60
DEFINING MOMENT: DECEMBER 28, 1944

When Maurice Richard attended his first NHL training camp, he was told by Montreal coach Dick Irvin that he would not be playing in one pre-season game. The fiery, black-haired Richard immediately displayed his famous temper by slamming the door shut as he left the arena in a rage. It would not be the last time the Habs would see an enraged Richard. It was, in fact, his great passion for the game that helped him come back from possible disaster.

Richard grew up in the north end of Montreal as a fan of the Canadiens and admired players like Howie Morenz and Hector "Toe" Blake (who would later become a teammate). He spent most of his time playing hockey but did not really think he was going to be a professional player. However, he had a natural instinct to score goals and kept playing on higher-level teams as he got older. When he played junior hockey for the Verdun Maple Leafs, Richard's play caught the attention of the Canadiens, who would invite him to play in the Quebec Senior Hockey League. Up until that time, young Maurice had experienced little or no difficulty playing hockey. But this was soon about to change and cause him to have great doubts about his future in the game.

Richard's first injury came when he and another player fell together, with Richard sliding into the boards at full speed. He met the boards with a thud and cracked an ankle. "The pain was terrible and I knew right then and there that I'd be out the rest of the season," Richard recalled. Incredibly, he was able to return for the playoffs, which helped ease, his mind, at least temporarily. He was playing for the Senior Habs the next season and was beginning to think a pro career was a possibility when he broke his wrist as he was squeezed on a play near the net. The sound of bones cracking, yet again, sickened Richard and put more concerns into his mind. "I began asking myself whether this was worth all the pain and frustration," Richard said.

Luckily for Richard, he was able to find work as a machinist as World War II raged on in Europe. This job took a little bit of the pressure off. Richard was already a married man, so having steady work made life easier—but he was in no way ready to give up on hockey. The Canadiens invited him to their training camp for the 1942–43 season as they tried to ice a team that had so many of their regular players serving overseas. Having broken an ankle and wrist in just two years of pro hockey, Richard knew he was hardly a sure thing. "I was rapidly developing an image of an injury-prone athlete, the kind major league scouts usually ignore." He made the team despite not understanding much of what Montreal coach Dick Irvin was saying (Richard spoke virtually no English at this point), but in his first 16 games, he had five goals and six assists. Then disaster struck again: in a game against Boston, a defenseman body-checked him heavily and then fell on top of Richard. His ankle snapped one more time. Soon afterward, Montreal newspaper journalists were writing that the right winger was far too brittle to play in the National Hockey League. However, they did not yet understand Richard's burning desire to win. It was a personal crusade each and every time he laced up his skates.

Still, it was a bleak time for Richard who, at this point, believed his playing career might be over. There was even talk that the Canadiens might trade him (since the New York Rangers showed an interest). However, Richard returned to the ice for the 1943–44 season. He would score 32 goals in 46 games. He was also outstanding in the playoffs with 12 goals (including 5 in one game against Toronto) and 17 points in just 9 games as Montreal won the Stanley Cup. To prove that the performance was no fluke, Richard had an outstanding year in 1944–45, with his best night of that season coming on December 28, 1944, against the Red Wings.

Richard spent game day moving his family into a new home, which involved hauling furniture up and down the stairs all day long. He showed up to the rink tired and complained of a sore back. But a good massage seemed to do the trick. He hit the ice flying, easily living up to his nickname of "the Rocket." He was unstoppable on this night and made life miserable for young Detroit goalie Harry Lumley (who would go on to have a Hall of Fame career). Richard opened the scoring after just 1:07 of play and then assisted on a goal by Blake before the first period was over.

As the second period began, Richard scored his second goal at the 1:19 mark, followed by another just eight seconds later! After setting up teammate Elmer Lach for a goal, the Rocket was back at Lumley's doorstep with another shot that found the back of the net. The third period saw Richard score his fifth goal with his best effort of the game. He started off by breaking up a Detroit rush at his own blueline, then taking the puck all the way down the ice, deking Lumley out of position before putting the puck into an empty net. Another assist capped off his record-setting eight-point night (seven points was the previous NHL record). Richard would go on to score 50 goals (the first NHL player to do so) in 50 games (the length of the regular season) during that '44–'45 campaign. His performance forever erased any doubts that he could not come back from injuries; in fact, he went on to become the most beloved player in the history of the Montreal Canadiens.

Maurice Richard won 10 Stanley Cups with Montreal and scored 544 career goals. He was elected to the Hockey Hall of Fame in 1961.

ROD GILBERT
BORN: MONTREAL, QUEBEC
NHL SEASONS: 1960–61 TO 1977–78
**DEFINING MOMENTS: APRIL 3, 1962, FEBRUARY 24, 1968
& APRIL 23, 1972**

The New York Rangers have won only four Stanley Cups (only one since 1940) in team history and do not have many Hall of Fame players to show for their futility. But there's one Ranger from the past who had a stellar Hall of Fame career: right winger Rod Gilbert. And if Gilbert had not shown the courage and determination to come back from debilitating injuries and near death, it would have been one less Blueshirt in the hockey shrine.

The Rangers were looking forward to having the youngster Gilbert join their team after he had enjoyed a brilliant junior career. They had discovered the 5'9", 180-pound right winger—one of the very few French-Canadian players to escape the clutches of the Montreal Canadiens—in his native province of Quebec (The Canadiens were Gilbert's favorite team growing up). He was assigned to play junior hockey in Guelph, Ontario, and was part of a Memorial Cup–winning team in 1960. He also led the OHA in scoring with 103 points the next season.

The New York club had rebuilt their team with many graduates of their junior program, and Gilbert looked ready to add his name to an impressive list of Rangers. But in his last junior game of the year, disaster struck. He was skating in on a rush, and when he stepped over debris that had been thrown onto the ice by fans, he lost control and crashed heavily into the end boards. Gilbert could not feel his legs and was told later in hospital that he had suffered a broken vertebra in his back. The terrified youngster had to face a spinal fusion procedure (done at the Mayo Clinic) in which a bone from his leg was moved to his back to tie vertebra together. To say his hockey career was in jeopardy at this point would be a great understatement.

The recovery did not go well as a blood clot developed in his leg. Very concerned doctors began hinting that they might have to amputate it. Gilbert worried every minute, but miraculously, his leg began to recover, as did the rest of his body. He was back playing in that 1961–62 season (after missing about half a season), and then got called up to the Rangers for the playoffs.

He acquitted himself very well while taking a regular turn with the big club. And he scored his first NHL goal on April 3, 1962, against Johnny Bower of Toronto in the semi-final series. "I danced around on the ice like a madman and then dived into the net to retrieve the puck. I wanted to save it for my collection, so I skated with it to the Ranger bench and handed it to our trainer, Frank Paice," Gilbert recalled of his first goal. The Rangers did not win the playoff series, but Gilbert now had the confidence he could play in the big league.

Gilbert scored 11 times in his first full season but then had 24- and 25-goal seasons to establish himself as an NHL sniper. However, part way through the 1965–66 season, Gilbert had to go back and have another operation because the graft in his back had loosened. Gilbert nearly died after this second operation, but a doctor was able to restart his heart. He then once again had to go through a lengthy and painful rehabilitation process.

He came back to the Rangers at the start of the next season, fit and ready to go. He scored 28 goals in just 64 games. The 1967–68 season saw Gilbert make good use of his strong shot to connect for 29 goals, with the best night of this lucky man's tremendous career coming on February 24, 1968, in his hometown of Montreal.

Gilbert and his teammates had been beaten rather badly by the Canadiens in New York just a few days earlier and were looking for revenge during this Saturday-night contest. If there was a time and a place to shine, it had to be in the Montreal Forum. By the time the game was over, Gilbert had beaten Rogie Vachon for four goals, with the Rangers winning by a 6-1 margin.

Gilbert's first goal came on a power play when he was fed the puck right in the slot and whipped home a drive to give New York a 2-1 lead in the first period. His next goal came on a two-on-one break as he slapped in a pass from Jean Ratelle. A slap shot from about 50 feet out fooled Vachon again for the third goal of the opening period. Gilbert's final goal came after he knocked in a Ratelle rebound. In total, Gilbert had fired 16 shots on goal during the contest, which had the media searching the record books.

"My linemates (Ratelle and Camille Henry) were feeding me," Gilbert told reporters after the game as he posed for pictures, "and I just kept shooting. I'll have to read about it in the papers before I believe it really happened. Don't forget we were bombed by the Canadiens just last Wednesday by a score of 7-2, so it was nice to come in here and sort of give it back to them on their own ice."

Gilbert had a 30-goal season in 1970–71, but the next season was his best—he scored 43 times. He was also very good in the '72 playoffs in which the Rangers finally broke through to make it to the Stanley Cup finals for the first time since 1950. Gilbert had a four-point game (one goal, three assists) as the Rangers eliminated the Chicago Blackhawks on the night of April 23, 1972, in the second round of the playoffs, with a four game sweep. New York coach Emile Francis paid tribute to Gilbert after the game saying, "They all played well and the line of Rod Gilbert, Bobby Rousseau, and Vic Hadfield broke loose to lead us in scoring." The Rangers all believed they could win the Stanley Cup, but Boston, led by Bobby Orr, proved to be too much. The series marked the only time Gilbert (who had seven points in six games versus Boston) played in the finals.

Gilbert finished with 406 career goals—all of them scored as a New York Ranger. And he was the first player in team history to have his sweater (number 7) retired. It was a just reward for all the determination required to come back from such potentially devastating injuries.

Rod Gilbert was elected to the Hall of Fame in 1982.

TED GREEN
BORN: ERIKSDALE, MANITOBA
NHL SEASONS: 1960–61 TO 1971–72
DEFINING MOMENT: FEBRUARY 25, 1971

It was one of the worst incidents in the history of the National Hockey League. The Boston Bruins were playing the St. Louis Blues in a pre-season game in Ottawa the night of September 21, 1969. Late in the first period, Blues forward Wayne Maki speared Bruins defenseman Ted Green in the mid-section after the Boston player had shoved him near the net. Green swung with his stick and struck Maki a blow up in the shoulder area, which appeared to stagger the Blues player. Maki then raised his stick and swung it vigorously, striking Green in the head with an ugly thwacking sound that sent him to the ice. Green's head was twitching uncontrollably until he was helped off the ice. The results of tests at a local hospital revealed a compound skull fracture, a very serious injury. Good work by the doctors got Green repaired quickly (the operation took more than two hours) and he was not in mortal danger initially.

However, due to the nature of Green's injury, there was always the possibility of brain hemorrhage. Eventually, it happened, and Green once again had to undergo an emergency operation. This time, his whole left side was paralyzed. The possibility of him dying was now very real. But Dr. Michael Richard again worked brilliantly to save the patient. It was still feared he might not recover from paralysis, but through hard work and great determination, Green eventually returned to normal. A steel plate was inserted into his scalp as the final procedure to close the physical wounds of this incident, yet Green was left to deal with the mental and emotional issues from one of hockey's ugliest episodes. Green missed out on the Bruins' 1970 Stanley Cup win, but he was going to try and return to hockey for the 1970–71 season.

It was ironic that Green would be out of the lineup just as the Bruins became champions. He had been with the Boston club since 1960–61 and had experienced many lows playing for a mostly terrible team. Green, Ed Westfall, Eddie Johnston, and Johnny Bucyk had all been with the Bruins for many losing seasons and were now happy to be with a winning club that was changed the moment Bobby Orr arrived on the scene. The sad-sack Bruins became the "Big, Bad, Bruins" and nobody symbolized the Bruins toughness more than the man they once called "Terrible Teddy Green." He came to the Bruins after they plucked him out of the Montreal organization, and he quickly developed a tough guy reputation in the minors (including two lengthy suspensions). He was a regular with Boston starting in 1961–62 but struggled with his skating at first. However, he showed the Bruins he was a tough competitor. In fact, recording over 100 penalty minutes was rather easy for the 5'11" 185-pound blueliner since he was always quite willing to drop the gloves and fight. He also had a bit of a reputation for using his stick, and it was rather cruel irony that the stick of an opponent would cause such damage years later. But Green also showed he could play the game, and in 1968–69, he was named to the NHL's second all-star team with 8 goals, 38 assists, and 99 penalty minutes that season. He was now among the NHL elite.

After the injury, Green managed to get into 54 games for the powerful Bruins in '70–'71. He was also able to keep up with his fast-moving teammates—especially on the night of February 25, 1971, when he proved to himself that Ted Green was really back.

The Bruins were hosting the Vancouver Canucks, who they defeated 8-3 behind a record-setting splurge in the third. The Canucks held the Bruins to a 2-2 tie after two periods, but Bucyk scored before the five-minute mark of the third to get Boston ahead. Just 12 seconds later, Westfall scored his 20th of the year and then, after taking a pass from Derek Sanderson, Green let a shot go that beat Vancouver goalie Dunc Wilson over the shoulder on the far side. Green let his drive go just as he crossed the blueline eight seconds after Westfall's tally. Three goals in 20 seconds established a new NHL team mark for fastest three goals (beating the mark first set by Chicago in 1952 by one second).

"From late February on, I was much more myself," Green recalled about his comeback. "At first, I wasn't hitting guys, partly because I didn't think I was ready for it and partly because I didn't feel like hitting anyone. I purposely avoided contact. Later, however, I started giving good, clean body checks, a defenseman's stock-in-trade." As for his first on-ice meeting with Maki, Green refused to speak to his opponent but stated, "The Maki episode actually started when he speared me with his stick and I retaliated with mine. Except I don't think I shall ever do so again. I realize now, more than anyone else in the NHL, what can happen." From 1970 on, Green never came close to the 100-penalty-minute mark ever again.

Green was used less and less by the Bruins, but his last game in a Boston uniform saw the team win the Stanley Cup for the second time in three years when they beat the Rangers right in New York's Madison Square Garden on May 11, 1972. Green then jumped to the new league the following season and captained the New England Whalers at the first WHA championship. He also won two WHA titles with Winnipeg before he retired in 1979.

Green's impressive return to the playing ranks of professional hockey was amazing, considering he nearly did not survive that infamous night back in 1969.

Ted Green became an assistant coach with the Edmonton Oilers and was a part of five Stanley Cup wins between 1984 and 1990.

HOWIE MEEKER
BORN: KITCHENER, ONTARIO
NHL SEASONS: 1946–47 TO 1953–54
DEFINING MOMENT: JANUARY 8, 1947

When Howie Meeker entered the military during World War II, it meant he would go to England and be away from playing hockey for the next two seasons. While he was in training, a grenade exploded right at his feet and did extensive damage to his legs. Meeker's concerns were made even worse as gangrene set in because of all the metal now inside his body. He was also in great pain as he lay in hospital for the next eight weeks.

While in hospital, Meeker took the time to write Toronto coach Hap Day, suggesting that his name be taken off the team's list. "I

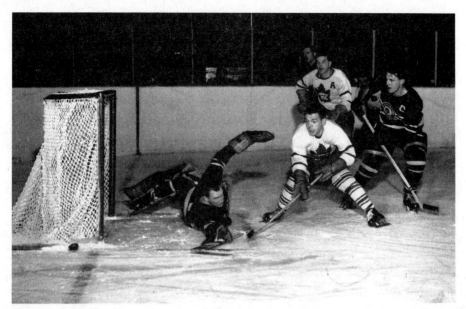

Al Rollins, Howie Meeker, Bill Gadsby, c1954. Photo credit: Imperial Oil-Turofsky/Hockey Hall of Fame

didn't think I'd be playing hockey any more. I didn't think I'd be doing much of anything for a while," Meeker recalled. However, the doctors who attended to him had done a good job and his injuries were not as catastrophic as was first believed. As time went on, Meeker became very determined to get better. He had strong legs and soon found himself on the road to recovery. He stayed in Europe (mostly in England) and took a physical education course that also helped him get back into good shape. Meeker's tour of duty came to an end in late 1945, and he came home a better and more disciplined person.

Meeker had shown promise as a teenager, before the injury. He had a pretty good year as a 16-year old with the hometown Kitchener Greenshirts, scoring 13 times in just 9 games during the 1941–42 season. The next year saw him play junior B in Stratford, Ontario, where he scored 29 goals in just 13 contests. The next season still found him in Stratford but now he was playing junior A and the Leafs were keeping an eye on this developing right winger (he had 6 goals in 6 games during the 1942–43 season). One day,

Meeker was invited to practice with the Leafs, and he acquitted himself very well. But then came the war.

He was not sure what to expect from a hockey point of view upon his return, although he had managed to play a little hockey while he was in Europe. He played senior hockey in Stratford and the Maple Leafs took note of his fine performance (eight goals and 13 points in just seven games). Meeker then got a phone call from Leafs owner and manager Conn Smythe—Toronto wanted to get the gritty winger under contract. Smythe had also been seriously wounded in World War II and liked Meeker's determination and ability to recover. However Smythe balked at Meeker's money demands. Not having much bargaining power pretty much forced the hockey player to take what Smythe offered ($4,500 a year for two seasons, plus a $1,000 signing bonus). Smythe did, however, give Meeker an extra $1,000 when he found out the 5'9" 165-pound winger was about to get married!

Having made it this far back, Meeker was not going to let anything stop him from making the team for the 1946–47 season. "Nobody was going to stop me from making the club," he said, "I had gotten this far and I was going to make the Toronto Maple Leafs or die trying." Meeker did well in training camp and the Leafs were determined to give many new players a chance to make the team. It ended up well for Meeker because he would go on to score 27 times in his rookie year (a very high total for rookies in this era of close-checking hockey) and take the Calder Trophy as the best first-year player in the NHL—beating out, among others, Gordie Howe of Detroit for the award!

Meeker's definitive night as a rookie came on January 8, 1947, when the Leafs hosted the Chicago Blackhawks. The revamped Leafs were in first place with 20 wins and 44 points, while the Hawks were in last place with 18 points and only 7 victories. Chicago opened the scoring, but Meeker scored to even it up by whacking in a loose puck in front of the Chicago net. The Hawks took the lead once more, but Meeker scored again to make it 2-2. Meeker then converted an easy pass to give himself three goals on the night so far and the Leafs a 4-2 lead. In the third, Meeker scored his fourth of the night. "(Ted) Kennedy slips it over to me and I knock it into the open net. I basically did nothing and had my fourth goal of the night." Kennedy made another pass to Meeker, which he converted into his fifth goal of the evening. The wild scoring affair ended 10-4 in favor of the Leafs, who had just seen the best goal-scoring night a rookie had ever enjoyed in the NHL.

Years later, Meeker reflected on his great night. "At that time a five-goal game was really something special. A hat-trick was great, just to score a goal meant something back in those days when 20 goals in a season got you an all-star rating. Twenty goals, you were a heck of a hockey player, 30 goals and you were a superstar. So to get five in one night certainly helped my career."

The Leafs went on to win the Stanley Cup in 1947, 1948, and 1949. Meeker was a part of all those teams and also picked up one more championship in 1951. Meeker's NHL career was not especially long (346 games) but it was *very* successful. And who would have thought it even possible at all when he was in hospital in 1943? His great comeback from serious injuries inflicted during a time of war is a tribute to the man and soldier.

During the 1970s, Howie Meeker became one of the best and most energetic hockey analysts on *Hockey Night in Canada.*

TEEMU SELANNE
BORN: HELSINKI, FINLAND
NHL SEASONS: 1992–93 TO 2010–11
DEFINING MOMENT: MAY 20, 2007

To put it simply, Finnish-born Teemu Selanne exploded onto the NHL scene in 1992–93 with the Winnipeg Jets. Selanne scored an NHL rookie record 76 goals and added 56 assists for 132 points, also an NHL record for first-year players. It was clear he was destined for superstardom and for many years, the player known as the "Finnish Flash" did not disappoint. Years later, the superb skating right winger was injured and down, almost out of NHL options. However, many of the truly great players in NHL history have made unexpected recoveries, and Selanne proved he belonged in this elite group.

Selanne was originally selected by the Winnipeg Jets 10th overall in the 1988 Entry Draft but had trouble reaching a contract with the team. Eventually, the Calgary Flames signed him, but the Jets quickly matched the offer (about $400,000 per season—a very high total at that time). Jets fans quickly came to understand why they paid such a high price. Selanne won the Calder Trophy as best rookie and also made the NHL's first all-star team—a rare achievement for a player in just his first year. His main strength was his explosive skating; he was also gifted with a great shot. He saw plenty of ice time in Winnipeg, and the 6', 190-pound winger was not afraid to use his body to create scoring chances. After four great seasons in Winnipeg, Selanne was dealt to the Anaheim Ducks when the Jets decided they could not afford to keep him under contract. He had 51, 52, and 47 goal seasons for the Ducks but was dealt to San Jose after a 33-goal effort in the 1999–2000 season. He was with the Sharks for a little more than two seasons before becoming a free agent.

Selanne then signed with the Colorado Avalanche for the 2003–04 season, and it was expected he would post his usually high numbers. He went to Colorado because his good friend Paul Kariya (a teammate when they played in Anaheim) was also joining the team, and both accepted smaller, one-year deals to be together again. However, things did not go well for Selanne, who played in 78 games but only scored 16 goals to go along with 16 assists—totals well below his average production (he had scored over 50 goals twice and more than 100 points four times over his career). A knee injury was more bothersome than he let on and he was also 34 years of age by the time the '03–'04 season was over. He had off-season surgery in 2004, but the 2004–05 NHL season was wiped out due to the owner's lockout. Selanne wanted to play in Finland during the work stoppage, but the rehabilitation on his knee took longer than anticipated. He missed the entire season and when it was time to return to the NHL, there were few teams willing to take a chance on the former superstar.

As the summer of 2005 wore on, Selanne was still without a contract. Then one of his previous teams decided to give him another chance. It took until almost the end of August for Selanne to sign with the Ducks, but it was one of the best free-agent pick-ups of the year. His knee stayed strong and Selanne's play was rejuvenated as a result. He scored 40 goals and added 50 assists in 2005–06 to re-establish himself as one of the better players in the NHL. The Ducks were improving each year, and by the 2006–07 season, the team was ready to make a serious run at a championship. Anaheim won 48 games during the regular campaign and recorded 110 points, good for first place in their division. Selanne was outstanding once again with a 48-goal, 94-point campaign at the ripe old age of 36. The Ducks knocked off Minnesota and Vancouver easily in the first two rounds of the playoffs but faced a much better team in Detroit for the Western Conference championship. The series was tied at two games each, with the fifth game in Detroit on the afternoon of May 20, 2007. It was the spotlight Selanne needed to tell the hockey world he was back.

It was a very tight contest, with Detroit holding a slim 1-0 lead late in the third period. Selanne got the puck over to defenseman Scott Neidermayer with 47 seconds to go, and a deflected shot somehow eluded Detroit netminder Dominik Hasek. The power-play tally with the goalie on the bench sent the game into overtime. Then, at 11:57 of extra play, Red Wing defenseman Andreas Lilja lost the puck near his own net and Selanne pounced on it quickly. Making a smart split-second decision, Selanne got Hasek down with a move and lifted the puck over the prone netminder for a 2-1 win and a 3-2 series lead. "Everything happened so quickly," Selanne said. "But I've been practicing that move my whole life. I knew I had to get it up. He (Hasek) goes down and covers up everything down low." The Ducks won the next game to eliminate the Red Wings.

Anaheim then beat Ottawa in five games to take their first ever Stanley Cup. Selanne rejoiced in the glow of his first NHL title. "Obviously, we have to wait a long time for something unbelievable. And it really makes it even more special. I can't imagine to be getting the (final) win in our own building. I'm so proud of my teammates. We've been like brothers. And we have had one dream together and that's why it's so special." Then Selanne said as he cried in the dressing room following five goals and 15 points in 21 playoff games in the '07 post-season, "I was so happy that my parents were here, my brothers, my friends and there are so many people who deserve this as much as I do."

Nobody deserved it more than the modest Selanne who thought his career might be over just three short years before his Stanley Cup win. It made his comeback to stardom all the more sweet.

Teemu Selanne has scored 637 goals and recorded 1,340 points in 1,259 career games.

ROBYN REGEHR
BORN: RECIFE, BRAZIL
NHL SEASONS: 1999–2000 TO PRESENT
DEFINING MOMENT: APRIL 22, 2004

Robyn Regehr has developed into one of hockey's premier defensemen, a hard hitter who makes opponents think twice before venturing onto his side of the ice. But Robyn Regehr almost did not make it to the National Hockey League at all. On July 4, 1999, just a few months after his junior career ended, Regehr nearly lost his life. An oncoming vehicle crossed over to his side of the road and smashed head-on into his Chevy Nova. Two people in the other car were killed, and Regehr broke the tibias in both his legs. With his hockey future in serious jeopardy (doctors initially thought his hockey career might be over), he put himself through very intensive rehabilitation. "I did whatever little things I could do," he said about the slow process of getting back to playing hockey. "I did it every day for as long as I could." Only a few months after the accident and with two screws in his left leg, he had recovered enough to join the Calgary Flames AHL farm team in Saint John, New Brunswick. And by late October, after only five games there, he was back in the NHL to stay.

Regehr is the only player in the NHL who was born in Brazil. His parents were Mennonite missionaries. He lived in Brazil and Indonesia until the family moved to Rothern, Saskatchewan, when he was 11. A strong work ethic, physical presence, and decent skating skills made Regehr a sought-after property among junior scouts. After playing junior A for Prince Albert, he made the major junior Kamloops Blazers, arriving in the fall of 1996—just after future teammate Jarome Iginla had left for the pros.

Regehr was drafted by the Colorado Avalanche in 1998, after his second year of junior hockey. The Avalanche had stockpiled draft picks, and although he was taken in the first round (19th overall), he was Colorado's third choice in that draft. All that extra young talent made for attractive trade packages, and in February 1999, Regehr was swapped to Calgary (who insisted the big 6'3", 225-pound defenseman be included in the deal) with Rene Corbet, Wade Belak, and two draft choices for Theoren Fleury and Chris Dingman. Five months later, he was involved in the horrible car crash. But the same work ethic that characterized his on-ice play helped Regehr overcome his injuries more quickly than anyone predicted. By the first anniversary of the crash, he had played 57 games for the Flames.

Regehr scored his first NHL goal in his second week in the league against San Jose's Mike Vernon, and totaled five goals (the most he scored until his sixth season). He was the Flames nominee for the Masterton Trophy—and the youngest nominee in the history of the award, which recognizes his perseverance and dedication to hockey. In Regehr's sophomore season (2001–02), he finished fourth on the team in penalty minutes, second in hits, and first in blocked shots. Although the Flames were in the midst of a seven-year playoffs drought, Regehr was gaining notice. In his third season, he played in the Young Stars game during the NHL All-Star weekend. On March 18, 2003, he scored what is referred to as a "Gordie Howe Hat Trick," recording a goal, an assist, and a fight in a 4-1 win over the Los Angeles Kings.

Regehr and the Flames really came into prominence in the magical year of 2003–04, when Calgary went to the seventh game of the

Stanley Cup final before losing to Tampa Bay. It was the team's first appearance in the playoffs since 1996, and Regehr made the most of the exposure, finishing third in scoring among defensemen, with nine post-season points. He got the underdog Flames heading in the right direction by scoring their first playoff goal in eight years, against Detroit on the night of April 22, 2004. The Flames had just come off a very long seven game series against Vancouver and many thought they were a spent force. It sure looked that way in the first two periods of the opening game against the Red Wings in Detroit. The shot count was 22-11 for the Wings at the end of two periods. Then Regehr fired a blast over the shoulder of Detroit netminder Curtis Joseph to even the score before the end of the second. There was no scoring in the third period, but Calgary got a goal from Marcus Nilson in overtime to take the game 2-1.

After the game, Calgary captain Jerome Iginla said it was goals from unexpected sources like Regehr and Nilson that was making the difference for the Flames in the '04 post-season. "That's part of what's been so much fun this year. It's been somebody different scoring a big goal each night. That's why we're at where we're at." Coach Darryl Sutter added, "We knew we were going to be tired. We basically played eight games in two weeks coming into tonight to play a well-rested team. But at the same time we showed grit by hanging in the first period and doing what we always do—digging down and fighting back." The words of the Calgary coach were a perfect description of the life and times of the best Calgary defenseman in '03–'04, Robyn Regehr.

Robyn Regehr scored into an empty net for the clinching goal of the Western Conference final in 2004 against San Jose. Flames coach Darryl Sutter showed his confidence in Regehr by making him an assistant captain early in the 2003–04 season. The defenseman then went on to record career highs in assists (14), points (18), and games played (82), and was a plus player (plus

14) for the first time in his career. Robyn Regehr was traded to the Buffalo Sabres prior to the start of the 2011-12 season.

PATRICE BERGERON
BORN: ANCIENNE-LORETTE, QUEBEC
NHL SEASONS: 2003–04 TO PRESENT
DEFINING MOMENT: JUNE 15, 2011

It was a brutal hit from behind that felled Boston Bruins center Patrice Bergeron on the night of October 27, 2007. Bergeron was nailed squarely from behind and into the boards by Philadelphia Flyers defenseman Randy Jones. The crushing blow sent Bergeron down to the ice immediately. He did not move for quite some time, and he was carried off on a stretcher in one of those horrible scenes everyone hates, but which have seemingly become commonplace in hockey. For his reckless hit, the 6'2", 210-pound Jones was suspended for all of two games, while the victim of this unnecessary assault suffered a severe concussion. For Bergeron, it was the start of a long nightmare that would make the simplest of tasks difficult.

Bergeron missed the rest of the 2007–08 season and his career appeared to be in jeopardy. Certainly, the thought that he might never play hockey again crossed his mind as he fought nausea and constant headaches. Merely getting up in the morning was difficult, and much of his day was spent lying down in a dark room. This went on for months, but the 22-year old was amazingly able to return to play in the NHL for 64 games in the 2008–09 season. However, he was not the same productive player he had been. He scored a mere eight goals and rarely played like the young man who had joined the league as an 18-year old right out of junior hockey. It looked like this might be the best Bergeron could do in his post-concussion state. However, with time and youth on his side, Bergeron was eventually able to re-capture much of his old form.

Selected 45th overall by the Bruins in 2003, the 6'2", 194-pound Bergeron surprised everyone by making the Boston club on his first attempt. He scored 16 times as a rookie and totaled 39 points in 71 games played. The lockout season saw him play in the American Hockey League, where he racked up 61 points in 68 games, playing against many veteran players. His minor-league experience paid off the next season in Boston where he scored 31 times and notched 73 points. Bergeron had another good year in 2006–07 with 70 points in 77 games, but then the concussion felled him for all but 10 games of the '07–'08 season. After a below-average season in '08–'09, Bergeron showed he was recovering his touch with a 19-goal season in 2009–10, a year that also saw him play for Team Canada at the 2010 Winter Olympics.

Getting selected for Team Canada seemed to give Bergeron even more of a boost, and he was even better during the 2010–11 campaign in which he scored 22 times and set up 35 others (he has always been an excellent passer) for a total of 57 points in 80 games. He missed just two contests from the 82-game schedule. He had now proved he was able to survive the rigors of a long season and was a more focused player on the defensive side of the game. However, that was just the beginning, as Bergeron saved his best hockey for the 2011 post-season which saw the Bruins re-capture the glory of the 1970s.

The Bruins did not have an easy time advancing to the Stanley Cup final and had to beat Montreal and Tampa Bay in an exciting seven-game series along the way. Boston also defeated Philadel-phia, erasing the bad memory of blowing a three-games-to-none lead just the previous year. The Vancouver Canucks would also prove to be a very difficult opponent in the final, and the Bruins were down 2-0 in games before going back home to tie the series. The two teams each won at home again to force a seventh and deciding game in Vancouver the night of June 15, 2011.

It looked like the first period would end 0-0, but late in the stanza, Bergeron redirected a pass by Canucks netminder Roberto Luongo for a 1-0 Bruins lead. It turned out that was all they would need, but it was still a very tight contest. After Boston scored to make it 2-0, a penalty call to the Bruins threatened to give Vancouver some life. Bergeron put any thought of that to rest by breaking away to score another goal on Luongo. It was not the prettiest goal and had to be reviewed, but his effort to get down the ice with a defenseman on his back was sheer determined effort. The puck somehow skittered and bounced past Luongo, but it seemed like a justifiable ending to a superb individual play. Bergeron had not scored in the final until this game, but his two goals (the first being the Stanley Cup winner) could not have come at a more opportune time.

"It is an amazing feeling," Bergeron said after the game. He then took time to reflect on his journey back to playing hockey. "I had to work so hard to get back. This is all about the medical staff that made sure I took the time to get back. It is about the whole team. What a feeling." On his second goal of the game, Bergeron said, "We'll take that bounce. It is a lucky bounce but I worked hard to get there, to go to the net." His 2011 playoff totals were 6 goals and 14 assists for 20 points in 23 hard-fought games.

Teammate Brad Marchand (who also scored two goals in the seventh contest) paid this tribute to Bergeron after the game. "You have to know what he's had to go through and how he's come back—he won an Olympic gold and now a Stanley Cup. It just shows what a great player he is to have on our team. We wouldn't have won if he wasn't here with us."

By the end of the playoffs, Bergeron firmly established himself as one of the best two-way centers in the game, and now he was also a Stanley Cup champion—quite the comeback for a player who was worried he might not ever play hockey again. It also gives hope to all those who suffer sports concussions—that there is the possibility of recovery and a successful return to the game they love so much.

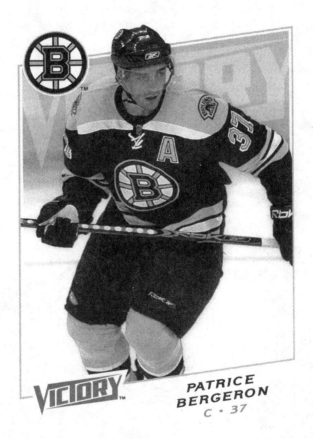

Patrice Bergeron has recorded 337 points in 456 games as of the end of the 2010–11 season. He has also recorded 40 points in 54 career playoff games to date.

Luke Schenn
Toronto Maple Leafs D

VICTORY BRUINS
TIM THOMAS G 30

ALEXANDER OVECHKIN LW-CAPITALS
NEXT IN LINE

Vintage
Martin Brodeur Goaltender
NEW JERSEY DEVILS

30 GOALTENDER
TERRY SAWCHUK

HENRI RICHARD CENTER
MONTREAL CANADIENS

GREATEST OLYMPIANS
XIIIth WINTER GAMES-1980 LAKE PLACID
U.S.A.
MIKE ERUZIONE

O-Pee-Chee
STEVE SMITH
EDMONTON OILERS

INSPIRED BY

Hockey players are by nature very motivated people. They are driven by a wide variety of reasons to play hockey at a very high level. Some have been inspired to do their best by great tragedy, while some want to prove others right or wrong. Some players are influenced by a hero (or heroes), others by an opportunity to seize the moment. In this chapter, we'll focus on the stories of those who were "Inspired."

Steve Smith
Ted Kennedy
Mike Eruzione
Henri Richard
Denis Potvin
Terry Sawchuk
Martin Brodeur ✓
Tim Thomas
Luke Schenn
Alex Ovechkin ✓
Kevin Weekes

STEVE SMITH
BORN: GLASGOW, SCOTLAND
NHL SEASONS: 1984–85 TO 2000–01
DEFINING MOMENT: MAY 31, 1987

On the night that Edmonton Oilers defenseman Steve Smith turned 23, he suffered his worst moment as a hockey player. After knocking off the Vancouver Canucks in three games in the opening round of the 1986 playoffs, the Calgary Flames became the next team to challenge the Oilers supremacy. It was another instalment of the "Battle of Alberta" and it went down to the seventh and deciding contest. Smith was hoping to celebrate his birthday with a big win; instead, disaster struck. With the score tied 2-2 in the third, Smith, who had the puck behind his own net, attempted to making a cross-ice to a teammate. Instead, the puck hit the back of the leg of Edmonton netminder Grant Fuhr and bounced into his own net. Smith slowly crumpled to the ice upon realizing what had transpired.

There was no Edmonton goal to rescue Smith from the humiliation and embarrassment of his tragic clearing attempt. The Oilers tried their best, but Calgary goalie Mike Vernon made all the saves, dashing Edmonton's hopes for another Cup. Smith left the ice in tears for all to see. He was sobbing in the dressing room. The Oilers had lost, and it was his fault.

However, Smith did manage to speak to the media. "I just tried to make a play up the ice. The puck hit Grant's pad and went in. The guys worked so hard, they deserved better. Sooner or later I've got to face it—and the sooner, the better. The sun's going to come up tomorrow and I've got to live." For a young player, such a mistake could have been devastating—and potentially, career ending. But the 6'4", 215-pound bruising defenseman realized there was still a great deal of hockey left in him, too much to let one mistake become insurmountable. The Oilers also helped by taking the blame as a team and vowed to make amends the next season.

Smith was a late-round Oilers pick (111th overall in 1981). He was a rookie in the 1985–86 campaign, cracking the lineup of the defending Stanley Cup champions. He played 55 games, recording a very respectable 24 points. Smith played in 62 games the next season. The Oilers won 50 games that year, but everyone knew all eyes would be on their playoff performance. The Los Angeles Kings planted more seeds of doubt by winning the first playoff game right in Edmonton, but that only served to wake the Oilers up. They won the next four games to take the series in five, with Smith playing a strong hand in one of the victories. Next, the Oilers knocked off Winnipeg and Detroit to make it all the way back to the finals where they would tangle with the Philadelphia Flyers.

The Oilers had plenty of depth on defense during the '87 postseason, which meant that Smith was in the lineup for only three of the seven games played. It looked like Edmonton was going to win as easily as they had in 1985 against the Flyers, but a 3-1 series lead quickly evaporated and a seventh-game showdown was scheduled for Edmonton the night of May 31, 1987. Smith had not played since the first two games of the finals but was going to be in the lineup for the game that would decide the Stanley Cup. In the face of what happened just a year earlier, it was unclear how Smith would respond. But as the game unfolded, all concerns would dissipate.

Philadelphia opened the scoring but that was all they would get on the night as the Oilers scored the next three goals to take the game 3-1. Smith was on the ice for Edmonton when Jari Kurri scored the game-winning goal; Smith was a solid presence on defense throughout the game. He was also the first player captain Wayne Gretzky passed the Cup to after it was presented to the team by league president John Zeigler—a very meaningful moment for the hard-luck defenseman of one year ago. "No matter what you do in this game, you're only as good as your last shift. That's something I learned last year," Smith said afterward. "What happened last year is over now. This is the ultimate. This is the biggest thrill of my life. I was ecstatic when I heard I was going to play."

Smith would go on to win two more Stanley Cups with the Oilers with his improved play catching the eye of teammate Kevin Lowe. "Despite the 1986 experience, Steve Smith was encouraged and gradually became a force with us. By the time we reached the 1988 finals, Smith began to remind me of a young (Hall of Fame defenseman) Larry Robinson. He skates well, moves the puck and is capable of throwing the big check like Larry did in his early days." Smith's success was possible not only because he learned to deal with failure, but because he was inspired to overcome it.

Smith would also play for the Chicago Blackhawks and the Calgary Flames (where he was captain for two seasons) before he retired. All together, he played in 804 career games, recording 375 points and 2,139 penalty minutes.

TED KENNEDY
BORN: HUMBERSTONE, ONTARIO
NHL SEASONS: 1942–43 TO 1956–57
DEFINING MOMENT: APRIL 19, 1947

Theodore "Ted" Kennedy was thrilled to be offered a deal by the Maple Leafs but insisted that he speak with his mother before accepting the contract. He was very close to his mother, since he had never known his father, and he sought her advice on just about everything. His mother wanted him to attend the University of Western Ontario, but she knew his heart was set on trying to become a pro hockey player. "If I had my way, you'd stay in school and forget about hockey. But you're a grown boy now, son, and you will have to decide for yourself. No matter what you do, I'll be standing right behind you," Mrs. Kennedy told her son. "I know that, Mom," Ted replied. "I've made up my mind that I'm going to be a hockey star. I only hope I don't let you down." Kennedy's promise to his mother was a driving force and the inspiration for the youngster who would go on to have, perhaps, the greatest career in Leafs history.

Kennedy was born in the small town of Humberstone, Ontario, in 1925 but never had the opportunity to meet his father, Gordon, who was tragically killed in a hunting accident just a few days before Ted came into the world. The task of raising four children fell to his mother, Margaret, who took on an additional job at a hockey arena concession stand to help pay the bills. Kennedy was very much a hockey player who followed the fortunes of the Toronto Maple Leafs. When he was just seven years old, a family friend took him to a playoff game at the Gardens. Kennedy immediately took a liking to Leafs star Charlie Conacher. Like his new-found hero, Kennedy hoped to one day play for the Leafs as well.

Kennedy played all his minor hockey in Port Colbourne, Ontario, and was captain of the team called the Lions when they won the midget championship in 1941. The 15-year-old led his team to victory with a five-goal effort, two of which were described as coming off individual rushes. The next season saw him score seven goals in one game and six in another contest. Hockey scouts started to notice the youngster who played with great determination. However, it was the Montreal Canadiens who approached Kennedy and put his name on their negotiation list. The Canadiens managed to convince Kennedy and his mother to give their organization a chance, but after a short time in Montreal at a training camp, he was unhappy and eventually returned home.

Now 17, Kennedy played for the Port Colbourne Sailors and scored 23 goals in 23 games during the 1942–43 season. The Sailors were coached by former NHL great Nels Stewart, a high-scoring center during his playing days, and he taught young Kennedy a great deal about how to play the game properly from the center-ice position. Montreal once again tried to get Kennedy to sign with their team, but he refused. He thought afterward that his chances of getting into the NHL were over. However, Stewart got the Maple Leafs interested in the 17-year old, and a trade was completed with Montreal for his playing rights—perhaps the best deal ever completed by the Toronto club in its long history.

In his first full season (1942–43), the 5'10", 170-pound center scored 26 times and followed up with a 29-goal season the year after in a season that saw the Leafs win the Stanley Cup. Kennedy had seven points in seven games when the Leafs beat Detroit for the title in '45, and he was just as good in the '47 finals when Toronto faced Montreal for the championship. It was during this series that Kennedy would have one of his truly inspirational performances. Toronto took the series lead from the Canadiens with an overtime win at the Forum in the fifth game, returning home the night of April 19, 1947, with a chance to win the Cup on home ice.

Montreal opened the scoring early by getting a goal just 20 seconds into the contest. The Leafs finally tied it in the second period when Kennedy set up teammate Vic Lynn for the equalizer. The game remained tied till late in the third, when Kennedy seized the opportunity and let go a long, low shot that eluded a screened Bill Durnan in the Montreal net, with under six minutes to play. The Canadiens challenged the Leafs, but Toronto was able to turn back every Montreal chance and hang on to a 2-1 victory and claim the Stanley Cup once again. At age 21, Kennedy became the youngest player to score a Stanley Cup–winning goal.

After another successful season, on September 18, 1948 to be exact, Ted Kennedy was fittingly named captain of the Maple Leafs, replacing the great Syl Apps, who had retired after the Leafs won the Cup win in 1948. "I'd like to become as great a hockey player as Syl Apps and as great a captain and to gain the same respect that everyone holds for Syl. He's really a wonderful fellow," said an inspired Kennedy after being named to the prestigious position.

Kennedy won two more Cups with Toronto to bring his total number of championships to five, the last one coming in 1951. He retired by age 31, but was always remembered as the most industrious player on ice. He was never the fastest, but he was very smart and could control the face-off dot like no other center in the NHL before or since. He scored 231 career goals and totaled 560 points in 696 career games—all as a Maple Leaf. He still holds the team record for most points—23—in the Stanley Cup finals. Toronto owner and manager Conn Smythe once called Kennedy the greatest Leaf ever, and it would be hard to argue the point. Perhaps none of this would have happened had Kennedy not been inspired to keep the promise he made to his mother so many years ago!

Ted Kennedy was elected to the Hall of Fame in 1966.

MIKE ERUZIONE

BORN: WINTHROP, MASSACHUSETTS

SEASONS: 1973–74 TO 1979–80

DEFINING MOMENT: FEBRUARY 22, 1980

The clock was running down and the Russians were down by a 4-3 count to the American Olympic team. The 1980 Winter Olympic hockey tournament was not supposed to end this way, but the inspired United States team was about to pull off the one of the greatest upsets in sports history. Play-by-play broadcaster Al Michaels led the countdown on the television broadcast, and as the game ended, his well-chosen words perfectly captured the moment: "Do you believe in miracles? Yes!" The Americans then celebrated wildly on the ice surface of Lake Placid. They had just defeated the unbeatable foe. However, none of this might have happened had it not been for the efforts of U.S. captain Mike Eruzione, who had his own motivation that February afternoon.

Eruzione began playing hockey as a youth on a team that was part of the Greater Boston Hockey League. He captained his high school team in his senior year and eventually attended Boston University (BU) on a scholarship when another player dropped out of the program. The 5'10", 180-pound right winger put up some impressive numbers at BU, scoring 21, 27, 21, and 23 goals over his four seasons there. However, it was made clear to him that he was too small and too slow for the National Hockey League. But Eruzione was not ready to give up on hockey just yet and played two seasons for the Toledo Goaldiggers of the International Hockey League. He was named the best American-born first-year player for the 1977–78 season in which he scored 30 goals in 76 games. The Toledo team also won the Turner Cup that is given to the IHL champions. After another season in Toledo, Eruzione was all set to go back home and put his college degree to work when he got a call to tryout for the American Olympic team. He accepted, and it was a decision that would unequivocally change his life forever.

Not only did Eruzione make the U.S. Olympic team, he was named team captain. American coach Herb Brooks was looking, not for superstars, but for a group of players who would work hard and closely follow his instructions. No one expected the Americans to do much with the Russians so heavily favored to win gold. And playing in front of friendly fans was not considered a factor. But the Americans were very well prepared by Brooks, and soon, every person in the United States was cheering for them.

The Americans opened the Olympics with a 2-2 tie against Sweden and then hammered the Czechoslovakians 7-3, with Eruzione scoring the first American goal. An easy 5-1 win over Norway followed and an 8-2 win over Romania kept the American record unblemished. West Germany jumped to a 2-0 in the next game, but the Americans scored four straight to take the game 4-2. That victory kept the Americans unbeaten. But the Russians were up next as the medal round began. The Soviet side had a perfect 5-0 record, but the Americans somehow sensed that destiny was on their side.

The Russians were not very popular back in 1980, not only at the hockey rink, but around the world as well. The Russians had invaded Afghanistan, and the entire world condemned this action, especially the Americans under President Jimmy Carter. Cold War rhetoric was heating up and anti-communist sentiment was running deep at these Olympics. Thus, the contest between the U.S. and the Russians went beyond a hockey game and took on a whole new meaning.

Brooks knew he had to get his team mentally ready to play,

and his pre-game speech was one for the ages. He avoided political implications but made it clear to his team that he was tired of hearing how great the Russian hockey team was and that his team had no chance. The Russian team featured great players of course, including Vladislav Tretiak, Boris Mikhailov, Slava Fetisov, Valeri Kharlamov, and Aleksandr Maltsev—all stars in the 1972 Canada-Russia series. However, Brooks emphasized to his team that they deserved to be there and that the time of Russian domination was coming to an end. He told his team to seize the moment. Duly inspired by Brooks's impressive talk, the Americans took to the ice with surprising vigor.

It was not going to be an easy task, however, and the Russians scored first before 10 minutes had passed. The Americans tied it four minutes later, but the Russians took the lead once more. It looked like the first period was going to end 2-1, but the Americans got a late goal (only one second left on the clock) to not only tie the score, but also knock out goaltender Trekiak from the game. However, only the Russians scored in the second period to make it 3-2 going into the third. Outshot 30-10 at this point, the U.S. side was simply glad to be behind by just one goal against this veteran-laden team. Brooks told his team to keep playing its game and reminded the players that they had a full 20 minutes to go. The team once again listened to its mentor and got a goal at 8:39 of the third period to tie the game. Sensing that the Russians were back on their heels, the Americans pressed forward. The puck was passed to Eruzione right in the slot, and he quickly snapped a shot into the Russian net for a 4-3 lead with ten minutes to play! The Americans had seized the moment just as Brooks had told them to.

But the Olympics weren't over just yet. The U.S. still had to beat Finland to secure the gold medal. They quickly found themselves down 2-1 after two periods of play. Once again, coach Brooks provided the inspiration, telling his players very pointedly, that if they lost this game, it would haunt them the rest of their lives. Stirred to action once again, the Americans scored three times to win 4-2 and take their first gold medal since 1960—the only other time the U.S. hockey team had won the Olympics. As much as the United States had to beat Finland, it was really the Russian conquest that everyone remembers. And for scoring that winning goal, Eruzione has become part of American folklore. The goal is considered one the greatest moments in American sports history. "Six months ago we came together from different walks of life and ethnic backgrounds across America and we (g)elled into a team," Eruzione said after the Olympics were over. "It's been a tremendous thrill for me." In fact, it was so good for Eruzione that he decided to leave hockey behind at the age of 25, knowing he could never achieve such a high again.

The made-for-television movie *Miracle on Ice* (starring Karl Malden as Herb Brooks) showed a dressing-room scene where Eruzione tells teammate Mark Johnson his playing career was going to be over after the Olympics because he could never equal this moment. Eruzione said he wanted to go out in a blaze of glory after learning so much from Brooks in the past year. He then proceeded to score the most famous hockey goal in American history. It made for good TV, capturing well the fact that it might never have worked had Herb Brooks not been there to inspire his team—and captain Mike Eruzione—to new heights. The team went on to uplift a nation at a time when the United States needed a group of heroes to call its own.

Mike Eruzione became a broadcaster, an assistant coach at BU, and more often, a motivational speaker who talks about the goal that changed his life. Herb Brooks went on to coach in the NHL with the New York Rangers, New Jersey Devils, Minnesota North Stars, and Pittsburgh Penguins. Tragically, Brooks died following a car accident in 2003.

HENRI RICHARD

BORN: MONTREAL, QUEBEC

NHL SEASONS: 1955–56 TO 1974–75

DEFINING MOMENT: MAY 18, 1971

A coach will sometimes try something radical to get the best out of a player—even if that athlete happens to be a long-time veteran with a history of winning on his résumé. Such was the case with Montreal Canadiens coach Al MacNeil when he benched the iconic Henri Richard during the 1971 Stanley Cup final. The "Pocket Rocket," as Richard was known, had won *nine* Cups already, so he knew something about being a winner. Nonetheless, MacNeil did not like what he had seen from the long-time Hab center and decided to send a message. Richard did not exactly receive it well, but the point was made and the fiery competitor now had more inspiration than ever to show his coach how wrong he was. What MacNeil might have failed to realize was that Richard had always been a highly motivated player.

As a young boy growing up in Montreal, Henri Richard idolized his older brother Maurice "Rocket" Richard, who was a legendary player for the Montreal Canadiens. It was Henri's dream to one day play for the Habs, and to perhaps play alongside his famous brother, who was 15 years older. At first, the Canadiens management was not quite sure what to make of the younger Richard, but he was so good at his first training camp in 1955 that they had no choice but to sign him to a contract. Maurice represented his brother in contract discussions, but all Henri wanted was a chance to play for the big-league team. Montreal general manager Frank

Selke made sure the younger Richard was given a fair contract with a good signing bonus. It would never be a decision Montreal would regret.

Richard was on the small side at 5'7"and 160 pounds, but was he ever feisty on the ice. If anyone tried to take advantage of him, Richard was always ready to defend himself. One night in Boston, he took on three of the toughest Bruins players (who were all larger men) and more than held his own. At first, Maurice did his best to protect his young sibling, but he soon realized that Henri could take care of himself just fine. Henri scored 19 times as a rookie and totaled 40 points in 64 games, and then chipped in with four goals and four assists in the playoffs, which saw Montreal reclaim the Stanley Cup. In fact, the Habs won the Cup in each of Richard's first five years with the team, and he led the league in assists one year when he had 52 in 1957–58. Once Maurice retired in 1960, the most successful brother act in NHL history was no more—but Henri's career would climb to greater heights in the years ahead.

Montreal was a very good team between 1961 and 1964, but never played in the Stanley Cup finals during those years. The team was rebuilding and finally recaptured the championship in 1965 when they beat Chicago for the Stanley Cup. Richard scored the Cup-winning goal in overtime during the 1966 final versus Detroit, ending the series in dramatic style. The Habs took two more Cups in 1968 and 1969 and then missed the playoffs in 1970, which forced many changes the following year. Only Richard and Jean Beliveau were left from the great Montreal teams of the Fifties, but they still had a great deal to contribute during the 1970–71 season. Montreal was up and down that season but managed to finish in third place in the East Division. But all that got them was a meeting with the first-place Boston Bruins led by Bobby Orr and Phil Esposito. Montreal implemented a checking system to stymie Orr, and behind the superlative work of rookie goalie Ken Dryden, beat Boston in seven shocking games. The biggest goal of the series was scored by Richard (normally a center, but used on the right wing in this series) who notched a goal late in the second period of the second game to make the score 5-2 Bruins. The Habs were re-energized by the goal and came back to win that game 7-5—right in Boston!

After the Canadiens beat Minnesota in the next round, another finals meeting with Chicago was in order. The powerful Blackhawks, led by superstar Bobby Hull, won the first two games at home, but the Canadiens would not roll over and took the next two at home. In the meantime, back at home, Chicago won the fifth game 2-0 with Richard riding the bench—and ineffective (only one assist in the series) in the mind of the Montreal bench boss. The proud Richard was furious at his treatment and was very critical of the Montreal coach. Beliveau managed to calm his longtime teammate down somewhat, but the damage was done. "I got mad at MacNeil just because he didn't play me. That's the only reason," Richard recalled years later. "He didn't play me in a game in Chicago. After it was over I went into the room and said to myself that I wasn't going to say anything. But I was so mad that when the first newspaper guy came up to me and asked me how come I didn't play, I was so mad I said right away, 'He's the worst coach I've ever played for.' I didn't really mean it, but it came out because I was mad."

Mad or not, there was still a series on the line, and the Canadiens were able to force a seventh game after eking out a 4-3 win.

The night of the final game in this epic series was May 18, 1971. It was very warm in Chicago and the Blackhawks were even hotter, scoring twice and gaining a 2-0 lead in the middle stanza. Montreal did not do much of anything until late in the second, when Jacques Lemaire scored on a long shot that beat Chicago netminder Tony Esposito. Then Richard went to work. First, he tied the game 2-2 before the second period was over, and then in the third, he took the puck and raced around a Blackhawk defenseman before butting a shot over Esposito's shoulder for the winning goal. Chicago battled until the final buzzer, but to no avail. Montreal had won another Stanley Cup—and the 10th title for the player known as the "Pocket Rocket." "This is the best of the 10 Stanley Cups I've won," Richard said right after the game. Asked about his outburst against his coach Richard replied, "You can bet I'm relieved. This one is the best because we were so much the underdogs, it wasn't even funny." In the post-game celebration on the ice, the media noted that MacNeil and Richard hugged each other.

No matter whether Richard was inspired by his benching or his team's underdog status, he still proved to be the consummate professional whose inspiration kept him motivated and focused on the task of winning—a big reason why, with 11 victories, Richard has the most Stanley Cup wins of any player in NHL history.

Henri Richard recorded 1,046 career points (including 358 goals) in 1,256 regular season games played. He added 49 goals and 129 points in 180 playoff games. Richard replaced Beliveau as Montreal captain in 1971 and was elected to the Hall of Fame in 1979.

DENIS POTVIN
BORN: OTTAWA, ONTARIO
NHL SEASONS: 1973–74 TO 1987–88
DEFINING MOMENT: 1983 PLAYOFFS

Denis Potvin's father, Armand, was a pretty good athlete himself. The powerfully built Armand made it to a Detroit Red Wings training camp, but a back injury incurred at camp stopped his rise through the hockey ranks and derailed his chances of making it to the National Hockey League. Armand fathered three boys, Bob, Jean, and Denis. They would all share hockey equipment as they learned to play the game. Denis quickly developed as a hockey player and felt an inner urge to rush the puck up the ice. He was also gifted with a big body (he grew to an even 6' and 205 pounds) and was never afraid to use it. Since he had older brothers, he often played against boys who were more senior, which helped to develop his skills faster. Surprisingly, Potvin was cut from his high school hockey team by a coach who had no appreciation for his talents. He was very upset, but played with the local team and eventually was noticed by Ottawa's junior A team, the 67's.

Potvin played five years for the 67's (players could not be drafted into the NHL until they were 20 years of age at this point) and had a great year in 1970–71 when he scored 20 goals and totaled 78 points in just 57 games. In his last year of junior, he scored 35 times, and comparisons to the great Bobby Orr started to become commonplace. The New York Islanders, recently formed then, had the first pick of the 1973 Entry Draft and did not hesitate to select the multi-talented blueliner. "Being compared to Bobby Orr is nice but it's going to put pressure on me in my first year with the Islanders," Potvin told the media upon his selection as the top junior available. "I know I can cope with it. I hope the fans in New York can appreciate that playing in the NHL will be a whole new thing for me." The Islanders quickly became a good team as their top draft choices developed very well in those early years. They made the playoffs in 1975 and were a consistent contender from that point on, although it took a few efforts to achieve the ultimate.

One playoff disappointment after another frustrated the Islanders and their Norris Trophy–winning defenseman (Potvin was named the league best defenseman three times over his career) but finally in 1980, they edged the Philadelphia Flyers in six to take their first Stanley Cup. They repeated as champions in 1981 and 1982 without too much difficulty, with Bryan Trottier, Mike Bossy, Clark Gillies, and Billy Smith all in their prime years.

In 1983, they were hoping to add a fourth straight title. Always a key player in the post-season, Potvin was ready for another challenge to the Islander supremacy. But he also had something more serious on his mind. His father, to whom he had always been close, had cancer and was suffering badly from the medical treatments. So Potvin made a deal with his father that if Armand stuck closely to his treatments, the 1982–83 season would be dedicated to him. Potvin wanted to see his father enjoy another championship. "My dad and I kept talking about how it was improbable that I could win but I was going to give it all I had. He made the promise that he would do the same thing, that he would live through everything to see us bring home the Stanley Cup."

The Islanders began defense of the title by knocking off Washington in the first round of the playoffs, but had a harder time against the New York Rangers in the next series. Potvin got the Islanders off to a good start the night the best-of-seven series began at home. The game was tied 1-1 going into the third when Potvin shot home the winning goal with just 1:14 gone in the final stanza.

He pounced on a loose puck in the slot and put a drive past Ranger goalie Ed Mio for his 43rd career playoff goal. The goal by Potvin opened the floodgates and the Islanders added two more goals for a 4-1 victory. "That was a demonstration of a team that will win no matter what they have to do," Potvin explained after the game. "We'll play it to the very fullest and any way we have to (to win)." The Rangers were defeated in six games.

The Bruins were the next opponent, and once again, it was a difficult series. The Islanders eventually wore the Boston club down. On May 3, the Bruins hoped to tie the series at two games each, but the Islanders had other ideas. A 3-2 New York lead into the third period quickly turned into an 8-3 slaughter. In this game, the big defenseman scored twice and assisted on another to lead the New York attack. The Bruins never recovered and were gone in six games. The victory over Boston sent the Islanders to the finals for the fourth consecutive year. Their opposition this time was the upstart Edmonton Oilers led by Wayne Gretzky and Mark Messier. It was a battle between grizzled veterans and upcoming youth. It wasn't close. The more experienced Islanders made short work of the Oilers, taking the Cup in four straight games!

There was no doubt Potvin had been deeply inspired to bring some happiness to his father for one last time, and his playoff performance (20 points in the '83 playoffs) was certainly a strong indicator of his inspiration. Potvin took the Cup home after the final game and shared a few moments with his father as they closely examined the fabled silver trophy. They took pictures and remembered the past and did everything possible to make the moment last. "If it weren't for my dad, it (Denis's career) never would have happened. He made me a hockey player," Potvin once wrote about his father. Armand Potvin died during the playoffs the next season when the Oilers took the Stanley Cup from the Islanders with a five-game final series victory. Potvin never played in the finals again.

Denis Potvin was elected to the Hall of Fame in 1991. He had a great career with 1,052 points (310 were goals) in 1,060 games.

TERRY SAWCHUK
BORN: WINNIPEG, MANITOBA
NHL SEASONS: 1949–50 TO 1969–70
DEFINING MOMENT: 1952 PLAYOFFS

As Terry Sawchuk was growing up in Manitoba, he was generally known as an easy-going kid who was quick to make friends. His best friend was his older brother Mike, who played hockey as a goaltender. Young Terry would put on Mike's goalie pads at home and pretend to be like his brother or the legendary George Hainsworth, who played in the NHL with Montreal and Toronto. On occasion, Terry tried to play goal with his brother's equipment at the nearby rink, just to see what it felt like to be in net. Mike was considered a pretty good netminder, but tragically, as he was moving up in the minor hockey system, he incurred heart problems and died at age 17. Terry, who was now 10, was devastated and missed his brother terribly. Those close to Sawchuk recalled that he became obsessed with carrying on his brother's legacy as a goaltender. He refused to read books or look at movie screens for fear of damaging his eyes and making him less effective as a goalie! Sawchuk wanted to succeed, not just for himself, but also for the memory of his brother Mike.

The year of Mike's death saw Terry play organized hockey for the very first time. He was a goalie in his first year, but in his second season, he played center and won the scoring title. Sawchuk was a very good athlete and loved to play football (although he did suffer a serious elbow injury playing it), but one day a coach he knew needed a goalie. Sawchuk told the coach he had the necessary equipment already at home and started out to gather his goalie gear. He quickly became a star netminder.

Sawchuk was athletic—that much was clear. But he also knew how to play the angles, making him very difficult to beat because he was so good at getting himself set properly. He also worked on standing up as much as possible and developed a crouching position (while still up on his skates) to help him spot the puck. At age 15, Sawchuk played in goal for the Winnipeg Rangers, and his performance got the Chicago Blackhawks and the Detroit Red Wings interested in him. Since he was very familiar with one coach who worked for the Red Wings, Sawchuk signed with Detroit. Just two years later, at age 17, he was in Galt, Ontario, playing for Detroit's junior team. It would be the start of a long and mostly good relationship between the goalie and the Red Wings.

In short order, Sawchuk established himself as the best goalie prospect in all of hockey. He was thrilled to be signed to a pro contract and thought he had all the money in the world when he got a $2,000 signing bonus from Detroit. After junior, he was sent to the Omaha Knights of the United States Hockey League (USHL) and was promptly named rookie of the year for the 1947–48 season when he posted a 30-18-5 record. The next season saw him play in the American Hockey League, where he was named best rookie. His team won the Calder Cup with Sawchuk in the starring role. His performance made Detroit think about making Sawchuk their full-time goalie, even though star netminder Harry Lumley had led the Red Wings to a Stanley Cup victory in 1950. But Detroit had such faith in Sawchuk that they traded away Lumley to Chicago. The news surprised Sawchuk who said, "I was figuring on playing in Indianapolis again and I'm still not counting on simply walking into the job."

Sawchuk need not have worried. The Red Wings had added good defensive players in the trade for Lumley and the young netminder ended up leading the NHL with 44 wins in 1950–51. He was also named rookie of the year in one more league! The Red Wings were upset in the playoffs that year by Montreal, but the 1951–52 season would be one of the most memorable in Red Wing history. Sawchuk played in all 70 games and once again won a league-best 44 times, with Detroit finishing in first place with an even 100 points (the first team in NHL history to do so). Sawchuk also posted 12 shutouts as Detroit only allowed 133 goals against the entire year.

The Red Wings were primed for the '52 playoffs and easily beat the Maple Leafs in four straight games, with Sawchuk recording two more shutouts. After the first game, a 3-0 victory for the Red Wings, Sawchuk said, "I feel a lot better this year than I did in last season's playoffs. I felt nervous and jittery a year ago but I feel right at home now." The Red Wings now had another chance at the Montreal Canadiens in the finals.

Even though Montreal finished second (22 points behind Detroit), the first two games of the final were played at the Forum. The Red Wings won both games by a 2-1 score and returned home for the next two contests. Sawchuk did not allow a goal over the final two games, and the Red Wings swept the Canadiens and Maurice Richard in four straight. Sawchuk had to be very good in the last game as Montreal fired 26 shots at him during the heated contest. Detroit scored a goal in each period for their second consecutive 3-0 shutout. In total, Sawchuk recorded four shutouts in the playoffs, equaling a mark set by only two other goalies. Incredibly, Sawchuk did not allow a goal on home ice. "I wasn't worried about equaling the playoff shutout record. All I wanted to do was to get this series over with," Sawchuk said later. Richard paid a high compliment to Sawchuk when he said, "He is their club. Another guy in the nets and we'd beat them."

Sawchuk would go on to win three more Cups before his great career was over. He set a record that lasted 40 years when he notched his 103rd and final career shutout in his last NHL season. Through it all, the seven-time league all-star (three times on the first team) and four-time Vezina Trophy winner played through many injuries and recovered from more than one surgery. He was disappointed to be traded away by Detroit in June 1955, but was glad to return to the Red Wings in July 1957. He stayed in Detroit until the summer of 1964 when Toronto acquired his rights. He would win his final championship in 1967 as a Maple Leaf—the final great moment of his illustrious career.

There is no doubt Terry Sawchuk's brother would have been proud that he inspired one of the most legendary goaltenders in NHL history, and, in the eyes of many, the best ever!

Terry Sawchuk was elected to the Hall of Fame in 1971.

MARTIN BRODEUR
BORN: MONTREAL, QUEBEC
NHL SEASONS: 1991–92 TO PRESENT
DEFINING MOMENTS: JUNE 9, 2003 & DECEMBER 21, 2009

When players are asked about matching the achievements of their idols or setting new records, most will say they are not as good as their heroes and that they do not play for individual records. Goaltender Martin Brodeur would never say he was out to match the Stanley Cup championships mark of someone like Patrick Roy (a netminder he watched while growing up in Montreal), or that he was out to beat the shutout record of the legendary Terry Sawchuk. However, over his great career, Brodeur has nearly matched Roy's mark of four championships and, in the process, has surpassed the shutout mark first established by Sawchuk. As such, it is quite reasonable to assume that Brodeur was inspired to greatness by those who came before him.

Sports were a big part of Brodeur's upbringing. His father, Denis, played net for Canada at the 1956 Winter Olympics in Cortina, Italy. His older brother, Claude, was a pretty good baseball pitcher who was in the Montreal Expos farm system until an injury to a shoulder ended his career. Another brother, Denis Jr., liked to do stunts while riding a bicycle, until he too suffered a bad injury. So it wasn't surprising that Martin picked up his father's goalie equipment and, playing in the minor hockey system in and around the Montreal area, found that he liked the position. He became a big hockey fan, and when he was 14 years old, he saw the Montreal Canadiens win the 1986 Stanley Cup. He also recalled missing school to attend the parade afterward. He was never pushed by his father to be a player or a goalie, and the senior Brodeur never put pressure on his son to excel or give the boy undue advice. Young Martin subsequently thrived and climbed quickly up the ranks, but he did so without flash or fanfare. He was not considered the best goalie in junior hockey (that title went to Trevor Kidd, a netminder who never achieved much in the NHL), but the New Jersey Devils thought very highly of Brodeur and selected him 20th overall in the 1990 Entry Draft. It may have been the best choice in team history.

By just his third year in the NHL, Brodeur was playing in the semi-finals, losing a tight seven-game series to the New York Rangers, who went on to win the Stanley Cup in 1994. One year later, it was Brodeur who won his first championship when the Devils defeated the Red Wings in four straight games. Brodeur was averaging somewhere between 34 and 43 wins a season but was not back in the finals until 2000, when the Devils beat Dallas in overtime to win the Cup for the second time.

Brodeur was on the wrong end of a Game 7 loss to the Colorado Avalanche in the 2001 finals and took the defeat rather hard. Losing to fellow Quebecer Roy only added to the sting. His next chance at redemption was in the 2003 finals when the Devils faced the Anaheim Mighty Ducks for the title. The series went to a seventh game—only, this time, the Devils were at home. For Brodeur, the final and deciding game of the series was the ultimate challenge.

"Going into Game 7, I wasn't reliving 2001 (versus Roy and the Avalanche) at all although in an interview I said the pain of that defeat (in the seventh contest) never completely goes away," Brodeur recalled later. "I felt far more confident against the Mighty Ducks than the Avalanche, particularly since we had already shut them twice in our building." Brodeur was able to erase any doubts by backstopping the Devils to a 3-0 victory and his third Stanley Cup. He stopped all 24 shots directed his way, but the Mighty Ducks never seriously challenged the Devils once they got up by a 1-0 score. It was one of the very few times in NHL history that Game 7 ended with a shutout. Brodeur was inspired to play and win the game everyone dreams about when they are kids. "The romance of Game 7, the charm of being in that special place that every little boy imagines with his friends while chasing a tennis ball in a game of street hockey, seemed to overshadow the reality that nine months of hard hockey labour had been reduced to a single game. Win that game (and) the season was a success," Brodeur wrote years later.

Not only was Brodeur winning a lot of games in the regular season and playoffs, he was also posting a lot of shutouts each and every year. The Devils built their team around his superior goaltending, and a strong defensive system gave the stand-up goalie what he needed to record 10 or more shutouts four times in his career. It was once believed that Sawchuk's record of 103 career shutouts was unbeatable, but on the night of December 7, 2009, Brodeur did the unthinkable and tied the record when New Jersey beat Buffalo 3-0. Exactly two weeks later, on the night of December 21, 2009, Brodeur set out to top the mark established by Sawchuk. The game was in Pittsburgh, and the Devils got scoring out of some unusual players to defeat the Penguins 4-0. The game was not without suspense. Sidney Crosby hit the post late in the game and Brodeur had to make a big stop against Evgeni Malkin with just 42 seconds to play. Brodeur had stopped 35 shots to preserve the shutout.

"Tying it was pretty amazing in Buffalo a couple of weeks ago. Now surpassing him (Sawchuk) is a great honour (to be in that position), that's for sure," he said after his record-breaking game. "This record was held so long by Terry Sawchuk (who recorded his final shutout on in 1970). When you do break records and you see how long they've lasted, it's pretty cool," Brodeur added. The New Jersey netminder has never been too effusive about all the goaltending marks he has set over his illustrious career, but it was easy to tell that the shutout mark was special to him. Once he got close, it was the very idea of setting a new level of achievement for all future goalies that inspired him.

Whether it was a playing in a special game or going for a seemingly unbeatable record, there was no doubt that Martin Brodeur was inspired to do his best. Considering he has rewritten the record book for virtually all goaltending marks, it is safe to say Brodeur will be one of the all-time great goalies in NHL history.

Martin Brodeur has recorded 116 career shutouts as of the end of the 2010–11 season.

TIM THOMAS
BORN: FLINT, MICHIGAN
NHL SEASONS: 2002–03 TO PRESENT
DEFINING MOMENT: OCTOBER 28, 2010

When asked what kept goaltender Tim Thomas playing all these years in Europe and in the minors, he told a story about another goalie who inspired him to keep at it—the legendary Johnny Bower. Thomas first learned about Bower from a book on goaltending greats he read as a kid. "I had a goaltending book and I read about all the old goaltenders. Then somewhere in my mid-20s, when it was taking longer and longer for me to get a chance, his (Bower's) story stuck out to me because he didn't make the NHL until so late in his career," Thomas said of the Hall of Famer whose career really did not start at the NHL level until he was 33. Thomas said he had never met Bower as of yet. "I might have seen him up on the screen (at the Air Canada Centre) when we played there but it would be definitely nice."

Like Bower, the Bruins netminder has always had his doubters, but Thomas has learned to battle through and come out on top. In fact, at the end of the 2011 playoffs, which saw Thomas lead the Boston Bruins to their first Stanley Cup since 1972, many were calling Thomas the "modern day" Johnny Bower!

When Thomas was a young boy growing up in Flint, Michigan, he was very much affected by the United States gold at the 1980 Winter Olympics. The six-year-old decided then and there that he wanted to play in the Olympics for his country. However, it wasn't until high school that he gave much thought to playing in the National Hockey League—a dream that took a long time to achieve.

After attending the University of Vermont, Thomas was selected very low in the NHL Entry Draft (217th overall by the Quebec Nordiques). However, from the age of 23 to 27, the 5'11", 201-pound goalie played in Europe (in Finland and Sweden) where he was earning a good living. The Boston Bruins signed Thomas in August 2002, but he was assigned to the minors after training camp that year (although he did get into four NHL games, winning three of them). After the NHL lockout ended, he started the 2005–06 campaign in the minors but was called up for 38 games later in the year (winning 12 times). The 2006–07 season saw Thomas play in 66 games, posting a 30-29-4 record as the number-one Bruins goalie. Thomas had finally arrived in the big league at age 32.

By the 2008–09 season, Thomas had not only become an NHL first team all-star goalie, he had also won the Vezina Trophy awarded to the best goalie, two recognitions Bower also achieved during his career. Thomas also took home the Jennings Trophy for allowing the fewest goals during the regular season (shared with Manny Fernandez, Boston's other goalie that year). Thomas won 36 games while losing only 11 times in '08-'09, allowing only 2.10 goals a game and recording five shutouts. His great performance earned Thomas a new, lucrative contract, and it looked like he had settled into the Boston team quite nicely. But the next season did not prove to be so good for the unorthodox netminder, who really has no definitive style, but somehow stops the puck. Thomas got into just 43 games (because of a hip injury) in 2009–10 and posted a 17-18-8 record. Soon afterward, youngster Tuuka Rask was occupying the Bruins net in the games that mattered the most. There was talk that Boston was looking to move Thomas, but his new deal may have hindered any chance they had to trade him. However, Thomas was not about to give up and returned for the 2010–11 season, ready to battle for his job.

Rask got the first assignment of the '10-'11 campaign, but after a loss to Phoenix in the season opener, Thomas appeared in the next game and shutout the same Coyotes 3-0. Thomas then defeated New Jersey 4-1 before taking two from Washington by scores of 3-1 and 4-1. On October 28, 2010, the Toronto Maple Leafs came into Boston and Thomas promptly shut them out 2-0. Thomas had only 20 shots on goal, but he made some great saves along the way. The game marked his tenacity and will not only to stay in the big league, but also to succeed there. After the game, Toronto captain Dion Phaneuf commented, "Their goalie made some good saves. He was hot. We threw everything at him." Thomas, who was named the first star of the game, said he was ready to play. "I feel good. It's fun to play right now. It was easier to focus on a shutout because we couldn't afford to give up a goal and let them back in."

Two days later, on October 30, Thomas earned another shutout when the Bruins rolled into Ottawa and beat the Senators 4-0. In this game, Thomas stopped 29 shots for his 20th career shutout and was named the first star of the contest once again. "The effort in front of me was great," Thomas said after the game. "They're (his teammates are) making my life easy right now," he concluded modestly, heaping praise on his mates and not much on himself. On November 3, Thomas set a new team record for goaltenders with his seventh straight win from the start of the season when the Bruins beat the Sabres 5-2. Not only was Thomas a perfect 7-0, the Sabres were the first team to score more than one goal against him during the streak. He made 33 stops against hometown Buffalo and was named the second star of the match. After the game, Thomas said he remembered a similar start when he played one year in Finland during the 2004–05 season. "It was kind of something similar to this start. I was able to ride that the whole year, so I hope the same thing happens (this year)", said the 36-year-old. It happened just so as Thomas took the Vezina win and helped his team win the Stanley Cup championship that season.

Just how long Thomas will play is uncertain, but Johnny Bower played until he was 45, and that's probably inspiration enough. "I don't know how Johnny felt (at this age) but I feel pretty good. And I have a mask, so I have an advantage on him."

Tim Thomas has won 161 games in 319 NHL appearances to date. In the 2011 playoffs, Thomas won in Game 7 three times (over Montreal, Tampa Bay, and Vancouver) and was awarded the Conn Smythe Trophy after the Bruins beat the Canucks in the seventh game of the Stanley Cup final.

LUKE SCHENN
BORN: SASKATOON, SASKATCHEWAN
NHL SEASONS: 2008–09 TO PRESENT
DEFINING MOMENT: JANUARY 31, 2009

For such a young man, Luke Schenn has always handled himself well in front of the Toronto media, who are an inquiring lot most of the time. He quickly became a focal point when he started a new tradition by donating $10,000 for a program that has come to be known as "Luke's Troops." Schenn's program allows Canadian servicemen and women to attend Leaf home games as his guest. A different Armed Forces person is honored each game and it has become a part of all games at the Air Canada Centre. Most of those recognized have served in places like Afghanistan and the Middle East, places filled with strife and conflict.

The son of a firefighter, Schenn certainly understood the sacrifice men and women make when they put their lives in danger for others. "A lot of times people don't recognize what they do over-seas for us," Schenn said, adding that he is not surprised at how the crowd responds with a standing ovation whenever the sol-diers are introduced and shown on the big screen. "I don't think there's any other way to react. It's well deserved. Lots of times I get to meet soldiers who come to the games and they say thanks for bringing them to the game but I think it's the other way around. I say thanks for the work they're doing overseas. They're the ones doing the real work. We're just having fun." The good times started for Schenn the minute he became a Maple Leaf.

Toronto was determined to add a quality defenseman at the 2008 NHL Entry Draft. They were slated to pick seventh overall, but realized any of the better blueline prospects would be gone by then. Leafs general manager Cliff Fletcher decided he had to make a move, so he sent two later draft choices to the New York Islanders to move into fifth position. The focus of the Leafs at-tention was Schenn, the big, bruising, 6'2", 229-pound stay-at-home defenseman from Saskatchewan, a province that has been the birthplace of more than one great Maple Leaf (Wendel Clark, Bobby Baun, and Johnny Bower, for example). Schenn had caught the attention of all the NHL scouts with his play for the Kelowna Rockets of the Western Hockey League (WHL). He was also im-pressive playing for Team Canada when the juniors won the gold medal at the world tournament in 2008. The Leafs were pleased to select the youngster, but were not sure he would make the big team for the 2008–09 season.

However, Schenn quickly showed that he was very mature for an 18-year-old, and his ability to make a pass out of his own end impressed the Toronto coaching staff. It was decided to keep the youngster and not send him back to junior, a move that some thought would actually hurt Schenn's development. Schenn played in 70 games, scoring two goals and adding 12 assists for a team that was clearly not a playoff contender during the '08–'09 season. On many nights, Schenn was the best defenseman on the team, and he showed flashes of what might be expected to come. He was always at his best when he was physical, and with a large frame, he could make life difficult for opposing forwards. If his program honoring the troops inspired Schenn to do his best, it was certainly in evidence in his best game as a rookie when the Pittsburgh Penguins came into Toronto on the night of January 31, 2009.

Schenn took over the contest. He was all over the ice and helped the Leafs gain a 5-4 victory over the Penguins, a team that had been in the Stanley Cup finals the previous spring. Schenn sent Pittsburgh star Evgeni Malkin reeling with a hit along the boards and then pounded out a decision over Tyler Kennedy who challenged the Toronto defenseman over his bodycheck on Malkin. In the third period of the game, Schenn set up teammate Matt Stajan for a goal, and at the end of the contest, he was named the first star.

Schenn also impressed his teammates with his performance. "He's definitely got the makings of a leader," said veteran defenseman Mike Van Ryn. "When they say he's a future captain, he definitely is," Leafs coach Ron Wilson added. "I don't think the experience he had tonight he could have got in 100 games in the WHL or the world (junior) championship." The game was indeed a confidence builder for Schenn, who scored his first NHL goal a week later in Montreal. "I hadn't scored a goal yet this year, so it was definitely nice to get it and there's no better place than in Montreal versus the Canadiens on a Saturday night." At the end of his first year, Schenn was named to the NHL's all-rookie team.

His second season was much harder for Schenn, and he struggled early in the 2009–10 campaign, but rebounded to score five goals and add 12 assists in 79 games played. He was also a plus 2 on a team that was generally terrible at the defensive aspects of the game. The Leafs missed the playoffs once again, but Schenn had established himself as a top-four defenseman on the Toronto club. He was strong right from the start of the 2010–11 campaign and had his best point total with 22. The Leafs also put more on Schenn's shoulders after long-time veteran Tomas Kaberle was dealt to Boston during the season.

"Luke's Troops" continued to be a Maple Leaf tradition during the '10–'11 season. The Armed Forces, who proudly wear the maple leaf on their uniform, inspire all Canadians with the service they provide to their country. One player with a large Maple Leaf on the front of his blue-and-white sweater is especially inspired by the troops to do his best every game. His name is Luke Schenn.

Luke Schenn was just 21 during the 2010–11 season and has already played in 231 games as a Maple Leaf.

ALEX OVECHKIN
BORN: MOSCOW, RUSSIA
NHL SEASONS: 2005–06 TO PRESENT
DEFINING MOMENT: JANUARY 16, 2006

The day Alex Ovechkin celebrated his 10th birthday, his oldest brother was involved in a car accident. It was a very a significant event in Ovechkin's life—it affected him greatly and would also inspire him to become the best he could at his chosen sport.

At first, everything seemed to be alright with his 24-year-old brother Sergei. He looked to be recovering just fine. But things suddenly took a turn for the worst when a blood clot in his leg caused irreparable harm. Sergei died, and Ovechkin's world was suddenly turned upside down. Amazingly, Ovechkin played in his scheduled hockey game the night his brother died, although his heart was not in the game at all. Through his tears, Ovechkin skated through the entire contest as if he were in a fog. His mother, Tatiana, would attend Ovechkin's subsequent games, and he would see her crying in the stands and go to her and say, "Mama, don't cry." Sergei had encouraged his youngest sibling to play the game, and young Alex would not forget what his brother had done for him. Although it was very difficult to keep playing hockey, Ovechkin kept going and used the tragic circumstances to motivate and inspire himself to achieve at the highest levels of hockey.

Ovechkin first tried skating when he was seven years old and did not take to it very well. "I tried skating for a while and I took some lessons but after four months I'd had enough. I decided I didn't like it," Ovechkin said in an interview in 2007. Ovechkin's parents were both very athletic people and were not going to let young Alex simply walk away—not without some more encouragement. His mother was a very good national team basketball player and a very driven individual. His father was a good soccer player. So it only seemed natural that their offspring would be drawn to sports. But not quite. The firstborn son, Sergei, was a wrestler for a while, but it soon became clear that he was not going to be a star in that endeavor. Another boy, Mikhail, was not the least bit interested in competitive sports. The only one who could fulfill an athletic destiny was Alex, and he wasn't doing all that well with hockey.

The main problem was that Ovechkin was a poor skater, so he was held out of close games. He would only play when the game was no longer in doubt. So his mother arranged for her son to get individual coaching, and those lessons started to pay off. By the time he was 12, Ovechkin broke the record of Pavel Bure, another famous Russian-born player, when he scored 59 times in a season. Not only could he score, his skating improved dramatically and he was soon a dominating player. During his teen years, Ovechkin was clearly on the verge of stardom, and everyone noticed how he approached each game with great passion and desire. Soon, Ovechkin and his entire family were committed to seeing him make it to the National Hockey League.

In the last year before he was eligible for the NHL Entry Draft, Ovechkin played in 53 games for Moscow Dynamo, recording 13 goals and 24 points. His performance at the world junior tournament was more impressive, but the hockey scouts all seemed to agree beforehand that he had the most potential of any player who was going to be selected in 2004. The Washington Capitals agreed and took Ovechkin first overall. They waited for the NHL lockout to end before unleashing the talented Russian on the rest of the league.

The 2005–06 season saw Ovechkin produce one of the best seasons a rookie has ever enjoyed in the NHL. He would score 52 times and total 106 points as he almost single-handedly took the Capitals back to respectability. His power-laden game struck fear into all opposing teams, and he could seemingly score at will. However, there was one goal that stood out, and it came on the road against the Phoenix Coyotes on the night of January 16, 2006. The Washington club had the game well in hand in the third period, but Ovechkin was not quite done. With about eight minutes to go, Ovechkin came down the right wing with Phoenix defenseman Paul Mara backing up with the 6'2", 229-pound Washington power-forward, who was determined to score a second goal in the game. Mara took Ovechkin down and the Capitals star briefly lost control of the puck as he hit the ice. However, Ovechkin swung his stick as he sprawled and rolled across the ice surface on his back, sending the disk into the net past a startled Coyotes netminder!

No one could believe what they had just witnessed—not even Wayne Gretzky, the Coyotes coach. "That was pretty sweet. You know he's a pretty phenomenal player and he's a tremendous influence in the game. It's great to see because he is that good." As for Ovechkin, he simply said, "The best goal I ever scored. I just went down and shot." The goal was a sensation on YouTube and has been viewed many times over since the goal was scored. Even those on the other side do not seem to mind being a part of a special goal, including goalie Brian Boucher, who was with the Coyotes at the time. "Now, looking back, it was a (great) goal by him. I guess I'm proud to be a part of it. He's a world-class player. You know my son certainly gets a kick out of looking at it," said Boucher few years later. It was merely the beginning of many highlight-reel goals Ovechkin would score in his first few years of NHL play.

Ovechkin was named rookie of the year for the 2005–06 season, the first of many awards the right winger has won since entering the league. He has been a first team all-star six times and has taken the Hart Trophy on two occasions so far. He has scored 50 or more goals on four occasions already, and is clearly one of the most gifted goal scorers in league history. It is great to see that Alex Ovechkin has developed his hockey talent this far—and to think it all started with the death of a loved one who inspired his dedication to the game.

Alex Ovechkin has scored 301 goals and 614 points in 475 career games for the Washington Capitals as of the end of the 2010–11 season.

KEVIN WEEKES
BORN: TORONTO, ONTARIO
NHL SEASONS: 1997–98 TO 2008–09
DEFINING MOMENT: JANUARY 27, 2004

Goaltender Kevin Weekes was born in Toronto to parents who had arrived in Canada from Barbados. Carl and Vadney Weekes were glad their son had an interest in hockey but knew he would face challenges as a black youngster in a sport that had virtually no people of color. But Kevin was inspired by Edmonton netminder Grant Fuhr, a star goalie for the Oilers who would become the first black player to be elected to the Hockey Hall of Fame. Weekes started playing in net as a result, and when he was just in the second grade, Weekes wrote that he wanted to one day play in the NHL. He started out by playing street hockey and eventually convinced his parents to let him try the game on ice. On occasion, Weekes would hear some rather inappropriate racial remarks, but he was undeterred from pursing his ambitions to be a hockey player. If Grant Fuhr could put this stuff behind him, so could he.

As he got older, Weekes was a part of some well-known teams in the Toronto area (St. Michaels and the Red Wings) and his good play got him noticed by the Owen Sound Platers of the OHL. The 6'2", 215-pound netminder was selected by the Florida Panthers (41st overall) in the 1993 Entry Draft. At age 19 and after two seasons in Owen Sound, he joined the Ottawa 67's for his final year of junior hockey. He had never posted a winning season with either junior club, which meant that he needed to find more experience in the American Hockey League. He played in 60 games for the

Carolina Monarchs and posted a 24-25-8 record, his best showing to date. In 1998–99, he was playing in the IHL for the Detroit Vipers and won 19 times while losing only five games.

Florida traded his rights to Vancouver as part of a major deal (Weekes appeared in 11 games for Florida during the 1997–98 season). He was a Canuck long enough to post six wins before being dealt away again, this time to the New York Islanders. Another move to the Tampa Bay Lightning saw Weekes get his first serious chance. He posted a 20-33-3 record for the team that only won 24 games in total during the 2000–01 season. Just when it looked like he had found a home, Weekes was traded to the Carolina Hurricanes. General manager Jim Rutherford, a former NHL goalie, had always liked Weekes from his junior days and looked forward to giving the still-developing netminder a chance. "I started watching Kevin in the juniors when he was 16 and I liked him then. Fundamentally he was good. He still had things to work on but everyone does at that age. He has good size, takes up a lot of net and has exceptionally good reflexes." The Carolina manager was not the least bit concerned that Weekes had been moved so often so early in his career. Rutherford believed the netminder had not been put into the right situations.

Weekes made his first great impression in Carolina when he filled in for regular starter Arturs Irbe in the 2002 playoffs. The unexpected playing time saw Weekes record a series-ending 1-0 shutout against New Jersey in the first round; then he beat the Canadiens 2-0 in the first game of the next series. Irbe reclaimed the starting role during the Montreal series, but without Weekes's efforts, the Hurricanes might not have made the Stanley Cup finals.

Carolina slipped back the next season and Weekes's record took another beating—he went 14-24-9 for a team that missed the playoffs. However, in 2003–04, Weekes played in a career-high 66 games and posted a career-best 23 wins to go along with six shutouts. One of those shutouts took place on the night of January 27,

2004, when the Hurricanes visited the Maple Leafs in Toronto. The local kid came back home to blank the Toronto side 2-0 at the Air Canada Centre, stopping 32 shots in the process. "It's very gratifying to come back here and win," Weekes said after the game. "There are 20 or 25 million people who would love to play here." Weekes made two spectacular saves on Leafs captain Mats Sundin who had eight shots on goal during the game. Hurricanes coach Peter Laviolette summarized Weekes's night best by simply saying, "He played real well. He was very sharp."

The shutout in Toronto may have been the last great moment of Weekes's NHL career. He was dealt to the New York Rangers, with whom he played out the last four years of his career to finish with a 105-163-39 record in 348 appearances with 19 career shutouts. But the netminder was not through with hockey just yet.

After his retirement, Weekes became the first black Canadian to be named an analyst on *Hockey Night in Canada*. It was his hope that his being on *HNIC* would inspire other young, black hockey fans to consider a career in broadcasting games. Weekes also took the time to recall how he had looked up not only to Grant Fuhr, but to other heroes as he grew up. "Grant was so important to me. So were Pokey Reddick, Freddie Brathwaite, and Joaquin Gage (all black goaltenders as well). Had it not been for those guys I might not be here today."

It's quite likely someone will say the same about Weekes one day.

Kevin Weekes continued to work as a game analyst for *Hockey Night in Canada* during the 2010–11 season.

SIDNEY CROSBY
PITTSBURGH PENGUINS®

JONATHAN TOEWS
C - 19

NICKLAS LIDSTROM
DETROIT RED WINGS®

JEAN BELIVEAU / CENT. MONTREAL CANADIENS

WAYNE GRETZKY
OILERS

MAPLE LEAFS

DARRYL SITTLER
CENTER

Husky

mario **LEMIEUX**
pittsburgh PENGUINS • C

LEADERSHIP

Wearing the "C" has always been considered a very important and prestigious honor. Being named team captain at any level is one of the greatest moments a player will ever achieve in his career. While all team captains have many of the same characteristics, only a few are truly exceptional leaders. In this chapter on "Leadership" we'll focus on the following players who truly excelled in their leadership roles:

Nicklas Lidstrom
Sidney Crosby ✔
George Armstrong
Trevor Linden
Mario Lemieux ✔
Wayne Gretzky ✔
Darryl Sittler
Jonathan Toews
Jean Beliveau
Mark Messier ✔

NICKLAS LIDSTROM
BORN: VASTERAS, SWEDEN
NHL SEASONS: 1991–92 TO PRESENT
DEFINING MOMENT: 2008 STANLEY CUP FINALS

It seems funny now, but many people actually believed that a European-born captain was not capable of leading his team to an NHL championship. This all changed on the night of June 4, 2008, when Swedish-born Nicklas Lidstrom accepted the Stanley Cup from Commissioner Gary Bettman after a 3-2 Detroit win, forever erasing all doubts.

Since his arrival in the NHL, Nicklas Lidstrom has played a quiet, steady game on the Red Wing blueline. He is not at all flashy, but he rarely loses any one-on-one battles. He is a superb skater and executes a highly intelligent game by stressing positional play in his own end. He has good size at 6'2" and 190 pounds, but is hardly the physical type. Lidstrom will not shy away from the heavy going, but he likes to move the puck up quickly to Detroit's very capable forwards. With his two-way skills (much like those of his idol, Hall of Famer Borje Salming), Lidstrom is in on virtually every important situation for the Red Wings. When fellow blueliner Vladimir Konstantinov's career tragically ended in a car accident only days after the Red Wings won the Cup in 1997, Lidstrom's value to the Detroit club skyrocketed.

Lidstrom began his NHL career in 1991–92 after being selected 70th overall by Detroit in 1989. He scored 11 goals and 49 assists that first year. His numbers slipped slightly the next season (only

41 points), but he quickly recovered in 1993–94 to post 56 points. In 1994–95, the rebuilt Red Wings got their first taste of success when they made it to the finals. Lidstrom led the way with 16 points in 18 playoff games. He followed up with a great regular season in 1995–96 with 17 goals and 50 assists, but the Wings lost in the playoffs to the Colorado Avalanche. Detroit, however, was ready for the 1996–97 season. Lidstrom had contributed 57 points that season and would rack up another eight points in the playoffs, helping the Wings win the Cup in four straight games. In the sweep, Lidstrom and partner Larry Murphy effectively shut down the explosive Eric Lindros and his Flyer teammates to clinch the championship.

The stellar defenseman was outstanding in 2000–01, when he finally won the Norris Trophy (15 goals, 56 assists) after three straight years as runner-up. He won it again in 2002 and in 2003 to become the first three-straight winner since Bobby Orr. When the Red Wings won the cup again in 2002, he won the Conn Smythe Trophy as playoff MVP.

As the Detroit club aged (especially on defense), the team relied more and more on Lidstrom. In 2002–03, he led the league in ice time per game (29:20 minutes), the highest of his career. He was also named a first-team All-Star, becoming the only defenseman besides Orr and Doug Harvey to be selected for six consecutive seasons.

Lidstrom had a rather dismal season in 2003–04 when he recorded just 38 points (his lowest full-season total since he joined the Red Wings). However, he came back strong in 2005–06 (after taking the lockout year off from hockey) to score 16 goals and rack up a career-high 80 points. Urged to shoot more by new Detroit coach Mike Babcock, the consistent Lidstrom heeded the advice and worked his power play magic. He averaged 28:06 minutes of ice time each contest and proved to be durable by playing in 80 games. The Red Wings won the Presidents' Trophy for leading the league in the regular season, but were upset by the Edmonton Oilers in the first round of the '06 playoffs. Lidstrom had an especially difficult time in the post-season, but he did help Sweden capture the gold medal at the 2006 Winter Olympics.

The next year, Lidstrom was named Detroit's new captain to start the 2006–07 season. The Wings faced the agony of another playoff exit when Anaheim knocked them off in the Conference final in 2007, but in 2007–08, Lidstrom led his team to the best record in the NHL (contributing 70 points during the season) and then to the championship with playoff wins over Nashville, Colorado, and Dallas. The Lidstrom-led team would meet Pittsburgh for the Stanley Cup.

When the Red Wings won the third game of the '08 finals in Pittsburgh, it looked like they would capture the Stanley Cup rather easily. During that May 31 contest, Lidstrom scored on the power play to even the score 1-1 before Jiri Hudler put the game away in the third. The Red Wings captain was named first star and played 28:23 minutes in the tightly fought contest. But after the game was over, Lidstrom cautioned his teammates like a good captain should. "We know we haven't won anything yet. We won three games. We have to win four to win the Cup." The Penguins won the next game after a long overtime session, but Detroit was still determined to win it all—even if it meant doing it on the road.

There were those who questioned if the super-smooth Lidstrom had enough fire in him to take a team all the way. There should have been no concern about Lidstrom's hockey abilities. To be sure, he is one the greatest defensemen in NHL history, but doubts about a European captain remained. So it's a safe bet that Lidstrom really relished being the first European captain to lift the trophy high over his head. "It's something I'm very proud of," Lidstrom said. "I've been over here for a long time. I watched Steve Yzerman win it as our captain and I'm very proud to be captain of the Detroit Red Wings and to win the Stanley Cup again (his fourth). It felt great to be the first guy to touch the Cup on our team." He then passed the Cup to teammate Dallas Drake, a long-time NHL veteran who made it to the finals for the first time in 16 seasons—a classy move by the Red Wings leader.

Coach Babcock would say this about his captain: "Nicklas Lidstrom, in my opinion, is a phenomenal leader and captain with his poise and his skill." Enough said.

Nicklas Lidstrom has won the Norris Trophy a total of seven times. In June 2011, Lidstrom announced he would play in his 20th NHL season in 2011–12.

SIDNEY CROSBY
BORN: COLE HARBOUR, NOVA SCOTIA
NHL SEASONS: 2005–06 TO PRESENT
DEFINING MOMENT: 2009 PLAYOFFS

When the NHL's lottery draft was held in the summer of 2005, the Pittsburgh Penguins were hoping history would repeat itself. Way back in 1984, the Penguins were fortunate enough to have selected Mario Lemieux first overall, a move that saved their floundering franchise. At that time, the Penguins had been assured the first selection simply by finishing last the previous season—but times had changed. Since the Penguins had the worst record in 2003–04, the last year before the lockout, they would be part of a lottery that determined the draft order. The smile on Lemieux's face (he was now a part-owner of the team) said it all when it was announced that the Penguins had won, and would indeed have first selection.

And they were ecstatic, of course, to select Sidney Crosby, a native of Cole Harbour, Nova Scotia first overall. The Penguins—and maybe the entire National Hockey League—had a new savior.

Nobody ever has had greater expectations of themselves than Sidney Crosby, and he has maintained these expectations ever since he first put on skates before turning three years old. His prodigious goal-scoring made him a hockey phenomenon and got him noticed early. The attention was not always pleasant, but it helped give Crosby a mental toughness that has helped him become hockey's highest achiever. He was so focused on exceling that it never bothered him that others might want to see him fail. As he kept rising up the ranks, it became clear he was going to be an NHL star. He started off by recording 102 points (39G, 63A) in his rookie season. And then, to prove he was no fluke, he notched a league-leading 120 points in his second year. Comparisons were made to Wayne Gretzky and Mario Lemieux, but those gifted players had the benefit of starting their careers in an era where goals were plentiful, making Crosby's achievements (572 points in 412 career games to date) all the more remarkable.

Crosby also knew that his career would be measured by how many Stanley Cups he would win, and in the 2008 playoffs, he missed his first opportunity when the rebuilt Penguins were edged out in the finals by Detroit in six. A television commercial had previously run with the young Pittsburgh captain (Crosby was given the "C" to start the 2007–08 season), stating he would not want to be looking at another team skating off with the coveted silver trophy. Losing in the final was, therefore, a real turning point. Crosby realized more than ever that it was up to him to lead his team to victory and become "the new Mario Lemieux" in Pittsburgh—not an easy role to fill. To his credit, Crosby never shied away from the demands. In fact, he excelled because of them, and there is no better instance of this than in the 2009 playoffs, where Crosby had a playoff best—15 goals scored (totaling 31 points in 24 post-season games)—and then raised the Cup when the Penguins came back to defeat Detroit in a seven-game final. No one should ever doubt that Crosby will do what he sets out to accomplish!

The Penguins had a difficult time with the Philadelphia Flyers but eventually wore down their state rivals in six games in the first round of the '09 playoffs. The second round would prove to be even more difficult as the Washington Capitals held home ice advantage and Crosby would have to face his long-time nemesis—Alex Ovechkin—for the title of the NHL's best player. The series came down to the seventh game; the Penguins survived in amazing fashion with a 6-2 win, with Crosby scoring two goals. Crosby scored the opening goal of the game on a Pittsburgh power play as he stood beside the Washington net. The Penguins never looked back. Crosby assisted on the Penguins' third goal and then stole the puck from Ovechkin to score his second of the night in the third period to put the Penguins up 6-1. When "Sid the Kid" was asked about beating his archrival "Alexander the Great" in such an important game, he chose to focus on his team instead. "It feels good just because of how the series went, not particularly because it was me and him," said Crosby, who was named first star of the game. "I just said, 'Great series.' There were a lot of eyes on the series. It was a battle for both teams. Individually we both wanted to make sure we did a great job," Crosby told the assembled media about the post-game handshake with Ovechkin. Both players did indeed want to excel, but only one came out the true victor and that was Pittsburgh captain Sidney Crosby, who seized the moment to lead and excel.

Given his history of scoring big goals, was anyone surprised when Crosby scored the "Golden Goal" at the 2010 Winter Olympic Games? As overtime began between Team Canada and Team United States, somewhere around 34 million Canadians held their collective breath. There had to be a certain calm among those players wearing the Maple Leaf that somehow, Crosby would find a way to score the winner. Just past the seven-minute mark, Crosby yelled for a pass from teammate Jarome Iginla and, with one quick swat from his magical stick, the puck was in the American net. The conquering hero was mobbed by teammates and adored once again by all those who live north of the 49th. Teammate Joe Thornton may have expressed it best for every Canadian hockey fan after the game when he said, "You're just happy Crosby is on your team. You're happy he was born in Canada."

The pressure to win gold at the Olympic Games may have produced one of the most tension-filled moments in hockey history, but for Crosby it was just another highlight in a career filled with great opportunities to succeed. Well mannered, polite, and giving of his time, the 5'11", 200-pound Nova Scotian is by no means the biggest player in the NHL, but he does have the greatest will to win, and he wants to do it over and over again. He is everything a great hockey player should be and the best of role models for youngsters. Crosby is now the face of the NHL—and that might be the best thing to ever happen since the days of Gretzky and Lemieux. As he approaches his mid-twenties, Crosby has plenty of time to keep adding awards and championships to his ever-growing list of achievements. And this list will continue to grow, due in no small part to the great leadership skills that he will carry along the way.

Sidney Crosby was named the NHL's most valuable player for the 2006–07 season, a year that saw him win the Art Ross Trophy as well. He scored 51 goals in 2009–10 and had 66 points (including 32 goals) in only 41 games during 2010–11, when a concussion ended his season early.

GEORGE ARMSTRONG

BORN: SKEAD, ONTARIO
NHL SEASONS: 1949–50 TO 1970–71
DEFINING MOMENT: MAY 2, 1967

Toronto Maple Leafs owner Conn Smythe loved George Armstrong's approach to the game of hockey, and in one of his last moves as the Leafs boss, he named the man they called "Chief" (largely due to his Native background) team captain in 1957. Smythe knew something of great leadership, having named Hap Day, Syl Apps, and Ted Kennedy—all superb Stanley Cup–winning Leafs and Hall of Fame players—to the role of Leafs captain. As great as many of his predecessors were, however, Armstrong was the only Leafs captain to lead Toronto to four Stanley Cups!

Armstrong grew up in Falconbridge, a small town near Sudbury in northern Ontario. His mother was of Algonquin heritage while his father, who earned his living working in the mines, was of Scottish descent. Young George developed his hockey skills locally and eventually caught the eye of Toronto scout Bob Wilson. He played for the Copper Cliff Redmen as a 16-year-old in 1946–47, but really became a prospect when he scored 33 goals and totaled 73 points in just 36 games with Stratford the following year. The Maple Leafs assigned Armstrong to their main junior team—the Toronto Marlboros—and the 6'1" right winger promptly scored 29 goals and 62 points in just 39 games. It was determined, however, that he was not quite ready to play in the NHL, so he played senior hockey for one year, recording 115 points over a 45-game schedule and helping the team win the championship in 1950. Armstrong then played most of the following two seasons in Pittsburgh in the American Hockey League before finally sticking with the Leafs for good in 1952–53.

It was quickly determined that Armstrong was not going to be a great goal scorer or point producer—but he was going to be a solid professional. He would score anywhere between 15 and 20 goals most years (his highest goal total was 23) and usually around 40 to 55 points. He was renowned for his wonderful sense of humor, and served as an important buffer between stern coach Punch Imlach and the Leaf players for the next ten years. Armstrong was never fast on his skates, but he was rarely out of position. He was also one of the most determined checkers in team history. He could stickhandle out of the corners with ease and his 184 pounds made him hard to handle. Armstrong was especially good in the playoffs (60 points in 110 career games), helping lead the Leafs to four championships in the Sixties. One of the most magical playoff moments for Armstrong came in the 1967 finals when the Leafs and the Montreal Canadiens met for the last Stanley Cup in the era known as the "Original Six."

The 1966–67 Maple Leafs had a very up-and-down regular season with a team record 10-straight losses at one point, but a strong finish landed them in third place. The powerful Chicago Blackhawks were expected to demolish Toronto in the semi-final, but the resilient Leafs got some great goaltending from Terry Sawchuk to defeat the first-place team in six games. Armstrong missed three games of the series with an injury but battled back in time to face the high-flying Canadiens in the finals. Montreal opened the series with a 6-2 win and made the Leafs look old and slow (there were 12 Leaf players who were 30 or older. Johnny Bower and Allan Stanley were in their 40s). But Johnny Bower filled in for Sawchuk in the next game and shut out the Habs 3-0. He was also in net when the Leafs won a long overtime game 3-2, but Sawchuk had to go back in and got bombed 6-2 in the next game. The Leafs never lost their ability to bounce back throughout this post-season and took the fifth contest 4-1 right in Montreal. The Leafs would have the chance to win the Cup on home ice on the night of May 2, 1967.

It was a very tight game, but Toronto opened the scoring in the second period with two goals while Sawchuk held the Canadiens off the scoreboard. Montreal got one back early in the third on an individual effort by Dick Duff. The Leafs then set up a blue wall and dared the Canadiens to get past them. Sawchuk turned all Montreal drives aside and with just 55 seconds to play, the Leafs iced the puck. Imlach sent out five veterans, including Armstrong, to protect the lead. The tension in the building was high, as all fans knew the Habs—with the likes of Bobby Rousseau, Henri Richard, Jean Beliveau, and Yvan Cournoyer—had the ability to strike quickly. But the Leaf senior players were on the ice because they were cool, seasoned professionals who would be able to deal with the moment at hand. They did not disappoint.

The Leafs won the draw and got the puck to Armstrong as they skated up the ice. He made sure he crossed center (to avoid an icing call) before taking a long shot that went right into the middle of the empty Montreal net. It was Armstrong's only goal of the finals and marked the end of a special era of hockey. It was also Armstrong's last great moment as captain and leader of the Maple Leafs—and their last Stanley Cup to date.

Armstrong did something unusual as he accepted the Stanley Cup from League president Clarence Campbell—he brought along his son Brian. The youngster helped his father take the Cup as the silver trophy was swarmed by blue sweaters. After the game Armstrong, as team captain, spoke to Ward Cornell of *Hockey Night in Canada*. "It was a thrilling game for us, especially in this Centennial Year, and to beat a great hockey team like the Montreal Canadiens. Their fans should be proud of them. And we're proud that we were able to beat them. Anybody that can win the Stanley

Cup is a great team, and we are a great team also. We went out there and did the best we could, and we came through and won, and certainly it was not easy. That team never stopped until the last bell went." When asked about why all the older Leafs (nobody under 30) were out on the ice to close out the game, Armstrong quipped, "That's because we don't get out of position as fast as the younger guys do. We stay in position a bit better."

It was speculated during the television broadcast that Armstrong might be playing his last game as a Leaf. However Armstrong came back to play four more seasons to bring his totals to 1,187 games played (still a Leaf record), 296 goals, and 713 points—all earned in a Toronto uniform. Conn Smythe once called Armstrong the best captain the Maple Leafs ever had and few could argue that point. It was a great compliment for Armstrong—one of the most humble people in hockey.

George Armstrong was elected to the Hall of Fame in 1977.

TREVOR LINDEN
BORN: MEDICINE HAT, ALBERTA
NHL SEASONS: 1988–89 TO 2007–08
DEFINING MOMENT: JUNE 14, 1994

The Vancouver Canucks were a pretty bad team at the end of the 1987–88 season. Winners of only 25 games in an 80-game schedule, the Canucks recorded just 59 points. Only Minnesota (51) and Toronto (52) notched fewer in the regular campaign, but because the Maple Leafs were in the same division as the North Stars, they managed to pick up a playoff spot. As a result, the Canucks held the second pick of the 1988 Entry Draft. Mike Modano and Trevor Linden were the most prized prospects going into the draft, but it made sense for the Minnesota club to select the American-born Modano. When Minnesota selected the slick center from Michigan, the Canucks were happy to take Medicine Hat native Trevor Linden, who had just come off two Memorial Cup championships with the hometown Tigers. Even though the Stars (who later moved to Dallas) did quite well with Modano in their lineup (for the next 21 years!), Linden was not a choice the Canucks would ever come to regret.

From the moment Linden joined the Canucks as a rookie for the 1988–89 season, he showed a maturity rare for anybody 18 years of age. He scored 30 times in his first year and recorded 59 points, gaining second place in the rookie-of-the-year honors (he was beaten out for the Calder Trophy by New York Ranger defenseman Brian Leetch). If his on-ice performance was impressive, so was the way he conducted himself off the ice. "He seems like that squeaky-clean, all-Canadian boy," said Canucks general manager Pat Quinn, who selected Linden in the draft. "He's a very nice young man who seems to know where he's going at a very young age. While others his age are still growing up, he seems to have grown up. His people skills are amazing." Vancouver coach Bob McCammon predicted great things for Linden. "When you think of the kind of player Trevor Linden is, 30 goals is amazing," he said after the '88-'89 campaign. "He plays as hard in his own end as he does in the other. He goes into the corners and makes plays. He'll never be a (Wayne) Gretzky or (Mario) Lemieux (in terms of scoring) but you win Stanley Cups with guys like Trevor Linden." Russ Farwell, who knew Linden well in junior as the general manager of the Tigers, added this about the youngster: "He plays hard every night and does whatever he has to win. There's only one way with

Trevor—he plays the game head on. He'll be captain in Vancouver one day, no doubt."

By the 1990–91 season, Linden was one of three players who wore the "C," and the next year saw him take over the captain's role on his own. He became a consistent 30-goal scorer and a 70- to 80-point player, which was right about where a player of his skills should have been from a production point of view. The Canucks made the playoffs in 1993–94, but they had not won more than one round in the playoffs since unexpectedly making the finals in 1982. The Canucks had only posted a 41-40-3 record during the '93–'94 regular season, but a trade late in the year netted them two mobile defensemen, Bret Hedican and Jeff Brown, and a utility forward, Nathan LaFayette. The move set the team up with great depth. Linden and his sublimely talented teammate Pavel Bure led the way in post-season, getting the team as close to the Cup as they had ever been. It was a new level of achievement for the Canuck organization, which entered the NHL in 1970–71. And it would not be matched until the 2011 playoffs (when the Canucks once again lost the seventh game of the final).

To open the playoffs, Vancouver came back from a 3-1 series deficit to sneak by Calgary in seven games. Linden scored an overtime winner to clinch the sixth game, with Bure closing out a thrilling seventh game with another OT winner. From that point on, the Canucks steamrolled over the Dallas Stars (in five games) and the Toronto Maple Leafs (also in five) to reach the finals against the New York Rangers. Once again, Vancouver fell behind three games to one but battled back to even the series, forcing a deciding contest in New York. It was the night of June 14, 1994—and Linden would shine.

Linden, in fact, had the game of his life in this epic contest, but it was still not enough to get the Canucks the coveted Stanley Cup. The Rangers were under enormous pressure to end their 54-year drought and took a 2-0 lead in the first period. But Linden was just as determined to lead his team back, and scored Vancouver's first goal as he broke in on Ranger netminder Mike Richter. Linden fought off defenseman Brian Leetch by going to his backhand, and then switched to his forehand as he approached the net. Linden's superb short-handed effort suddenly gave the Canucks some life. However, Ranger captain Mark Messier would score to make it 3-1 before the end of the second period.

Linden once again got his team back into the game when he scored a power-play goal before five minutes had passed in the third period. He knocked home a shot past Richter as he stood beside the Ranger net. The Canucks tried as hard as they could to tie the game (one late-game shot beat Richter but hit the post) and the Rangers hung on to win 3-2. After the game, Linden sat down with a blood-stained towel over his shoulder and said, "It was a battle. I was asked if we got beat by a better team. I don't think we got beat by a better team. It could have gone either way." Linden had 25 points (including 12 goals) in 24 playoff games (second only to Bure's 31 points) and had clearly shown he was the leader everyone had predicted he would become years ago.

Vancouver traded Linden away in 1998 (largely due to the free-agent signing of Messier by the Canucks), but he was never as good a player as he had been in a Canuck uniform. However, the popular Linden was brought back to Vancouver to close out the final five years of his career—a proper ending for Vancouver's best captain and finest leader.

Trevor Linden still holds the Vancouver Canucks team record for most seasons played (16) and most games played (1,140). His number 16 was retired by the team in 2008.

MARIO LEMIEUX
BORN: MONTREAL, QUEBEC
NHL SEASONS: 1984–85 TO 2005–06
DEFINING MOMENTS: MAY 17 & MAY 25 1991

Mario Lemieux had been one of the most dominating players to ever play junior hockey. In 200 games for the Laval Voisins of the QMJHL, the 6'4", 230-pound center scored 247 goals and a total of 562 points. He was also a superb playoff performer as a junior (98 points in just 44 games) and took the Laval club to the Memorial Cup. Lemieux's soft hands made many of his goals look like works of art—a prelude to things to come in the NHL. Many hoped the native of Montreal would play for the hometown Canadiens, but there was no way the Penguins were going to trade away their first pick. They expected the elegant Lemieux to lead them to the top of the NHL—and, eventually, to the Stanley Cup.

The Penguins were an absolutely dreadful hockey team by the end of the 1983–84 season. Their record was 16-58-6 and the future of the entire franchise seemed to be in doubt. Attendance was dwindling and the Penguins had never come close to winning anything since they had begun playing in the NHL, starting in the 1967–68 season. Sure, they had produced some high-scoring, entertaining teams in the 1970s, but nothing close to championship caliber. By 1984, there was a special player available to draft in June, and the Penguins made sure they were in a position to take Mario Lemieux. The Penguins did everything they could to finish dead last overall (barely edging out the New Jersey Devils by three points for the dubious honor), thereby securing the first overall draft selection (the draft lottery had not been introduced at this point). Some accused Pittsburgh of trying too hard to be the worst team in the league (like using a minor league goalie for many games). Nevertheless, on June 9, 1984, their fortunes took a turn for the better.

Lemiuex and his representatives soon realized what he meant to the team and were not very happy with the way his contract discussions were going. While he attended the draft at the Montreal Forum, he refused to go to the table of the team that selected him. He stood when his name was called and waved to the crowd, who gave him a warm reception, but he did not put on the team's jersey as was custom for all players being drafted. "I didn't go to the table because negotiations aren't going well," he explained. "I didn't want to put on a Pittsburgh sweater because they don't want me badly enough." It was an act of defiance, to be sure, but young Lemieux was not afraid to stand up for what he thought was right.

The Penguins eventually worked out a contract that got Lemieux in a Pittsburgh uniform. He scored a goal on his very first shift in the NHL, finishing with 43 goals and an even 100 points as an 18-year-old rookie. For the next five seasons, Lemieux would record 107 points or better (199 points was his highest count in 1988–89) and would score 48 or more goals each of those years (an incredible 85 goals in one season was his career high).

As well as he was producing, the great frustration for Lemieux was that the Penguins were out of the playoffs almost every season. When they finally made the post-season in 1989, the Penguins blew a 3-1 lead to Philadelphia in the second round. But Lemieux was still determined. "I know I'll drink from that Cup one day. I just know it," he said in the aftermath of that loss.

The Penguins missed the post-season again in 1990, but in 1991, they made it all the way to the final round after defeating Washington, New Jersey, and Boston. Lemieux had missed much of the regular season with a back injury, but he was ready for the playoffs. So was the rest of the Pittsburgh club. The Penguins faced the surprising Minnesota North Stars for the Cup and lost the first game at home. The next game was played in Pittsburgh on the night of May 17, 1991. Down 2-1, the North Stars were pressing for the equalizer when Lemieux went into action and scored the most memorable goal of his career.

Lemieux took the puck right up the middle of the ice and moved in on two North Star defensemen. One of the defenders moved away slightly, putting Lemieux up against Shawn Chambers in a one-on-one situation. Lemieux charged toward the net. He slid the puck past Chambers with a brilliant move through the legs that completely froze the North Star player. The Penguins captain was now in all alone on goalie Jon Casey. Using his long reach to great effectiveness, Lemieux kept the puck away from Casey, who had made a move to stop him. Lemieux then swept around the netminder before backhanding a clean shot into the empty net! Minnesota never recovered from Lemieux's spectacular effort, losing the game 4-1.

"The first time I came down on Chambers, I tried to go outside and he caught up with me. This time, I went outside but then I brought it back at the last second. He thought I was going outside again. Then I just beat Casey on a backhand," Lemieux said matter-of-factly. "They'd played better than us in the first half of the game and though we had a 2-1 lead, I thought we were in a lot of trouble," he continued. "So it (the goal) was a really big one. I mean this was a game we absolutely had to get."

The series went back and forth, but the Penguins eventually took a 3-2 series lead back to Minnesota. The Penguins opened the scoring just two minutes in when Joe Mullen scored. Then Lemieux scored another one of his breathtaking signature goals to make it 2-0. The Pittsburgh captain would then set up three more tallies as the Penguins romped to an 8-0 win. Lemieux finally won the Cup—just like promised. "This means everything to be a part of a championship team," Lemieux said. "This is the ultimate dream." There was no doubt who led the Penguins to their first championship, and, to prove it was no fluke, Lemieux took his club to another Cup in 1992—winning the Conn Smythe Trophy on each occasion!

Mario Lemieux was elected to the Hall of Fame in 1997.

WAYNE GRETZKY
BORN: BRANTFORD, ONTARIO
NHL SEASONS: 1979–80 TO 1998–99
DEFINING MOMENT: MAY 19, 1984

The Edmonton Oilers were set to play their 99th game of the year as they took to the ice on the night of May 19, 1984. The hometown Oilers were greeted with wild cheers from an adoring crowd who sensed that Edmonton was about to put an end to the New York Islanders dynasty—winners of the Stanley Cup for the previous four seasons. The young Oilers held a 3-1 lead in games and were just one win short of wresting the championship. But the pressure was on Edmonton this night: they needed to win on home ice or face having to go back and play the last two games of the series in front of a hostile New York audience. Even though the Edmonton crowd hungered for a win, there was a sense of unease in the air. The Oilers had never taken it. With Gretzky, they had contended for at least three years, and even lost in the final just a year earlier to the same Islanders in four straight games. But tonight?

The spotlight would, of course, be on Wayne Gretzky. The superbly talented Edmonton center had been held scoreless versus New York in the 1983 finals, and had only recently started to produce in 1984's showcase. A couple of goals in the fourth game helped carry the Oilers to a resounding 7-2 win, but now the Cup was on the line. Could "The Great One" do it?

Gretzky had been named captain in 1983, but questions remained—could he lead his club to the ultimate victory? Could the Oilers finally silence all the critics? These were questions that would be asked until the Oilers finally put all doubts to rest.

Edmonton boasted an all-star lineup of young, fast, and highly skilled players who could score virtually at will (especially Gretzky) but still couldn't capture the final piece of the puzzle—the title of champions.

Gretzky was used to great pressure and always had to lead from the moment he first put on skates. His sublime hockey skills had made him the centerpiece of any team he had played on since the time he was about nine years old. When he joined the NHL (Gretzky was never drafted—his rights were retained from the days when the Oilers played in the WHA), there were people who did not believe the slightly built (6', 185-pound) Gretzky could survive in the rough-and-tumble NHL. He proved these critics wrong when he tied Marcel Dionne for the points championship in his rookie year (when he was just 19), and then began demolishing the NHL record book with one great year after another. He was only 23 at this point, and the only thing he had left to do was lead his team to the Holy Grail. Tonight the kid from Brantford had a chance to show he was a leader.

It turned out there was no need to worry. Gretzky had been waiting for this moment his whole life and was not going to let it pass without his absolute, greatest effort. He scored two first-period goals, one on a breakaway and another when he ripped home a pass from teammate Jari Kurri. The Oilers added two more in the second, taking a 4-0 lead going into the third. The Islanders put a little scare into the crowd with a pair of markers early in the third, but the Oilers got good goaltending from Andy Moog. Soon the clock was winding down and as the Edmonton crowd was in a total frenzy, the Oilers added an empty net goal to make it 5-2. The Oilers jumped for joy and as the clock ticked off the final seconds, *Hockey Night in Canada* announcer Bob Cole exclaimed, "The Oilers have won the Stanley Cup!"

The relieved Edmonton club mobbed their goalie. Each player had a huge smile on his face. The Stanley Cup was brought out for NHL president John Ziegler to present to the Oilers. Gretzky gave Ziegler a quick hug and then took the big trophy and raised it over his head. The Oilers leader took the Cup around the ice with a mob trailing along.

As reporters gathered around him, Gretzky was almost at a loss for words: "I don't know how to describe it.. When the NHL president gave me the Cup on the ice, my mind flashed to a picture I'd seen of Jean Beliveau receiving the Cup one time when Montreal won it. Now it's me. A dream come true." As champagne was poured over his head, Gretzky added, "We played well the whole series. We played tremendous hockey." Then he remembered to congratulate the opposition. "The Islanders are great champions. We hope we can be as good as they are."

The Oilers would indeed prove to be great champions, creating one of greatest dynasties of the NHL behind the leadership and great play of Gretzky. He would have many more great nights in the NHL, but few would ever match the night he led his team to the Stanley Cup for the very first time.

Wayne Gretzky is the NHL's all-time leader in goals (894), assists (1,963), and points (2,857). He was elected to the Hall of Fame in 1999.

DARRYL SITTLER

BORN: KITCHENER, ONTARIO
NHL SEASONS: 1970–71 TO 1984–85
DEFINING MOMENT: FEBRUARY 7, APRIL 22 & SEPTEMBER 15, 1976

When Darryl Sittler arrived for his first training camp with the Toronto Maple Leafs in the fall of 1970, the team had a surprise waiting for him. In his dressing room stall, the team had placed sweater number 27 for the rookie they had chosen eighth overall in the '70 draft. Sittler certainly appreciated the gesture, since he knew the player who wore number 27 with great distinction for the Leafs was none other than Frank Mahovlich. He also realized that this meant great things were expected of him, and that he was going to be cast in a leadership role in the very near future. Sittler was a natural center, but began his first year in Toronto playing left wing. He only scored 10 times in '70-'71 in an injury-shortened year, but upped his goal-scoring total to 15 the next season. Starting with the 1972–73 season, Sittler was moved back to center and responded with a 29-goal effort. From then on, Sittler was usually in the 80 to 100 points range while scoring 36 to 45 goals between 1973 and 1981. His most impressive performances all took place in the calendar year of 1976; moments that not only defined his scoring prowess, but also his ability to lead an NHL team.

Sittler was named captain of the Maple Leafs to start the 1975–76 season (replacing Hall of Famer Dave Keon in the role which means a great deal in the hockey-crazy city of Toronto). Some, however, were questioning his leadership abilities, including bombastic owner Harold Ballard. Then came the high-flying Boston Bruins into Maple Leaf Gardens on the night of February 7, 1976, just after Ballard had fired some uncalled-for salvos at the new captain. The always-outspoken Ballard suggested the Leafs needed a number-one center for their top line! Sittler responded to the job with the greatest single-game performance in NHL history, scoring six times and adding four assists in an 11-4 win over the shocked Bruins. After recording two assists in the first period, Sittler scored hat tricks in the second and third periods. He also found time to add two more helpers and, by the time the game was over, Sittler had broken a record first established by Maurice Richard. "Undoubtedly, Mr. Ballard will figure his little blast inspired me to set the record, but it just isn't that way," Sittler said after the game. "Maybe now he won't have to hunt quite so hard for the center he wants." Sittler would finish the '75–'76 year with 41 goals and an even 100 points.

The Leafs beat the Pittsburgh Penguins in the first round of the 1976 playoffs but faced a much more difficult foe in the second round—the Philadelphia Flyers, sporting the likes of Bobby Clarke, Bill Barber, and Bernie Parent on a physical team. Toronto was down 3-2 in games when they hosted the Flyers on April 22, 1976. A loss would knock the Leafs out of the playoffs, but a win would send the teams back to Philadelphia for a seventh-game showdown. The Flyers had done a good job of checking Sittler and linemates Errol Thompson and Lanny McDonald, the Leaf top trio. But before the night was done, Sittler had put an incredible five shots past Parent to lead the Leafs to an 8-5 victory over the hated opponent in a very ugly, penalty-filled contest. Sittler was typically modest about his great six-point performance. "Things weren't going well for me early in this series. I was testing Bernie (Parent) a lot but nothing was going in. Tonight was just one of those things." Sittler also told the gathered media that he was not the least bit happy about the way he was playing before this contest. "I was down on myself before the game. I was bothered I wasn't helping the team in the scoring department." When asked to compare this game to his 10-point outburst against Boston, Sittler replied, "This is more gratifying because we beat the Flyers and because it's the playoffs." The Leafs lost the seventh game against Philadelphia, but Sittler had now clearly established himself as the new leader of the Leafs.

If those memorable performances were not enough, Sittler had one more effort in '76 that would cement his name in the history books; a special winning goal scored the night of September 15. The Leaf captain had been selected by Team Canada to play the first Canada Cup Tournament. He was not to be the star center he was with the Leafs (because the ridiculously talented team featured future Hall of Fame centers like Bobby Clarke, Gilbert Perreault, Marcel Dionne, and Phil Esposito) but he accepted his new role at left wing without complaint.

Sittler played very well throughout the tournament, but saved his best effort for an overtime session against Czechoslovakia, who played Canada in a best-of-three final. A goal would give Canada the tournament, but the Czechs were very strong in this game, and if they scored, another sudden-death game would have to be played. But Sittler got a break down the wing and waited for goalie Vladimir Dzurilla to come out of the net, as was his custom. Sittler smartly held the puck and swept around the sprawled netminder before deftly depositing the puck into the open net. The crowd at the Montreal Forum went wild as Team Canada players mobbed Sittler, who had just secured the tournament championship with the goal.

"This is the greatest moment of my life. Not the fact I scored the (winning) goal but the fact I was able to play (on this team)," Sittler said. "In the third period (assistant coach Don) Cherry told us the guy (Dzurilla) was cutting down the angles and we should go wide on him. I moved wide along the boards and he came out of the net and made a lunge at the puck. It was just a matter of rounding him and aiming for the open net."

Sittler was named a tournament all-star, which capped a truly amazing year for a player who started 1976 with his leadership under fire and ended with great career-defining performances for his team and country.

Darryl Sittler recorded 1,121 points in 1,096 career games and was elected to the Hall of Fame in 1989.

JONATHAN TOEWS
BORN: WINNIPEG, MANITOBA
NHL SEASONS: 2007–08 TO PRESENT
DEFINING MOMENT: 2010 PLAYOFFS

A family Christmas photo of Jonathan Toews when he was about six years old shows the young child in a Chicago Blackhawks sweater. The picture features Toews, his brother David, his mom Andree, and dad Bryan, are all smiling. The photo was featured on *Hockey Night in Canada* as Toews talked about winning the Stanley Cup on the night Chicago broke a 49-year championship drought. There was no mention of why Toews was wearing a Chicago sweater in the photo, but it seemed to set the scene for a perfect circle. That night—June 9, 2010—the Blackhawks captain gathered around with his new Blackhawks family as photographers snapped shots of Toews in his Chicago uniform—this time with the Cup in the middle of the picture.

Actually, it was not the first time Toews had been a winning captain. When he was just nine years old, he captained a team to the city championships in Winnipeg, the town where he was born. Most hockey teams with nine-year-old players do not name a captain, but Toews was given his first "C" at this age because he was a natural leader—even at that early stage of his career. The team Toews was playing for at the time was a decided underdog, but that did not deter the youngster in any way. The other boys, inspired by their captain, worked very hard to overcome the odds and took the title in 1995. The coach of the team, Bob Saelens, recalled that Toews had more desire and dedication than the average kid. His mother remembers a son who talked about making it to the NHL, and how he dreamed about winning the Stanley Cup. By the age of 22, Toews had done just that while adding an Olympic gold medal in 2010 to check off another one of his boyhood goals!

Even though his greatest success came in the 2009–10 season, Toews was winning important awards well before then. In 2005, he captained the Canada West team (and was named the MVP of the tournament) at the World Under-17 Hockey Challenge. In 2006 and 2007, he won back-to-back World Junior Championships. He then played for Canada at the 2007 World Championships, notching seven points in nine games and taking home another gold medal. Toews' international experience was certainly noticed by Team Canada management when they selected the best NHL stars for the 2010 Winter Olympic Games. In the final game, Toews scored the opening goal (his only one of the tournament) in the gold-medal contest against the United States to finish with eight points in seven games.

In Chicago, the 6'2", 209-pound Toews is known as "Captain Serious" for his very strict approach to the game. If things are not going well, Toews will sit and analyze what went wrong and vow to do better and to do more as captain. He gets teased heavily by his Chicago teammates, who see their leader as someone who is

22 going on 40. Toews, however, is very mature and extremely focused on what he wants to accomplish.

It was the 2010 playoffs that really set him apart, showing the hockey world that this was a captain who could get the job done. Toews's best game of the playoffs came on May 7 when the Hawks were trying to take a 3-1 series lead on the Vancouver Canucks in the second round of the post-season. The Canucks were anxious to even the series on home ice, but backed by Toews's five-point night (3G, 2A), Chicago romped to a 7-4 victory. Toews got things going by setting up defenseman Brent Seabrook for a goal to give Chicago a fast 1-0 lead. A quick wrist shot from Toews in the face-off circle easily beat Vancouver goalie Roberto Luongo to make it 2-1 for the Hawks. In the second period, Toews redirected a pass right in front of the Vancouver goal to make it 3-2 and then assisted on Patrick Sharp's goal to make it 4-2. A five-on-three power play saw Toews score his third of the night from right in the slot. He got that shot away so quickly, Luongo could not move.

"It's one of those nights where you get some chances and you throw it on net and it happens to go in," a modest Toews said later. "It's nice to get those breaks. You work hard, and don't always expect to get lucky like that. I don't want to get too confident," he cautioned. His great performance earned Toews the first star of the game. The Canucks forced the series to six games, but Chicago knocked them out before beating San Jose in the Western Conference final. Their win over the Sharks set up a meeting with the Philadelphia Flyers for the Stanley Cup.

Toews nursed nagging hurts and had to contend with hulking Flyer defenseman Chris Pronger in the final against Philadelphia. However, when it was all said and done, Toews had set a Chicago playoff record for most points with 29 (7G, 23 A). He spoke about how he could not sleep the night before the last game of the 2010 Stanley Cup final, because he kept imagining how it would feel if the Blackhawks won the championship. He then went out and set up Chicago's first goal by Dustin Byfuglien, a very important goal in the Blackhawks' eventual 4-3 overtime victory to seal the title.

If Toews had not been so outstanding against Nashville, Vancouver, and San Jose, the Blackhawks would not have won their first Cup since 1961. Chicago is still relatively young and could dominate for a few years. And it is a certainty that Toews (chosen third overall in 2006) is staying in the "Windy City", and will likely captain the Chicago team to more championships. Chicago fans will likely not have to wait 49 years for another Stanley Cup!

Jonathan Toews was named winner of the Conn Smythe Trophy for his performance in the 2010 playoffs. He has scored 115 goals and recorded 267 points in 302 career games to date.

JEAN BELIVEAU
BORN: TROIS-RIVIERES, QUEBEC
NHL SEASONS: 1950–51 TO 1970–71
DEFINING MOMENT: MAY 1, 1965

The Montreal Canadiens had waited patiently for center Jean Beliveau to join their team. A large man (6'3", 205 pounds) in an era where most players were considerably smaller, the Habs were hoping Beliveau could score as he did in junior and when he played senior hockey for the Quebec Aces. He got off to a slow start during his injury-shortened rookie year (only 13 goals in 1952–53), but soon, he started to dominate. He scored 37 in his first full season, and then 47 in 1955–56 when he took the Art Ross Trophy and the

Canadiens took the first of five consecutive Stanley Cups. However, when team superstar and captain Maurice Richard retired in 1960, the Habs turned over leadership of the team to Beliveau. While he continued to play very well, the team had not been able to secure a Stanley Cup. The question then became, could Beliveau lead his team to a championship? In 1965, the Habs had another opportunity to reclaim the fabled trophy and give Beliveau a chance to lift the Cup as team captain for the first time. The Captain would not drop the opportunity.

"This is it, the seventh and deciding game. The winner gets the Stanley Cup," said legendary broadcaster Danny Gallivan as the *Hockey Night in Canada* broadcast began on the night of May 1, 1965. The Montreal Canadiens were at home to the Chicago Blackhawks. The Habs were favored to win the championship on home ice since the entire series to date had seen the home team win each contest. The Montreal crowd was nervous as the game began. But seconds after the puck was dropped, the Canadiens swarmed into the Chicago end. Beliveau, along with teammates Bobby Rousseau and Dick Duff, went on the attack and forced a turnover. Rousseau spotted Beliveau heading for the net and put the puck past Blackhawk goalie Glenn Hall after just 14 seconds! The puck hit Beliveau before bouncing past a startled Hall. A big smile then came to the face of the Montreal captain. It was Beliveau's 10th point of the finals.

A little while later Beliveau set up Duff with a perfect pass to make it 2-0. The Canadiens knew they had the Hawks on the run, and Montreal netminder Gump Worsley was having no trouble handling the Chicago attack, which featured stars like Bobby Hull and Stan Mikita. A penalty to defenseman Pierre Pilote gave Montreal a late power play, and they capitalized when the speedy Yvan Cournoyer scored to make it 3-0. Henri Richard made it 4-0 before the first period was over. Chicago could do little the rest of the way as Montreal coasted to an easy win.

Beliveau was out for the last face-off of the game. Then the crowd chanted off the final seconds of the game. He lifted his stick as the final siren went off, and galloped down the ice to where the Canadiens were mobbing Worsley. A youngster who found his way onto the ice during the celebration asked Beliveau for his stick. The ever-generous captain nodded his approval. He then skated over to the table where the Stanley Cup was sitting. Beliveau lifted the Cup straight up and down. He then accepted the inaugural Conn Smythe Trophy for the best player in the playoffs, becoming the first recipient of the coveted trophy. The organist then played "For he's a jolly good fellow."

A natural leader, Beliveau then addressed the crowd in both French and English. "It's a great pleasure for me to express on behalf of all my teammates and all members of the Canadiens how pleased we are to win the Stanley Cup, not only for us but for all of you, our great supporters." He then took the Cup and skated around the ice with the silver trophy, and posed for many photos. The Conn Smythe Trophy was once again presented to Beliveau for the benefit of the television audience. "It is certainly nice to win this beautiful trophy, but I want to thank all my teammates," he said graciously.

After the game, Beliveau spoke of the Habs' fast start. "I had a feeling before the game that this was our night. Coach Toe Blake told me our line was starting and I said to Duff and Rousseau, 'Let's give it a fast start.' I'm not saying I knew we'd have the winning goal after only 14 seconds, but I knew the puck was going into the Chicago zone right off the opening face-off." He also admitted his opening marker was a bit lucky. "I knew when I saw the puck I couldn't get it with my stick, so I put my legs together and coasted into it."

"Jean Beliveau is the best thing that has happened to modern hockey," said Conn Smythe, founder of the Toronto Maple Leafs, who was on hand to see the inauguration of the trophy named in his honor. It was very fitting that a great player like Beliveau was voted to take the Smythe Trophy, because it set the great precedent that all winners of this prestigious trophy would have to show great leadership when it counted most. And that is exactly what Beliveau did that night.

Jean Beliveau was elected to the Hall of Fame in 1972.

MARK MESSIER
BORN: EDMONTON, ALBERTA
NHL SEASONS: 1979–80 TO 2003–04
DEFINING MOMENT: MAY 25, 1994

The New York Rangers had acquired Mark Messier to win them a Stanley Cup. He was a major player on five championship teams with the Edmonton Oilers (the last as team captain) but was overshadowed by Wayne Gretzky. As the Oilers dynasty was breaking up in the late 1980s and early 1990s, Messier was a part of the exodus from Edmonton, a city once dubbed the "City of Champions." The Rangers, on the other hand, had not won a Cup since 1940 and had only appeared in the finals on two occasions (1972 and 1979). New York general manager Neil Smith jumped at the opportunity to acquire the tough-as-nails 6'1", 215-pound center, sending three players Edmonton's way to complete the deal.

By the time Messier arrived on Broadway, his reputation as a leader was well established. He was given the captaincy as he was introduced to the Rangers crowd for the first home game of the 1991–92 season, a great year that saw the 31-year-old record 107 points in 79 games. Even though the Rangers had finished first overall in the '91–'92 campaign, with a high-scoring team that included Brian Leetch, Mike Gartner, and Tony Amonte, they were defeated by the Mario Lemieux-led Pittsburgh Penguins in the second round of the playoffs. Messier had 91 points the next season but, incredibly, the team missed the playoffs. During the season, Messier essentially demanded that coach Roger Neilson be replaced. The Rangers' bench boss was fired. The Rangers eventually hired Mike Keenan to run the club for the 1993–94 season, which saw the club return to the top of the league with a 52-24-8 record during the regular season.

The Rangers were much more playoff ready as the '94 postseason approached. Smith had made all the moves requested by Keenan—giving up important prospects in the process—but they all paid off. The Rangers easily eliminated the New York Islanders (in four straight games) and then the Washington Capitals (in five), but faced a severe challenge from the New Jersey Devils. The Devils won the first game in overtime, but the Rangers bounced back to win the next game. The teams split the next two games in New Jersey, but the Devils won the fifth game at Madison Square Garden by a 4-1 score and had the Rangers facing elimination. At that point, Messier sensed he had to do something rather dramatic to get the attention of his teammates.

As the Rangers prepared for Game 6, Messier stood in front of all the reporters and declared that the New York team was going to win the next game. "We're going to go in there and win Game 6," he stated. "We've responded all year. We've won games we've had to win. We know we're going in there to win Game 6 and bringing it back for Game 7. We feel we can win it and we feel we are going to win it." Messier was not speaking in a loud or belligerent manner, but felt he had to set the tone for his team. The New York newspapers, however, decided to play up Messier's words to the hilt with headlines to match Joe Namath's assertion that the Jets were going to win Super Bowl III.

Messier's assertions created an electrified atmosphere as the Rangers rolled into New Jersey on the night of May 25, 1994. It looked like it was all going to backfire on Messier when the Devils took a 2-0 lead by the end of the first. The second period saw the Rangers get one back when Messier set up a goal by Alex Kovalev. Down 2-1 at the end of two periods, the Rangers season and their Stanley Cup hopes were on the line in the third. It was a moment when great players show leadership and rise to the occasion—and no one did it better than captain Mark Messier that night.

In the final stanza, Messier completely took over, taking six shots on goal and scoring three times to give the Rangers a 4-2 win. To put it simply, Messier assumed control of the game and young Devils netminder Martin Brodeur had no response to the Rangers leader. Messier's first goal came on a pass from defenseman Brian Leetch and he backhanded a shot past the Devils goalie to tie the game 2-2. The Rangers took the lead when Messier swept in a rebound from a Kovalev shot, and then he grabbed a loose puck deep in his own end and found the empty net with a long, accurate shot.

"What I said (before this game) was not cocky or arrogant, just me expressing confidence that we could keep the series alive and trying to help the team's confidence," said Messier. Coach Keenan kept his comments simple and very direct: "That had to be one of the most impressive performances, one of the greatest efforts in the history of this league."

The Rangers got by the Devils by winning the seventh game in overtime. They then faced the Vancouver Canucks in the finals. The Stanley Cup–winning goal in the 3-2 game-seven Rangers victory over the Canucks was scored by no other than Mark Messier—one of hockey's greatest all-time leaders!

Mark Messier was elected to the Hall of Fame in 2007.

GOLDEN SEALS

GOALIE

GILLES MELOCHE

CANADIENS

GOALIE

KEN DRYDEN

SABRES

GOALIE

GERRY DESJARDINS

TORONTO MAPLE LEAFS

PAUL HENDERSON

Justin Penner
Edmonton Oilers   RW

Maxime Talbot
Pittsburgh Penguins   RW

Patrick Roy   Goaltender

MONTREAL CANADIENS

O-Pee-Chee

DAVE POULIN
PHILADELPHIA FLYERS

UPPER DECK

MASTERPIECES

OUT OF NOWHERE

There are some players whose achievements pull them out of virtually nowhere and thrust them into the limelight. Some of these players were initially dismissed as rather ordinary, while others were lost among teams that never went anywhere. Some simply got written off as underachievers, while others were unknown because they had not been given a chance. But then, out of the blue, came an unforgettable performance that captured the attention all hockey fans. In this chapter, we'll focus on the following players who seemingly came "Out of Nowhere":

Ken Dryden
Paul Henderson
Lester Patrick
Dustin Penner
Maxime Talbot
Patrick Roy
Gilles Meloche
Dave Poulin
Gerry Desjardins
Martin St. Louis

KEN DRYDEN

BORN: HAMILTON, ONTARIO

NHL SEASONS: 1970-71 TO 1978-79

DEFINING MOMENT: 1971 PLAYOFFS

Ken Dryden was drafted 14th overall by the Boston Bruins during the NHL's second Amateur Draft in 1964. He was just 16 years old. The draft process was so secretive that the names of all players chosen (24 in total, or four for each of the NHL's six teams) were not publicly released. However, just 17 days later, the Montreal Canadiens made a four-player trade to acquire the rights to the young netminder and then tried to convince Dryden to play junior hockey for the Peterborough Petes. The lanky goalie who valued education had his own ideas about where he was going to play, and instead chose to attend Cornell University in the United States. It was an unconventional move at the time, especially defiant towards a pro team who wanted to train goalies their own way. Dryden's first season at the Ivy League school ended in a NCAA championship for Cornell. He would go on to play in 83 career games for his college team, winning 76 times and suffering just four defeats!

Dryden resisted pro hockey for a year, and instead played with the Canadian National Team in 1969–70. He eventually signed with the Canadiens for the 1970–71 season. Dryden was perhaps the best goalie at Montreal's training camp in the fall of '70, but the team wanted him to get some pro experience, so they assigned him to the Montreal Voyageurs of the American Hockey League. He posted a very impressive 16-7-8 record for the Voyageurs; at the same time, Montreal became disenchanted with veteran net-minders Rogie Vachon and Phil Myre. Quite late in the 1971 season, the Habs gave the 6'4", 205-pound Dryden a shot. He won his first start on March 14, when the Canadiens beat the Penguins 5-1 in Pittsburgh. Dryden would win five more starts (including one game where he faced and beat his brother Dave, a goalie for the Buffalo Sabres) to give him a perfect 6-0 record to finish the regular season. Montreal was to face the Boston Bruins in the first round of the playoffs, and nobody expected Canadiens coach Al MacNeil to chose Dryden as his starter. The more experienced Myre and Vachon had been on Stanley Cup winners in the past with Montreal, and it was assumed that they would play against the heavily favored Boston juggernaut. But two late season losses to the Bruins may have convinced MacNeil to give the untried Dryden a chance.

The opening game of the series went to Boston by a 3-1 score, although Dryden played superbly. The second game did not start out much better, with Montreal down 5-1 in the second. However, a great rally saw the Canadiens take a 7-5 win, and this spurred them to win the next contest at home by a 3-1 final. The Bruins took the next two games for a 3-2 series lead, and they looked like their old, dominating selves. But Montreal would not quit and won the sixth contest on home ice by a 5-2 score, thereby forcing a seventh game in Boston. The Bruins opened the scoring, but Montreal had a 2-1 lead by the end of the first. They made it 3-1 on a goal by defenseman J.C. Tremblay in the second, and the teams exchanged goals early in the third to make it 4-2. Montreal then defended as well as they could behind the superlative netminding of their rookie puckstopper. Dryden continually frustrated every Boston attack, with Bruins sniper Phil Esposito smashing his stick against the glass in disgust after Dryden made a great save with his arm. In total, Dryden faced 286 shots over the seven-game series from the likes of Esposito, Bobby Orr, Johnny Bucyk, and Ken Hodge, the top four players in the NHL scoring race with more than 100 points each that season. But Dryden never flinched. He did his best to hold his team in a series where the odds were stacked against them.

"Their entire team played well," said Esposito, "but Dryden decided the series. He never cracked, never appeared to lose confidence or be bothered by the pressure. He beat us." A rather modest Dryden replied that pressure was nothing new to him. "Maybe I appear very cool, but the pressure is there and I feel it. It's a relative thing, though. I felt it in college and international hockey in the big games. So pressure isn't exactly new to me. I think it took a couple of games for our club to realize how good we really are. In the second game we got behind (but) we never quit. We came back to win it and that told us we could win the series." If Dryden was concerned, he never showed it on the ice as he leaned on his goalie stick that he placed firmly under his chin. His stance as the puck was in the other team's end became as famous as his great saves.

After completing the impossible dream of beating the mighty Bruins, the Canadiens beat Minnesota to advance to the Stanley Cup finals. Another grueling seven-game series saw Dryden at his best in the deciding contest played in Chicago. His great work held Montreal in the game, even though they fell behind 2-0. Dryden then held off the Hawks, who swarmed his goal in a vain effort to tie the game. Montreal won the game 3-2 that May 18 night and the netminder, who was unknown to all but a few people in the hockey world just weeks earlier, was now a Stanley Cup champion. Dryden was named winner of the Conn Smythe Trophy as the MVP of the 1971 playoffs, just another honor that helped launch a great career.

Ken Dryden won a total of six Stanley Cups between 1971 and 1979 and was elected to the Hockey Hall of Fame in 1983.

PAUL HENDERSON
BORN: KINCARDINE, ONTARIO
NHL SEASONS: 1962–63 TO 1979–80
DEFINING MOMENTS: SEPTEMBER 24, 26 & 28, 1972

When left winger Paul Henderson left to attend Team Canada's 1972 training camp in Toronto in August, he was not sure of where he would place on the team. His fellow Toronto Maple Leafs teammate Ron Ellis would be there as well. Since they played on the same line, both were hopeful they would also play on a line together for Team Canada.

There were a total of 35 players invited to the camp. The competition to make the starting lineup for the first game in Montreal on September 2 would be fierce, and Henderson had to compete with top-notch NHL stars like Frank Mahovlich, Yvan Cournoyer, Dennis Hull, Vic Hadfield, and J.P. Parise to gain a spot on left wing. Not many experts were expecting him to do it, despite the fact that he had scored 38 goals for Toronto in the 1971–72 season.

If there was one thing in Henderson's favor, it was that he came to the camp in great physical condition. Normally in this era, most players would use training camp as a way to get in shape. But Henderson was smart enough to realize he needed every edge possible to make this team. He and Ellis were both very well prepared for training in the summer heat, and the upcoming series. However, the Toronto teammates were afraid they were going to be centered with the young, diabetic kid from Philadelphia named Bobby Clarke. The young Flyers center was just starting to establish himself (35 goals and 81 points in 1971–72), but he was still something of an unknown quantity. Their fears were re-alized right away as Clarke skated between the two Leafs as camp started, but it turned out to be the best thing that happened to all three players. The trio flew through the intra-squad games, clearly in better shape than all the other players. They played so well, in fact, that they gained the respect of coaches Harry Sinden and John Ferguson. They were also named to start the series against the Soviets in the first contest. But things did not go as expected. Canada's best pros were shocked to lose the opener 7-3, though Henderson and Clarke both scored, a fact that kept their line intact for the next game.

In fact, the line played in all eight games of the historic series. Clarke and Ellis used their smarts and checking ability to play a more defensive game, while Henderson would score a series-leading 7 goals (and total 10 points). Always one of the swiftest players in the game, Henderson played the greatest hockey of his life and was a constant concern for the Soviet team. His best hockey was played in Russia over the final four games of the series when the venue shifted to Moscow. He was nearly badly injured in the fifth game, but luckily he was wearing a helmet when he hit the end boards with a thud after being tripped. He suffered a concussion but continued playing—in fact, he scored two goals in the game. However, Team Canada lost Game 5; Canada had won only one game, the Russians had three wins, and there was one tie. Canada would have to win the next three games—in Russia—to take the series. Paul Henderson would amazingly score the winner in each of those next three contests.

His goal to win the seventh game was truly a spectacular individual effort. It was a four-on-four situation as Henderson took a pass from defenseman Serge Savard, but faced two Russian defensemen as he crossed the opposition blueline. He beat one defender with a move to the inside, but the other defenseman came to take Henderson out with a bodycheck. The speedy Canadian somehow managed to move the puck forward and get his stick free. Just as he was hitting the ice, he put a rising shot over Vladislav Tretiak for the winning goal. He was mobbed behind the net by his delirious teammates. There were only a little over two minutes to play in that truly memorable game, but Canada was to keep the Russians at bay.

"Of all the goals I scored, I never got that much satisfaction before," Henderson said after the seventh contest. "It's something to have 18 players like the ones on this team congratulating you," he added about the mob scene that took place behind the Russian net after he scored with just 2:06 to play. Henderson finished his impossible dream when he knocked in his own rebound with 34 seconds to play in the last game of the series, to give Canada a 6-5 win and 4-3-1 record over the eight contests.

After the final game, Henderson stated that it was the biggest thrill of his career to be named to Team Canada and that his second biggest thrill was actually making the squad after camp was over. "And now, three winning goals in a row. Who can believe it? This is the happiest moment of my career." Those thrills were easily surpassed by his winning goals (the last is forever etched in the mind of every Canadian who watched the final contest that Thursday afternoon). In fact, Henderson was so confident at the end of the series that he called teammate Peter Mahovlich off the ice because he was sure he could score the winning goal. "I let him on because he told me to get off, he was going to score a goal," Mahovlich said. Phil Esposito, who assisted on the winning goal, said, "I saw Henderson flying in. I fired on the net and the rebound went to Paul, and he put it away." Out of nowhere, Paul Henderson skated into the hearts of millions of Canadians to emerge the unlikely, but never forgotten, hero!

Paul Henderson scored 236 goals and 477 points in 707 career games in the NHL.

LESTER PATRICK
BORN: DRUMMONDVILLE, QUEBEC
NHL SEASONS: 1926–27 TO 1927–28
DEFINING MOMENT: APRIL 7, 1928

Lester Patrick was a defenseman in the early years of professional hockey before the National Hockey League existed. He was rather tall for the players of this era (6'1") and was also known for his toughness.

Patrick played on two Stanley Cup teams with the Montreal Wanderers (in 1906 and 1907) before moving out to western Canada to play in cities like Nelson, British Columbia, and Edmonton, Alberta, before settling into Victoria (B.C.) for almost all the rest of his playing days. He put up impressive numbers in the pre-NHL days, with 128 goals and 195 points in 191 career games. Patrick and his brother Frank were also responsible for many hockey innovations and for the development of artificial ice plants in Vancouver and Victoria. As soon as his playing career was over, the Patricks became involved in the business side of the game. Lester took over the New York Rangers as general manager and coach when they joined the NHL in 1926.

The Rangers had some great players such as goalie Lorne Chabot, defenseman Ching Johnson, plus forwards like Bill and Bun Cook, Frank Boucher, and Murray Murdoch in their lineup when they started the 1926–27 campaign. The Rangers played out of the Big Apple's Madison Square Garden and soon became the city's favored hockey team ahead of the Americans, who also played in Manhattan. Boston upset the Rangers in the '27 playoffs, but just a year later, the Blueshirts beat Pittsburgh 6-4 in a two-game total goal series and then did the same to the Bruins by a 5-2 count. The Rangers were now in the best-of-five finals series against the Montreal Maroons for the 1928 Stanley Cup. All the games were to be played in Montreal, since the circus had taken over Madison Square Garden at that time.

The Maroons took the first game 2-0 and hoped to go up by two games on the night of April 7, 1928. The game was scoreless in the second when New York goaltender Chabot was hit in the left eye area with a high rising shot taken by Nels Stewart. In this era, goalies did not wear masks, and Chabot had to be rushed to the local hospital. He would recover, but he would not play in this series again. Patrick had to find a replacement for Chabot (there were no back up netminders on the bench) and asked permission from the Maroons (a league requirement at the time) to use Alex Connell, who was sitting in the stands watching the game. Connell was the regular goaltender of the Ottawa Senators, but the Maroons refused to let him play for the Rangers. Patrick asked if he could use another netminder who was at the game, and again, he was refused. He asked his team if anyone would volunteer, but no player raised their hand. Time to make a decision was running out—when Boucher suggested that the coach take on the job. "Alright, I'll do it," the 45-year-old, grey-haired Patrick said. He put on Chabot's ill-fitting equipment and took to the ice. The Montreal crowd greeted him with applause, but there was more than half a game still to be played.

Patrick had not played hockey in a number of years and was not in the best of shape, especially for such an important game. But he instructed his players to check the Maroons closely and make sure they cleared rebounds whenever he gave one up. The second period concluded with no scoring. The Rangers breathed a sigh of relief as they went to the dressing room to catch their breath. Very early in the third period, Bill Cook scored a goal to give New

York the lead, but at 14:20 of the final stanza, Stewart, one of the best goals scorers in the league, finally beat Patrick with a shot to make it 1-1. The game went into overtime with the old coach Patrick struggling to hang on.

The Maroons sensed a chance to win it with Patrick looking like he was going to crack, but he turned back every shot he faced. Finally, the Rangers broke up the ice with Johnson leading the attack. Johnson faked and then passed it over to Boucher who put it into the Maroons net for the winning goal after 7:05 of extra play. The Rangers carried their "goaltender" off the ice and, with tears in his eyes, Patrick said, "I stopped maybe six hard shots altogether. The boys backchecked terrifically to save the old man." Patrick had actually faced 18 shots in the 46 minutes he played and had given up just the one goal. Even Stewart, who had the Maroons only tally, gave due credit to Patrick. "The old white-haired son-of-a-gun was terrific," he admitted.

Goaltender Joe Miller was brought in for the rest of the series, and the Rangers took their first ever Stanley Cup with a 2-1 win in the fifth and deciding game. It might never have happened if Patrick had not come out of nowhere to rescue his team with one of the most memorable and heroic performances in Stanley Cup history.

Lester Patrick was elected to the Hockey Hall of Fame (player category) in 1947.

DUSTIN PENNER

BORN: WINKLER, MANITOBA

NHL SEASONS: 2005–06 TO PRESENT

DEFINING MOMENT: JUNE 4, 2007

Dustin Penner always believed he could be a hockey player, but was rejected so often that he began to think he might be wrong. He began playing at the age of four and he strived to play the game at the highest level possible. But virtually every team he tried out for cut him. Penner did not even get to play triple A hockey or junior hockey for that matter. Instead, he had to settle for high-school hockey in hometown Winkler, Manitoba. When that was over, Penner contemplated leaving hockey altogether and got a job working at a local plant. But a series of events would change this unknown dreamer and eventually get him into the NHL.

The first was a phone call from a cousin who asked Penner if he had any interest in coming to junior college in nearby North Dakota. Not knowing anything else about the opportunity other than that it was a chance to play hockey, Penner drove the two hours to get registered at the school just before the deadline. He was in school the next day. The team at Minot State-Bottineau played in exhibition games only, and Penner was rarely used. He then suffered an injury that ended his season, but he came back the following year to score 20 times in 23 games to win the "Most Determined Player Award." The second event that affected Penner's life occurred while attending an evaluation camp in Saskatoon. It was there that he was spotted by an assistant coach at the University of Maine who offered Penner a scholarship. Although he had to sit out a year because of the transfer, he then helped the Black Bears get to the championship game of the NCAA tournament. He scored the game-winning goal in the semi-final against Boston College, but lost the title game 1-0 to Denver University. Penner realized that if he used his size (6'4", 245 pounds), he could be a very effective player.

Just as Penner was leaving after the final game against Denver, he experienced another life-changing moment when pro scout David McNab approached him. McNab was the assistant general manager of the Anaheim Ducks at the time and told Penner he had a chance to play professional hockey. McNab loved what he saw of Penner and thought he had played some great hockey during the tournament. Penner's confidence soared when he talked to McNab, and he felt that he finally had accomplished something significant. Since he had played so little at the highest levels, the Ducks were able to sign him as a free agent and assigned the left winger to their farm team in Cincinnati for the 2004–05 season. He scored 10 times and added 18 assists while compiling 82 penalty minutes in 77 games. The following season saw the Ducks farm team move to Portland, where Penner had a great year with 39 goals and 84 points in just 57 games. He also spent 19 games with the Ducks, scoring four goals and then getting called back up for 13 playoff games. One of the most unlikely players had finally arrived. The next season was a year that saw Penner take a big step forward with a 29-goal effort in the regular season. He then added three goals (two of which were game-winning tallies) and five assists in 21 playoff games.

However, the defining moment in this rags-to-riches story was still to come. Penner's most memorable winning goal came in the fourth game of the Cup final played on June 4, 2007, in Ottawa. A win would give the Ducks a chance to wrap up the series on home ice, but a loss would even the series with the Senators. Anaheim was without star defender Chris Pronger for this game, but they overcame that hurdle with hard play and hustle the Senators could not match.

With the score tied 2-2 in the third period, Penner took a perfect pass from teammate Teemu Selanne and one-timed a shot past Ottawa netminder Ray Emery. The Senators had over-committed to Selanne on the play, which left a pretty much wide-open net for Penner—who made no mistake. "We needed other people (like Penner) to step to the forefront," said Ducks coach Randy Carlyle, "and I thought as a whole our group did that." The Ducks beat Ottawa badly in the fifth game (by a 6-2 score) to capture their first ever Stanley Cup. It was once thought that a team based in California would never be able to win the NHL championship, but players like Penner, Ryan Getzlaf, and Corey Perry meshed well with veterans like Pronger, Selanne, Scott Neidermayer, and J.S. Giguere. In due course, they became a solid group who made sure the Ducks would never be laughed at again.

Penner's impressive performance in the post-season got him some rave reviews and a monster contract offer from the Edmonton Oilers that summer. It's easy to see what the Oilers liked in the young power forward. Penner is large, but has the touch of a much smaller man. He has a good, accurate shot, and he knows he needs to hang around the front of the net to be most effective. His skating has improved steadily and his toughness is not to be questioned. The Ducks were furious that Kevin Lowe, the general manager of the Oilers at the time, gave such a rich contract ($21.25 million over five years) to a player they felt was not yet a proven commodity—but no matter. Penner's rise to prominence in the NHL is unbelievable, considering he was about to leave the game behind just a few years earlier.

Dustin Penner got off to a difficult start with Edmonton, but finished first on the team with 23 goals in 2007–08. He only managed 17 tallies in 2008–09, but came back to score 32 times in

the 2009–10 season. Penner scored 23 times in 2010–11, playing for Edmonton and Los Angeles.

MAXIME TALBOT
BORN: LEMOYNE, QUEBEC
NHL SEASONS: 2005–06 TO PRESENT
DEFINING MOMENT: JUNE 12, 2009

The visiting Pittsburgh Penguins were most likely counting on Sidney Crosby or Evgeni Malkin, or perhaps Jordan Staal, to score the important goals going into the seventh and deciding game of the 2009 Stanley Cup finals. All three had been first-round draft choices, and people figured that this would be the game where they would shine the most. However, the great thing about a one-game showdown for the Stanley Cup is that almost anyone can emerge a hero. Max Talbot would be the strongest of the marching Penguins on this night—and would steal the Cup away from the Red Wings in their own building!

This unlikely hero was drafted 234th overall by the Penguins in 2004—and players drafted that low rarely get out of the minor leagues. Talbot had put up good numbers as a junior in the QMJHL, but as is the case with many players who work in that circuit, the statistics (299 points in 249 career games) are not always taken at face value by NHL teams. The 5'11", 190-pound Talbot was assigned to the Penguins farm team in Wilkes-Barre, Pennsylvania, where he played for two full seasons. He posted very average numbers, but the Penguins liked his gritty nature and brought him up to the NHL during the 2005–06 season. He had five goals in 48 games as a rookie, but then scored 13 the next season. He scored a total of 24 goals over the next two years and found his niche on the talent-laden Pittsburgh team by playing a mostly checking role and popping in an occasional marker.

Soon, he developed a reputation as a player who could hold the Penguins together with an industrious, hard-working style of game. His infectious personality also kept his teammates loose. His pre-game ritual with goalie Marc-Andre Fleury (a long-time friend and teammate going back to their days as youngsters in Quebec) took some pressure off the sometimes erratic netminder as the two engaged in mock fighting. If he was not kibitzing with a teammate, Talbot would be scoring important goals at the most opportune moments. He would even get into a scrap if he had to, and that endeared him to his fellow players even more. In 2008, he scored an overtime goal in Detroit, ending a long extra-session game that had given the Penguins another chance on home ice. They blew that opportunity, but were determined to have a different go at it on the night of June 12, 2009.

The last game of the finals was a very tightly played contest that was scoreless at the end of the first period. After just 1:13 of the second frame, Talbot put a shot through the pads of Detroit goalie Chris Osgood to give the Penguins a 1-0 lead. At 10:07, Talbot broke in on a two-on-one, rifling a shot over Osgood to make it 2-0. It would turn out to be the game-winning goal. Detroit got a late goal to make it 2-1 and attacked the Penguins net as the clock was winding down. But Fleury made a game-saving stop on Detroit's Nick Lidstrom to preserve the win and give the Penguins their first championship since 1992. Talbot and his teammates leapt off the bench to join the celebration around the Pittsburgh net. "This is the best day of my life," he said afterwards. "And I love saying that."

As the Penguins celebrated on the ice, Talbot was interviewed and gave credit to his teammates for the victory. "There is more than one hero tonight," he correctly pointed out. "Geno (Malkin) was unbelievable. I was lucky to be in the right place at the right time." He also talked about coming up big when it mattered the most, and the belief that he could do it. "When you get one goal and you learn to lead a team to a championship, which I was lucky enough to do in junior, and you score big goals throughout your career, it feels like it stays with you and people talk about it. You start believing in it and you just say to yourself that you're that type of player. You want to be there in big games."

Talbot certainly had all the Penguins players and coaches believing in him. Coach Dan Bylsma perhaps put it best when he said, "He's gritty, he's determined, and he's not scared to go after it." On this night, Talbot did indeed go after it, after virtually coming out of nowhere to capture hockey's greatest prize—the Stanley Cup.

As of 2011, Max Talbot has recorded 33 points in 66 career playoff games and has appeared in the Stanley Cup finals twice.

PATRICK ROY
BORN: QUEBEC CITY, QUEBEC
NHL SEASONS: 1984–85 TO 2002–03
DEFINING MOMENT: MAY 5, 1986

When goaltender Patrick Roy was just 15 years old, he was forced to play in net for a house-league squad due to a reorganization of teams in his area. He was also the last goalie cut from the competitive team he tried out for because the coaches wanted to go with a more experienced netminder. He was unhappy about the course of events (most good players are on traveling teams by this age), but he at least got to practice and play every week as a starting goalie.

One year later, Roy was back playing a higher level of competitive hockey in Ste-Foy, Quebec. It's a good thing he was wanted for the Ste-Foy team; if he had not landed that spot, he might have left hockey for good. The Gouverneurs won the championship in 1981–82 and Roy got noticed by the Granby Bisons of the QMJHL, who took the young netminder onto their team for the 1982–83 seasons. The Bisons were rarely a good team when Roy tended the nets, although he did manage to win 29 games for the team in 1983–84. Roy faced an inordinate amount of rubber while he played in Granby, and his goals-against average (as high as 6.24 and 5.58 in a couple of seasons) reflected the fact that he was on a pretty bad team. Roy, though, did not complain. He knew what he was in for night after night. He never backed down and always kept his highly competitive spirit intact.

As a result, the Montreal Canadiens took a chance on the tall (6'2") netminder by selecting Roy 51st overall in the 1984 Entry Draft. Montreal liked to stockpile goaltenders and certainly wanted to develop as many French-Canadian players as possible. Interestingly enough, Roy never dreamt of playing for the Canadiens. "I was never a Montreal fan. When I was a kid I hoped every team would win except Montreal. But I was happy when they drafted me because I didn't want to go somewhere far away," Roy said years later. He spent the 1984–85 season playing in Granby, but the Habs sent him to their farm team in Sherbrooke to give him some professional experience once the Bisons were out of the playoff race. Roy got into one regular season game and was not expected to play in the post-season, but circumstances surrounding the other goalies forced the young netminder into action. All Roy did was lead the Sherbrooke club to the Calder Cup championship by winning 10 of the 13 games he played. Winning the AHL title gave Roy some newfound confidence and he started the 1985–86 season with the big-league team.

Even though those in the Montreal organization felt they might have a budding star in Roy, few others at the NHL level knew much about him. He had won his first NHL game by making a third period appearance and stopping a grand total of two shots during the '84–'85 campaign, but that hardly qualified him for NHL stardom. Montreal used a total of three goalies during the year, but Roy was the best of the group, posting a 23-18-3 record. He got the nod to start the post-season for a team that had gone 40-33-7 over the regular season. Montreal was hardly the favorite to win the Stanley Cup, but they bested Boston 3-0 in the first round, a best-of-five series. The Habs barely got by the Hartford Whalers in the next round, needing an overtime goal in the seventh game to take the series. The New York Rangers had pulled off some upsets of their own to meet the Canadiens in the semi-final, but Montreal won the first two games at home to get the jump.

The Rangers hosted the Canadiens at Madison Square Garden the night of May 5, 1986, for the third game of the series. A win would give the Habs a 3-0 lead while a New York win would get them back into the series. This would be Roy's night, the perfect time to put on a netminding clinic.

Montreal got a late-third-period power-play goal from Bobby Smith to tie the game 3-3, forcing overtime. The Rangers launched an all-out assault on the Montreal net as soon as overtime started, forcing Roy to make 13 saves—many of the spectacular variety. The Habs were completely under siege for more than nine minutes, but then Claude Lemieux broke away and put a shot past John Vanbiesbrouck to give Montreal an incredible 4-3 win. Roy had turned away 44 Rangers' drives to secure the win, leaving both his teammates and opponents shaking their heads over his remarkable play.

"That save on (Mark) Osborne was my biggest," Roy said after the game. "I was beaten. I know I was but sometimes you get lucky. I talked it over with the coach (Jean Perron) before the game. We agreed we had to challenge the Ranger shooters a lot because they play close to the net. They did. Maybe I was lucky, but a goalie has to be. I was aggressive and when I get that way, my confidence grows. It was probably my best game." Teammate Mike McPhee, who set up the winning goal, added this about the Habs netminder: "He was unbelievable. I don't know how he plays that way."

Roy instantly became the talk of hockey as he took the Habs past New York in five games, and then defeated the Calgary Flames in five to win the Stanley Cup. He made one last save just before the final buzzer as the Flames stormed the Montreal net, looking for a goal to tie the game. Roy stood tall and turned away the drive, which looked to be labeled.

Roy played the same way the rest of his illustrious career, but he made his first great impression when he dropped in way under the radar to win his first of four Stanley Cups in 1986.

Patrick Roy is the only player in NHL history to win the Conn Smythe Trophy three times (1986, 1993, and 2001). He was elected to the Hall of Fame in 2006.

GILLES MELOCHE
BORN: MONTREAL, QUEBEC
NHL SEASONS: 1970–71 TO 1987–88
DEFINING MOMENT: APRIL 27, 1980

The *NHL Official Guide and Record Book* lists the all-time goal-tending leaders for most games won. Three columns to the right are all the losses incurred by the win leaders, and a careful look at that list shows that Curtis Joseph and Gump Worsley each lost 352 career games—surprising in many ways, since both of those netminders are fourth and seventeenth respectively on the victory list. The goalie with the next most career defeats is Gilles Meloche, who lost 351 times (although he did manage to win 270 games, ranking him 34th on the wins list as of the 2010-11 season). Goalies who play a long time are, of course, going to rank on both lists, but few goalies will get on either listing the way Meloche did over his 18 NHL seasons.

The 5'10", 185-pound Meloche played one season of major junior hockey in Verdun, Quebec, and was then drafted by the Chicago Blackhawks 70th overall in 1970. Chicago sent him to Flint, Michigan, to play minor league hockey for the 1970–71 season, but he also played and won the two games he was called up for by the Blackhawks. However, the Chicago club was steady in net with Tony Esposito and even though they hoped to keep Meloche as a backup, they were forced to trade him to the California Seals just as the 1971–72 season got underway. The trade gave Meloche a chance to be a starting NHL netminder but, unfortunately for their new goalie, the Seals were usually at the bottom of the league. In five full seasons as a Seal, Meloche never won more than 16 games in any regular campaign and lost 25, 32, 33, 27, and 23 games over that time period. When the sagging squad moved to Cleveland in 1976 and was renamed the Barons, things improved slightly with Meloche recording 35 wins over two seasons. However, he also registered 51 losses.

Meloche was still considered a good goalie despite all the losing (he often held his team in many games when they would have otherwise been out of the contest). He finally caught a good break when the Barons and Minnesota North Stars merged in 1978. Meloche enjoyed his first 20-win season in 1978–79 and just one year later, the refreshed North Stars were in contention. A combination of good veterans (like Fred Barrett, Al MacAdam, Mike Polich, and goalie Gary Edwards) and talented youngsters (like Bobby Smith, Steve Payne, Steve Christoff, and Craig Hartsburg) gave the Stars a new identity, and they posted a winning season with a 36-28-16 record. Meloche even had his first winning season with a 27-20-5 mark during the regular season. Minnesota then knocked off Toronto in three straight to start the 1980 playoffs, but nobody expected them to give the defending Stanley Cup champions, the Montreal Canadiens, much of a challenge in the next round. However, the Canadiens were somewhat depleted by injuries (superstar Guy Lafleur did not finish the series against the North Stars, for example), while the North Stars were playing extremely well. The series was tied at three games each when the clubs returned to Montreal for the seventh game on the night of April 27, 1980, at the Forum. And the goalie who had for so long been lost to the margins of expansion mediocrity had his first chance to shine on the big stage.

The teams battled hard for two periods, but were tied 2-2 late in the contest when Al MacAdam scored with just 86 seconds to play, giving the North Stars a lead they would not give up. The mighty Canadiens, winners of four straight Stanley Cups (and hoping to match their team record of five consecutive championships) were vanquished by the upstarts from Minnesota. After ten years in the NHL, during which he had never won a best-of-seven series, Meloche paused and thought about what had just happened after facing 24 Montreal shots in the final series contest. "To do this, right in this place (his hometown), I think it makes me forget California and Cleveland. I don't live in the past. I made a good living then. I never got ticked off. Who else could be 20 or 21 (years of age) and play 60 games a year? I never knew how good I really was. But maybe, everything was going according to fate to build up to this." The North Stars gave the Philadelphia Flyers a good series in the next round, but eventually lost in five games.

Minnesota won 35 games the next season, but the team was much more prepared for the playoffs in 1981. Boston, Buffalo, and Calgary all fell to the North Stars and that got the Minnesota club (who had seven rookies on the squad) to the Stanley Cup final for the first time in team history. They were no match for the Islanders dynasty that easily won the title in five games. The 30-year-old Meloche played in 13 playoff games that year and won 8 of them, including the only North Star win in the final. During the playoffs, he reflected on how far he had come from the early days of his career. "The merger (between Cleveland and Minnesota) was like moving from hell to heaven. The first year in Minnesota we could see an improvement (of 23 points). In last year's quarter-final we beat the champions. And this year (reaching the final)...this is the life's dream coming true."

Meloche never got back to the final, but did win 20 or more games for the North Stars for the next three seasons (including a career-high 26 wins in 1981–82). At this point he was hardly an unknown quantity, and had in fact established himself as a very reliable netminder. He finished his career playing three seasons with Pittsburgh, recording his final win and loss for them in 1987–88 when he was 37 years of age. Not many goalies could have withstood all the losing to achieve special moments if they did not have the character of Gilles Meloche.

Gilles Meloche has been the goaltending coach for the Pittsburgh Penguins for many years and was a part of all three Stanley Cup wins the franchise has recorded (1991, 1992, 2009).

DAVE POULIN
BORN: TIMMINS, ONTARIO
NHL SEASONS: 1982–83 TO 1994–95
DEFINING MOMENT: FEBRUARY 11, 1987

When Dave Poulin was in the ninth grade in Mississauga, Ontario, he weighed only 90 pounds. He played hockey, but when he tried out for the better teams in the area, he was usually cut. But he would not give up on the game, and eventually made a junior B team called the Dixie Beehives in 1977–78. The Beehives had a pretty good team, with many of their players recruited by U.S. colleges. Poulin had 59 points (28 goals, 31 assists), which got him noticed by Notre Dame, who came up to look at him play. A scholarship was offered and Poulin played the next four season for the "Fighting Irish." While he scored 89 goals in 135 games at Notre Dame, he also studied business administration and was all set to take a sales position upon graduation. However, he was invited to play hockey in Sweden for one year, and the 24-year-old decided to see a bit of the world while he was still young. .

Poulin was recruited to play in Sweden by a coach named Ted

Sator. The bench boss of the Rogle team made it a personal goal to give Poulin a chance at a pro hockey career. Sator also had the ear of the Philadelphia Flyers, who relied upon his expertise to inform them about any players in Sweden who might be NHL-worthy. Poulin had 62 points in 35 games during the 1982–83 season and was signed by the Flyers as a free agent in March 1983. While the 5'11", 190-pound center was not immediately deemed ready for the NHL, he did do very well in a minor league stint with Maine of the American Hockey League, collecting 16 points in 16 games. His performance earned him a promotion to Philadelphia, where he scored two goals in two games played. The next season saw Poulin make the Flyers right out of training camp and he scored 31 goals and added 45 assists to set a new club mark for points (76) for first year players. To prove he was no flash in the pan, Poulin recorded 74, 69, and 70 points over his next three seasons. He was becoming one of the best centers in the entire league. Poulin was also considered one of the best defensive players and a top penalty killer (with 39 career short-handed goals).

In addition to his top play on the ice, Poulin was recognized for his leadership skills by being named team captain in just his second year in the big league. In 1984–85, he was given the "C" because he was bright, articulate, a natural leader, and a feisty combatant in much the same way the previous captain, Bobby Clarke, was, although not anywhere near as nasty. He helped the Flyers reach the Stanley Cup final on two occasions, but the Flyers lost both times to the powerful Edmonton Oilers. If Poulin was a Philadelphia success story, he was still relatively unknown throughout the rest of the league until the Rendez-vous '87 two-game series between the best of the NHL and the best of the Soviet Union. The NHL decided to scrap their All-Star Game in 1987 and instead promoted a two-game series slated for Quebec City. Both rosters were dotted with great players. Poulin was listed as one of the centers on the NHL team which included other pivots like Mario Lemieux,

Wayne Gretzky, Dale Hawerchuk, and Mark Messier! The opening game on February 11, 1987, showed that Poulin deserved to really be among such powerful luminaries.

The NHL team took a 2-0 lead during the second period, but the Soviets tied it up in the third. Poulin set up Kevin Dineen to give the NHL a 3-2 lead, but the Soviets (led by Igor Larionov, Viacheslav Fetisov, and Vladimir Krutov) quickly tied the game once again. Then, with under two minutes to go, Poulin got himself behind the Soviet defensemen to direct a pass from Mario Lemiuex to give the NHL a 4-3 victory. "I was trying to take out both defensemen at once," Poulin said. "I tried to get as much of them as I could. As it turned out, I popped in free behind them." Messier was given "player of the game" honors, but Poulin was likely more deserving with a goal and an assist plus a great effort in shutting down one of the best Soviet scoring lines. If hockey fans were not as aware of Poulin as they should have been, they certainly knew who he was after this game. He had proven he could play with the best players in the world.

Not long after this, Poulin's offensive numbers declined a little. He was then dealt to the Boston Bruins and played in one more Stanley Cup final in 1990 (and was once again on the wrong end of the series with Edmonton). He also played two seasons with Washington before retiring with 530 points in 720 NHL games. Few would ever have given Poulin a chance at making the NHL— but hard work and dedication gave the centerman a terrific NHL career that came out of nowhere!

Dave Poulin was head coach at Notre Dame for a number of years and joined the front office staff of the Toronto Maple Leafs in 2009 as vice-president of Hockey Operations.

GERRY DESJARDINS
BORN: SUDBURY, ONTARIO
NHL SEASONS: 1968–69 TO 1977–78
DEFINING MOMENT: MAY 8, 1975

When Gerry Desjardins was a young boy growing up in northern Ontario, he was the kid who played in net because nobody else wanted to. A rather chubby youngster, he did whatever he could just to play hockey—and if that meant playing in net, that was fine with the shy Desjardins.

Desjardins first played organized hockey when he was 11 years old, but lacked knowledge of the finer points of goaltending. He developed an attitude that made him solely responsible for any puck which ended up in the net, and it was this attitude that fuelled a determined and competitive spirit. He did show some promise early on, but was in dire need of some coaching from someone who understood the position. By the time he was 16 years old, Desjardins had played for two teams and tried to soak up as much knowledge as he could. "I loved the game," Desjardins would later recount. "I was young. I didn't know what it was to be tired. I had nothing else I wanted to do. In fact, I used to find other games to play afternoons or nights after school."

After he won a local championship, Desjardins's confidence level soared. He was invited to try out for a Detroit Red Wing junior club in Sudbury, which the 17-year-old made as a back-up netminder. He saw limited action here. However, he impressed the Red Wings enough to get inhim to their main junior team in Hamilton, Ontario, the following year. The Hamilton club cut Desjardins twice and sent him back to Sudbury for further development, but the Detroit affiliate in Sudbury folded, and Desjardins soon found himself in the Toronto Maple Leafs organization. He was named the Most Valuable Player for his new team and then got an invitation to try out for the Leafs main junior team—the Toronto Marlboros. It looked like he was once again going to be rejected at the higher level of competition, but he stuck around Toronto and the coach, legendary netminder "Turk" Broda, gave the 5'11", 185-pound goalie another chance. "It seemed like I was just not good enough and maybe I should give up thoughts of making it big in hockey," Desjardins said years later. "However, I just couldn't bring myself to do it." It's a good thing he did not give up, because a good NHL career would have ended right there at the age of 18.

Broda was a big help, but Desjardins had to take a small step back to play junior B in London, Ontario, for awhile. He was selected as a first team all-star in 1963–64 when in London, and that got him to the Marlboros full-time for the 1964–65 season. The Leafs made the mistake of not protecting Desjardins's rights and the Montreal Canadiens scooped him up with a good offer. He was assigned to the Central Hockey League with Houston for a couple of seasons, and by the end of the 1966–67 season, he was seen as a top prospect. Montreal, however, had no place for him on the big team but managed to get two first round picks (one of which turned out to be future Hall of Famer Steve Shutt) from the Los Angeles Kings who wanted the goalie for their club.

Desjardins played one year in Los Angeles before going to Chicago in a multi-player deal. He backed up Tony Esposito for the next three seasons, winning a total of 17 games over that time. The expansion New York Islanders claimed his rights in 1972, and he won a grand total of 14 games over two seasons for a very bad team. He was then in the World Hockey Association for 41 games in 1974–75 when the Buffalo Sabres rescued him by acquiring his rights from the Islanders. He joined a very talented Buffalo squad to end the '74–'75 season, winning six of his nine appearances.

The Sabres had finished the year with 113 points. They easily swept past Chicago and now faced Montreal in the semi-finals. Suddenly, Desjardins was the main man in net after so many years of basking in anonymity. He now appeared ready for the challenge. The highlight of the series was Desjardins's play in the semi-final against the team that once owned Desjardins but never gave him a chance—the Montreal Canadiens. The Sabres clinched the series the night of May 8, 1975, when they invaded the Montreal Forum to play the sixth game of the series. By the end of the first period, Buffalo was up 3-1 and added another in the second to make it 4-1. Montreal got two past Desjardins in the third but that was all he allowed. He truly shone on the largest stage, beating star net-minder Ken Dryden in the process right in the Montreal Forum.

Desjardins had his best game of the series to close out the Canadiens. His save on Montreal's Yvan Cournoyer late in the first period was a key moment in the contest. "That was the big save for us because a goal at that time, near the end of the period, cutting our lead to 3-2, would have given them the momentum going into the second period," Sabres general manager Punch Imlach said in praise of his recently acquired netminder.

Desjardins had come out of virtual obscurity to take his team to the finals, posting a winning record of 7-5 in 15 playoff games. The Sabres could not quite match the Philadelphia Flyers for the Cup, losing it in six games. But Desjardins had given the team's loyal fans their first taste of what it was like to make it all the way to the finals. One local singer recorded a song during Buffalo's '75 play-off run entitled "Gonna win that Cup," which paid tribute to the rotund netminder with the lyrics, "We've got Desjardins making the saves." It just wasn't to be. Desjardins had two more excellent seasons in Buffalo (recording 60 victories in total) but could never get the Sabres back for another chance at the Cup. Injuries forced him to retire after the 1977–78 season.

Gerry Desjardins twice led the NHL in losses (34 in 1968–69 and 35 in 1972–73) but won 66 games in 116 appearances for the Buffalo Sabres. He was also named the rookie of the year in the American Hockey League for the 1967–68 season.

MARTIN ST. LOUIS
BORN: LAVAL, QUEBEC
NHL SEASONS: 1998–98 TO PRESENT
DEFINING MOMENT: JUNE 5, 2004

When Martin St. Louis first came to Tampa Bay for the start of the 2000–01 season, he was hoping to get the opportunity that had eluded him with the Calgary Flames. Undrafted by any NHL team, he signed as a free agent with the Flames but only played in 69 games for them, scoring a mere four goals. However, he made the most of his new opportunity with Tampa, scoring 18 goals and recording 40 points in 78 games. Despite his diminutive size (listed at 5'9" and 177 pounds), St. Louis now proved that he could play in the NHL. From that point on, St. Louis has accomplished more in his career than most can dream about. He has won a Stanley Cup (in 2004), has been named the league's best player (in 2003–04 when he had an NHL best 94 points), and was twice named an all-star (once on the first team and once on the second team). He also played with some of the best Lightning teams (he was on one of the best lines in team history with Brad Richards and Fred Modin) and definitely on some of the worst. Through it all, the courageous 35-year old-winger has been one of the best players in the NHL.

The road St. Louis took to the NHL was certainly one less traveled. He never played major junior hockey, but did attend the University of Vermont for four full seasons (1993 to 1997). He also captured NCAA all-star status. He recorded 267 points (91G, 176A) in 139 games, but nothing captured the attention of the NHL scouts. So St. Louis played for the Cleveland Lumberjacks of the International Hockey League in 1997–98, collecting 50 points in 56 games. The Calgary Flames finally took note and signed him as a free agent on February 19, 1998, assigning him to the Saint John (New Brunswick) Flames for the rest of the year (where he recorded 26 points in 25 regular season games plus another 20 points in the playoffs). He split the next two years between Calgary and Saint John (notching 114 points in 95 AHL games), but did not do enough to impress the Flames who simply let him go to free agency. It appeared St. Louis's career was going nowhere quickly—until the Lightning gave him one more chance.

Allowed to get significant ice time in Tampa Bay, St. Louis's numbers kept getting better. In fact, he became a consistent 30-plus goal scorer. His best year for the Lightning came in 2003–04 when he led the entire NHL in assists (56) and points (94). His plus/minus rating soared to a league-best plus 35 and he was soon considered one of the best two-way players in the game. He won three major awards for the '03–'04 season, but saved his best performances for the 2004 playoffs when the Lightning made it all the way to the Stanley Cup finals.

The Lightning won 46 regular season games in '03–'04, finishing first in their division and second overall. They quickly dispatched the New York Islanders and the Montreal Canadiens in the first two rounds. Philadelphia was a much harder opponent in the Eastern Conference final, but the Lightning squeezed past in seven. The Calgary Flames provided the opposition in the finals and the first four games were low-scoring contests that saw each side win two games. However, the Flames won the fifth game in

Tampa Bay with an overtime goal and went home for the sixth contest with the chance to clinch the Cup on home ice.

On Saturday night, June 5, 2004, it was expected that the hometown Flames, backed by a rabid fan following, would win their second Stanley Cup in team history. The game was tense throughout and went into overtime tied 2-2. The Flames nearly won when Martin Gelinas almost knocked one in off his leg, but the play was not even reviewed. The first extra period did not produce a goal. However, in the second extra session, an exhausted St. Louis finally ended the contest. Always an opportunist, St. Louis was at the right spot when the moment presented itself. He rapped home a rebound from a shot taken by teammate Tim Taylor that passed a helpless Miikka Kiprusoff in the Calgary net, setting off a mob scene around the tiniest Tampa Bay player. The goal was St. Louis's only shot of the game, although he did assist (his 24th point of the post-season) on the Lightning's first goal by Brad Richards. St. Louis's winning tally sent the teams back to Tampa Bay for the deciding match.

"We'll get a chance at a Game 7, what a feeling," said St. Louis after the game. "I was just trying to put it on net. At that point it's not a pretty goal that will win. I just thought 'throw it on net, you never know.'" The phrase "you never know" summarized St. Louis's career perfectly. The next game was also another tight contest, with Tampa Bay prevailing 2-1 for their first Stanley Cup title. It was all made possible because the smallest player, who came out of nowhere, scored the biggest goal of his career.

Martin St. Louis has scored 298 goals and recorded 778 points in 854 career games to date.

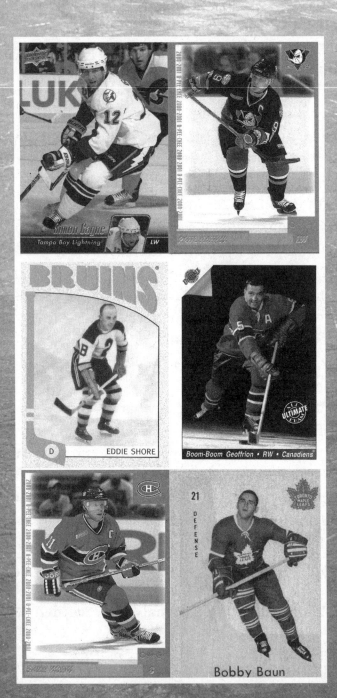

NOTHING CAN STOP US

Hockey players will do just about anything to stay in the game. Childhood mishaps, war wounds, and dreaded diseases are but a few of the things that hockey players have overcome to play the sport. Life threatening situations, broken bones, and even the weather are all obstacles to playing in a particular game or series. Hockey players are, obviously, a tough lot. In this chapter, we'll focus on a determined few who just couldn't be stopped:

Bill Gadsby
Bill Chadwick
Eddie Shore
Bob Baun
Bernie Geoffrion
Frank McGee
Simon Gagne
Paul Kariya ✓
Saku Koivu ✓

BILL GADSBY

BORN: CALGARY, ALBERTA

NHL SEASONS: 1946–47 TO 1965–66

DEFINING MOMENT: 1966 STANLEY CUP FINALS

Hall of Famer defenseman Bill Gadsby's life could have ended very early, and it goes without saying that he would then have never excelled in the National Hockey League. Right around the time he turned 12 years old, Gadsby and his mother boarded a passenger boat from Glasgow, Scotland, for Montreal. Mother and son had been in the UK, visiting relatives. They were aboard the passenger liner *S.S. Athenia*. It was September 1, 1939, and, unbeknownst to perhaps all the 1,103 passengers on the ship, World War II had broken out the day their ship left port. On the night of September 3, at around 9 p.m., a blast rocked the 13,581-ton ship. A wild, panic-stricken scramble ensued as the passengers tried to come to grips with what had happened—a German U-boat had tried to sink the *S. S. Athenia* with a torpedo. Gadsby and his mother were loaded into a lifeboat with other passengers and dropped into the Atlantic Ocean, in the hope that they would be rescued. Gadsby cannot recall exactly how long he was in the lifeboat, but he and his mother were saved when six rescue ships came to the aid of the surviving passengers. Gadsby recalled how cool his mother stayed despite all the chaos on board; he also recalled that she actually saved him, since she was able to get them both safely to the lifeboats. A reported 118 passengers were not so lucky; they perished that night. Perhaps not knowing exactly what happened while waiting to be saved made it a little easier for Gadsby to deal with it.

In fact, it was such a traumatic event that he and his mother rarely spoke about it ever again.

If that was not enough for Gadsby to endure, he was diagnosed with polio in 1952 at the age of 25. He thought he was just feeling bad when he woke up one morning, but it turned out to be something much worse. He had already played in six NHL seasons (all with Chicago) by this point and had just recently married, but doctors confirmed that he did, in fact, have the dreaded disease, which in many cases back then was a death sentence. He was also told that he had 49 polio-infected cells in his spinal fluid, and that 51 such cells usually meant paralysis for life. He was in hospital for two weeks and lost 15 pounds from his 6', 180-pound body. Fortunately, doctors told him he was lucky and was likely to make a full recovery. In fact, Gadsby played in 68 games during the 1952–53 season (recording 22 points), missing only two games of the Blackhawks schedule. He saw his first playoff action that year and was named to the NHL's second all-star team —quite a reversal from just a few months earlier when he was not sure he would even live!

If near-death experiences were not going to stop Gadsby from a great NHL career, neither was playing for the sad-sack Chicago teams of the 1950s. After eight full seasons as a Blackhawk, Gadsby was traded to the New York Rangers in a five-player deal completed in November 1954. Gadsby continued his fine play in New York (posting a 51-point season in 1958–59), but the Rangers were not much better than the Hawks. In another stroke of good fortune, a trade in the summer of 1961 sent Gadsby to Detroit, where he played the best five years of his career. The Red Wings were in the playoffs every year and made three trips to the finals with Gadsby a star on the Detroit blueline (they also finished in first place during the 1964–65 season).

Gadsby's defining performance in the playoffs came during the 1966 Stanley Cup finals when the Wings faced the highly favored

Montreal Canadiens. The series opened in Montreal on April 24, 1966, with the Red Wings stunning the Habs 3-2. Gadsby was nursing a very sore elbow (an injury he had picked up in the semi-final versus Chicago), but he scored a very important goal in the first game. He jumped into the attack and took a pass from Ab McDonald before ripping home a shot to give Detroit a 2-1 lead they would never relinquish. The teams exchanged goals in the third, but Detroit held on for the win. "The doctor figures it's a broken blood vessel," Gadsby said after the game about his sore elbow. "I'm sure I'll be okay for tomorrow night. You know, I didn't feel a thing when I was firing that goal but man, how it ached when we were protecting that lead in the final few minutes."

Gadsby did indeed play the next game, and the Red Wings took the second game by a 5-2 score to shock the entire hockey world. Gadsby set up Detroit's third goal in the final frame to give the Red Wings a 3-1 lead and believed his team was in good shape going home for the next two games. "This is the closest I've been to the Stanley Cup in 20 seasons," Gadsby reminded everyone after the contest. "And I'm not going to slow down until I sip champagne. This club is just reaching its peak. We gave them our one-two punch here in Montreal and they'll get the knockout drops Thursday and Sunday in Detroit. And then we'll celebrate." The Montreal side had other ideas, however, and the Canadiens proceeded to win the next four straight games, taking away Gadsby's dream of ending a long career with a championship. Gadsby retired after the season was over and even though he did not sip from the fabled Cup, his great career is truly a testament to the kind of determination that never lets anything stop you from doing what you really want in life.

Gadsby commented years later on his life in hockey, saying, "In reviewing my career, I'm proud that I left the NHL as the highest scoring defenseman in NHL history. I'm more proud of the fact that Gordie Howe and I were the first players to play in

1,000 games. I feel quite good that I left the game with a reputation of a man who played through many injuries. When the Red Wings acquired me at age 34 in 1961, Boston Bruins' great Eddie Shore said of the deal: 'He will play three to five more years. He is virtually indestructible.' That kind of praise means plenty to me because it meant that I never cheated on my effort."

Bill Gadsby played in 1,248 career games, scoring 130 goals and recording 568 points. He was elected to the Hall of Fame in 1970.

BILL CHADWICK
BORN: MANHATTAN, NEW YORK
NHL SEASONS: 1939–40 TO 1954–55
DEFINING MOMENT: NOVEMBER 20, 1941

Bill Chadwick was born in Manhattan, New York, on October 10, 1915. He was a pretty good amateur hockey player (he was named an all-star and won a scoring championship) when fate dealt him a terrible blow in March 1935, when he was just 19 years of age. He was at Madison Square Garden, about to complete a tryout for the United States national team. As he was just getting ready to step on the ice, an errant puck struck him in the right eye. Chadwick recalled the incident years later: "I remember stopping at the edge of the rink and looking out on the ice, thinking how good it would feel to step out there and glide away. I knew my dad was in the stands, watching, and I didn't want to embarrass him by flopping.

BILL CHADWICK

That's why my head was bent and my eyes were transfixed on the gray-coloured ice as I stepped from the rubber runner over the dasher boards. That's why I never saw that puck." After a long hospital stay, it was finally bad news for Chadwick, who was told the eye could not be saved. He would have no vision in it for the rest of his life.

Chadwick was surprised to learn he could not play baseball with his one eye, but was equally shocked to realize he could play hockey without too much difficulty. It would be hard for him to regain his star status, but he was still a useful player for the New York Rovers of the Eastern Hockey League, a team that often supplied players to the New York Rangers of the NHL. Chadwick was with the Rovers for nearly two seasons when, incredibly, a high stick cut him in the left eye—the one that had not been damaged. Chadwick was once again terrified by the sight of blood coming out his eye; fortunately, this time, it was just a cut that would eventually heal. However, the close brush with complete blindness made Chadwick realize something. "That horrible sinking feeling I had at that moment when I thought that stick had hit my good eye was just too much to take," Chadwick recounted. "I realized then and there that I was done with playing hockey. The risk was just too great." Chadwick still loved the game and would attend all the Rovers games. Then, fate intervened again.

One night, Chadwick was paged from his seat at the arena and asked to report to the timekeeper's box. Much to his surprise, he was asked to referee the game—the man who was supposed to wear the stripped sweater was stuck in a snowstorm and unable to make it to Madison Square. "That was all I had to hear. It was the game of hockey and if it meant trying to stand on my head, I would do it because it's the greatest game in the world," Chadwick said of his new opportunity. "Where's the whistle?" Chadwick then demanded.

Chadwick was told to keep his hands out of his pockets during play, so he found a new use for his 10 fingers during that first game. He started waving his hands all over, indicating who was being called for a penalty and then physically demonstrating the type of infraction the player was being called for. Hand signals helped him to communicate with timekeepers when the crowd was too loud. It also gave Chadwick a chance to work out some nervous energy. All said, Chadwick would soon set a standard for all hockey officials.

Chadwick started to referee (he was also a linesman) as many games as he possibly could, and his good work started to get noticed. At one point, he nearly gave up the idea of becoming an NHL referee, but the league recruited him to be a linesman for their games in New York while he continued with the EHL. In September 1941, there was an opening for a referee at the NHL level and Chadwick was hired for the job. His first season came in 1941–42, with his first assignment scheduled in his hometown between the Rangers and the Americans—both New York–based teams. It was November 20, 1941. Chadwick decided he would referee the game just as he had done in the EHL. He would call out the number of any offending player and indicate with his hand signals what the penalty was. For example, holding was indicated by one hand gripping the wrist, tripping was a hand slap going across the leg, high sticking was two hands raised, while charging was shown by rolling his arms. Chadwick was pretty good at putting on a bit of a show, but he was clearly in charge of the contest. The Americans won his first contest by a 4-1 score and he was especially busy in the first period, calling eight penalties. The second period included two more penalties, plus a fight, while the final period saw just two infractions.

Chadwick's work was well received and he was actually praised for his neutrality when he ignored Americans coach Red Dutton, who wanted to talk to him during the contest. Observers also felt Chadwick kept the game moving by telling the Americans captain to tell his coach to get his team on the ice or face a penalty.

At one point, Chadwick's eye problem became public. He took some heat, but it never really bothered him. Instead, he would joke and say the fans were "half right." However, he would add that his disability made him a better referee by forcing him to concentrate more. "Because it was always on my mind, I tried even harder not to make a mistake," Chadwick said. "I skated harder than most other guys." Finishing his first year in grand style, Chadwick was

chosen to referee the last two games of the '42 Stanley Cup finals—
the classic series that saw Toronto make a comeback from three
games to take the Cup with four straight wins!

Chadwick might never have refereed a single game if he had let
his eye injury stop him from the game he loved. Instead, he lived
his life to the fullest. His hand-signal system was a great contribution to the game of hockey and was "officially" adapted by the
NHL in 1956.

**Bill "The Big Whistle" Chadwick retired in 1955 after more than
1,000 NHL regular season and playoff games and a then-record
42 appearances in the Stanley Cup finals. He was elected to the
Hall of Fame in 1964.**

EDDIE SHORE
BORN: FORT QU'APPELLE, SASKATCHEWAN
NHL SEASONS: 1926–27 TO 1939–40
DEFINING MOMENT: JANUARY 3, 1929

People who grew up in the Canadian Prairies in the early part of
the 20th century were a tough and hearty breed. Not surprisingly, the province of Saskatchewan—the heart of the Prairies—was
where Eddie Shore grew up. Shore was not an especially good student, so he quickly learned to run a ranch like his father did. By age
15, Shore was already handling all aspects of ranching as well as
managing farmers who were tenants on the property owned by his
father. However, when his mother died prematurely, his father decided to send Shore to an agricultural college in Manitoba. Shore's

brother was already at the school, and he decided to try sports just like his older sibling. His brother tried to discourage Shore from hockey, but that only served to fire up the young Eddie, who boldly predicted he would play professionally one day.

Shore prepared himself physically by running every day to build up his legs for skating. He began playing—between the ages of 21 and 23—in his home province with teams in Melville and Regina. Shore then played for the Edmonton Eskimos of the Western Hockey League for the 1925–26 season, scoring 12 goals in 30 games. The defenseman had a reputation for being a hard, heavy hitter, but usually would deliver clean checks. The opposition did not always agree. Shore was, therefore, forced to fight in this era where the game was very physical and there was little help from the referee.

Shore was not afraid of anything, and even had to battle a veteran Boston player when the Bruins acquired him in an August 1925 trade with Edmonton. The tough-guy veteran was Billy Coutu, a big defenseman who did his best to make Shore's life miserable at training camp. Shore knew what to expect and took things in his stride for a while. "I took what I had to take for a long time. Then it was a fight to the finish between that old-timer (Coutu) and myself." Needless to say, Shore more than held his own during the inevitable fight, and soon he became a dominating presence on the Bruins blueline.

In his first five seasons of play in the NHL, Shore's goal scoring was in double digits each year (15 was his highest total in 1930–31), despite the fact that scoring defensemen were not in abundance in this era. He soon became a perennial first all-star team selection and was named the league's most valuable player a total of four times. In addition to his goal scoring, the most notable statistic on Shore's record was his penalty minute total —which was often over 100 minutes during a regular season that was usually shorter than 50 games. Shore was loved in Boston and Bruins fans revered his physical approach to the game. He was an important player when the Bruins won the Stanley Cup in 1929 because he was dedicated, energetic, and always played with great heart. He would carry on through injuries that would disable others, and his pain threshold knew no bounds. He would also do anything to help his team win, and that included a wild trip through a raging blizzard to get to a game in Montreal.

The Bruins beat Ottawa on New Year's Day, 1929. Their next game was in Montreal two days later. Shore was riding with a friend to the train station to join his teammates when his car broke down. He arrived at the station, but the train had already departed for Montreal. He tried to charter a plane, but was told that there was no way he could land in Montreal due to a snow storm. Incredibly, Shore talked a taxi driver into driving him the 300-plus miles (500 km) north for $100. But the road became treacherous as weather conditions worsened. Shore was able to purchase a snow shovel and ice pick from someone who was driving a truck, but the taxi really needed tire chains. The taxi driver wanted to turn back because he was afraid of driving in the bad weather—so Shore was forced to take over behind the wheel.

Shore got chains at an all-night gas station, but they quickly wore out. The taxi then went off the road. Shore managed to get the vehicle back on the road and the journey to Montreal resumed. The windshield had also given way at one point, so Shore had the elements of the storm hitting his face as he drove. He came upon a construction camp next and was able to get another set of tire chains, but they also wore out. "We wound up in a ditch and the cabbie quit right there," Shore recalled of his harrowing drive. "I found a farm house a mile or two up the road. The farmer hitched up a sleigh and drove me to a connecting train line. I made it to Montreal in 22 hours and so I was there at 6 o'clock the night of the game." His eyes were practically shut and his face was badly weather-beaten, but Shore was going to play against the Maroons.

Shore was able to rest briefly before the opening faceoff, and he then proceeded to score the only goal of the game to give Boston a 1-0 victory. The Boston defender also took a penalty for going after Montreal's Hooley Smith, a noted tough guy. Bruins coach Art Ross commented on Shore's game that night at the Montreal Forum: "He (Shore) had a couple of steaks, took about a half hour's rest and then played one of the greatest all-round games I've ever seen." Ross also fined Shore $200 for missing the train out of Boston but that never bothered Shore, who well understood he was wrong to be late.

Through sleet, snow, and freezing rain, the determined Shore would not let the weather stop him from playing in a hockey game—a contest that only added more lore to his legendary career.

Eddie Shore played in 550 career games, scoring 105 goals and recording 284 points. He was elected to the Hall of Fame in 1947.

BOB BAUN
BORN: LANIGAN, SASKATCHEWAN
NHL SEASONS: 1956–57 TO 1972–73
DEFINING MOMENT: APRIL 23, 1964

Bob Baun was always a tough man who played hockey the same way. One night at Madison Square Garden in 1960, he had his throat slit by a skate and merely put a towel on the wound as he walked to the infirmary. Baun and the Maple Leafs were playing the New York Rangers that night, and a scramble in front of the Toronto net saw Camille Henry's skate come up and slice Baun across the throat, just missing his jugular. He was stitched up and went back out to play the third period, even though he was told not to go back to the game. On the team bus that night, Baun suddenly was unable to breathe because he was hemorrhaging and his tongue was being pushed back down his throat. It was a life-and-death situation, but the Leafs managed to get Baun immediate medical attention. It took two operations to fix the problem. When finally allowed to go back home, he was admitted to hospital in Toronto—where he met his new son, who had just been born in the same facility! One week after his release from hospital, Baun was in a playoff game against Detroit on March 20. It would not be the last time Baun would show his true mettle.

Baun had a very successful junior career that included winning the Memorial Cup twice in 1955 and 1956. He nearly made the Leafs on his first attempt after turning pro but was a late cut. He was upset to be assigned to Rochester of the AHL, but did not stay there very long. He was there for 46 games in 1956–57, but was also a Maple Leaf for 20 games that same season. He vowed then that he would never play in the minors again. He made the Leafs the next season, a year that saw the club finish last in the six-team NHL. However, Baun was seen as an important part of the Leaf rebuilding efforts and Toronto owner Conn Smythe said to a reporter that "Bob the Bomb" was the best defenseman to be on the Leafs since the days of Bill Barilko, a tough defenseman who had been with the Leafs for four Stanley Cups wins. It was hoped Baun could fill the same role.

Smythe was always a very shrewd judge of hockey talent, and he was right on with his assessment of Baun. The Leafs developed a group of young players like Baun and mixed in the right amount of veterans to become consistent contenders. In 1959 and 1960, the Leafs were already back in the Stanley Cup finals, and two years later, they took their first championship since 1951. The Leafs re-peated as winners again in 1963, capping a great end to the 1962–63 season that saw them finish in first. Baun was a low-scoring defenseman who made life miserable for opposing forwards who dared to challenge him in the Toronto end of the ice. Paired with the talented yet enigmatic Carl Brewer, the Leafs hardrock defen-seman was always ready to be physical—but Baun could carry the puck out of danger just as well.

The Leafs were hoping for a third consecutive Cup in 1964, but had a much harder time at it than in the two previous seasons. They edged Montreal in seven games in the semi-final (with Baun scoring a rare but important goal in the sixth contest—a game the Leafs needed to stay alive). However, Detroit was ready for Toron-to in the finals, going up 3-2 in games. Then came the night the Leafs met the Red Wings on April 23, 1964, at the Detroit Olympia.

The Leafs opened the scoring, but Detroit would take a 2-1 lead before Toronto tied it again. Gordie Howe put the Red Wings up 3-2, but Billy Harris tied it for the Leafs late in the second. The third period was scoreless, although Detroit tried very hard to end it before their hometowns fans. At one point, Baun took a Howe blast off the ankle. Although he tried to keep playing on it, he eventually collapsed on the ice and had to be carried off on a stretcher. Incredibly, Baun returned before the final period was over after having his ankle taped tightly and frozen with a needle. For most other players, their season would have ended there. But not for Baun.

When overtime began, Baun was ready for his first shift. The puck came to him at the point in the Detroit end; it was rolling a little, but Baun did not try to stop it. He let a shot go that hit a Red Wing stick in front of the net and it went over the shoulder of net-minder Terry Sawchuk. Just 1:43 into overtime, the game was over, and the Leafs had forced a seventh game with the 4-3 win. "I forgot all about the pain when I saw my blooper shot hit the shaft of (Bill)

Gadsby's stick and shoot up into the top of the Detroit goal," Baun said later in the dressing room. "I just managed to make it to the blueline in time or it would have thrown our guys offside. Then I fired in the general direction of the goal." When asked if he would play in the seventh and deciding game in Toronto, he answered, "You think a little thing like this is going to make me miss the last chapter?"

The "little thing" was a broken bone in his lower leg and while extremely painful, Baun was assured he could do no more damage to it. Once again he was taped and given a painkiller and took to the ice, receiving a roaring ovation from the Toronto crowd who jammed Maple Leaf Gardens on Saturday night, April 25, 1964. The Leafs scored early and then hung onto a 1-0 lead into the third, and then proceeded to add three more goals to make it a 4-0 final and take their third straight Stanley Cup. Baun did not miss a single shift, although his ankle had to be frozen again during the final period. "I couldn't feel a thing from the knee down," Baun revealed after the game. "I stopped a couple of shots with my skate and didn't even feel the puck hit the blade. The only time it bothered me was when I tried to skate backwards."

Baun often wondered how he had been able to play in such agony, but he realized that he had an uncommonly high pain threshold. He was also able to block out the pain mentally, which helped him overcome his injury. Years later he wrote of his famous playoff goal that it "was the high point of years of determination, dedication and desire." There was no way a man like Baun was going to let a little broken bone in his leg stop him in any way—not with the Stanley Cup on the line!

Bob Baun was with the Leafs when they won another Stanley Cup in 1967. He also played for the Oakland Seals and the Detroit Red Wings before returning to Toronto in 1970.

BERNIE GEOFFRION

BORN: MONTREAL, QUEBEC

NHL SEASONS: 1950–51 TO 1967–68

DEFINING MOMENT: APRIL 20, 1958

When Bernie Geoffrion was a young boy growing up in Montreal, he learned to play hockey on outdoor rinks. He did not care how cold it was outside because his one goal in life was to be an NHL hockey player, and Geoffrion realized practice was the only way to get there.

Geoffrion started playing for a local church team and cheered for the Montreal Canadiens, especially Maurice "Rocket" Richard. He met his hero one time, and Richard wished young Bernie luck in pursing his hockey career. The one thing Geoffrion was good at was scoring goals, which he did very well because of his hard shot. He used a full windup to deliver his drive, making him the first player to use the "slap shot" instead of the wrist shot most commonly used. "I would bring my stick back in an arc and then— POW!—I'd whack it like a golf ball. I could tell immediately that I had a better and harder shot than anyone else." His shot made such a loud sound when the puck hit the boards that one witness said he could hear a couple of "boom, boom" echoes. It was decided Geoffrion would be called "Boom, Boom" from that point on, and the nickname stuck for the rest of his life.

By the time Geoffrion was playing junior hockey, his goal scoring prowess was more than impressive. In five seasons in the Quebec Junior Hockey League (QJHL), Geoffrion scored 174 goals and recorded 310 points in just 167 games. The rebuilding

Canadiens owned Geoffrion's playing rights, inserting him into their lineup for 18 games in the 1950–51 season (scoring eight goals and totaling 14 points). He was still considered a rookie the following season and won the Calder Trophy as the best first-year player with 30 goals and 54 points in 67 games. His goal total dipped slightly in 1952–53 to 22 but the Canadiens won the Stanley Cup that season, the first of Geoffrion's six championships. Geoffrion won the Art Ross Trophy during the 1954–55 season with 76 points (with a league-leading 38 goals), but it came about because "Rocket" Richard received a lengthy suspension near the end of the season. Montreal fans wanted to see Richard win his first scoring title, and were not pleased that another member of the Canadiens took the award!

Geoffrion's career was moving along quite nicely with the Habs, who were used to winning one championship after another. However, it all came to a crashing halt when Geoffrion attended a Montreal practice on January 28, 1958. He collided with a teammate and suddenly felt a burning sensation, and soon afterward he collapsed on the ice. Although many of his teammates thought Geoffrion was just joking, the 5'9", 166-pound right winger could not breathe properly. He was rushed to hospital, where it was discovered he had a ruptured bowel. Geoffrion was wheeled into surgery and doctors were able to save his life—but it was close for a while. Geoffrion had 27 goals at the time of his injury, but his season was done due to the surgery. He was told to rest and he promised his wife (the daughter of Canadiens legend Howie Morenz) that he would not play hockey anymore. It was a promise he really hoped to keep. But on the night that the playoffs opened, Geoffrion went down to the Montreal Forum to visit his teammates.

Somehow, he convinced Montreal coach Toe Blake to let him take the pre-game warm up. Blake agreed and the Forum crowd let out a tremendous roar when they saw Geoffrion on the ice! Perhaps Geoffrion was inspired by teammates like Maurice Richard (bad cut on his leg) and Dickie Moore (broken bone in his wrist), who had also come back from serious injuries. So Geoffrion stayed on the ice. Montreal then beat Detroit in four straight games to advance to the finals once more—this time to face the Boston Bruins. The series went back and forth early on, but Montreal had a chance to win the Cup right in the Boston Garden on the night on April 23, 1958. It was the sixth game of the series.

Just 46 seconds into the contest, Geoffrion scored to give Montreal a quick 1-0 lead. A high pass from Jean Beliveau was knocked in by Geoffrion to get Montreal off to the good start. The Rocket added another soon afterward, but Boston answered back with one before the first period ended. Beliveau scored one to give Montreal a 3-1 lead and then Geoffrion went to work again. He poked the puck past Boston defenseman Leo Boivin and broke in alone on Bruins goalie Don Simmons. Geoffrion faked a slap shot and went to his backhand to score a brilliant goal, giving Montreal a 4-1 lead. It turned out to be the Stanley Cup–winning goal. Boston got two back in the third, but Montreal added an empty net goal for a 5-3 win.

"Toe (Blake) and these guys deserve as much credit as I do. Blake is the greatest coach I've ever played under. He knew I wasn't right when I came back and he let me play on power plays and gradually work my way up to a full turn. For a time I thought I might have to quit. But gradually I got stronger. I felt the team needed me," said Geoffrion, who scored five times versus Boston and totaled eight points in the six-game series. Bruins captain Fern Flaman said it was Geoffrion who did the most damage: "Geoffrion was their big guy in this series. Not only did he kill us tonight but he got big goals...but for him we'd be sipping champagne from the Cup." Coach Blake marveled at how well Geoffrion played: "He came back only two months after a major operation that usually requires a four- or five-month recuperative period. He got the first goal and that big fourth one that locked up the game and the Cup for us. I've never seen him play a better game."

Years later, Geoffrion wrote, "Considering my physical condition, I consider my playoff production one of the most amazing things I ever accomplished. In 10 games I delivered 6 goals and 5 assists. This from a guy who said he would never play again." Geoffrion might have added: from a player who would not let a near-death experience stop him from playing for the Stanley Cup!

Bernie Geoffrion finished his career with 393 goals (including a 50-goal season in 1960–61). He was elected to the Hall of Fame in 1972.

FRANK MCGEE
BORN: OTTAWA, ONTARIO
SEASONS: 1899–1900 TO 1905–06
DEFINING MOMENT: JANUARY 16, 1905

Scoring a lot of goals in a playoff game is bound to get some attention, but when the player doing the scoring has only one good eye, the attention gets even more intense. Such was the case for the man known as "One-Eyed McGee", who, many years ago, set a record that still stands today. It will never be broken.

Frank McGee was born into a prominent Canadian family on November 4, 1880. He was the sixth child of eight born to Elizabeth and John McGee. His uncle, Thomas D'Arcy McGee, was one of the Fathers of Confederation. McGee grew up to be a very good athlete, playing sports like lacrosse and football, but he was also a very good hockey player.

FRANK McGEE

McGee learned to skate along the Rideau Canal, and the sturdy
5'6", 140-pounder would play for the Ottawa Aberdeens at 19. On
the night of March 21, 1900, McGee was playing in a charity game
when he was struck in the eye with a puck that someone had lifted
too high. The eye was injured and could not be repaired, but that
did not stop McGee from continuing his hockey career. He was fast
on his skates and could score goals, which helped him overcome
his eye injury. He played in 23 games for the Ottawa senior hockey

club (the "Ottawas" as they were known) between 1903 and 1906 and scored a remarkable 71 goals—or about 3 goals per game. He started off this run by scoring a pair in his first game against Montreal AAA and then scored five times in one contest versus the Montreal Victorias.

Reviews of McGee's play were favorable. The *Ottawa Citizen* wrote, "(McGee) showed that he was qualified to stay with the finest in the land and finish strong. He followed up fast and was always in the vicinity of the puck." McGee helped the Ottawa team (soon renamed the Silver Seven because they had seven players on the club and because the board of directors had given the players silver nuggets to commemorate their first championship) win the Stanley Cup in 1903, 1904, 1905, and 1906. By all accounts, his eye injury did not hinder him in any way: he was a very competitive player who had a deadly shot. McGee was also a good playmaker and had a way of playing his best when it mattered most. In 1903, he scored seven times in four games as Ottawa beat two teams to claim the Stanley Cup. During the 1904 playoffs, McGee scored five times in one game versus the Toronto Marlboros and had another big game against a team from Brandon, Manitoba. It was obvious that any team that faced Ottawa had to know where McGee was at all times, since he was clearly the best goal scorer on the Silver Seven.

Still, all of McGee's scoring exploits were quite minor compared to what he did the night of January 16, 1905, in Ottawa. A team from the Yukon, the Dawson City Nuggets, had traveled to Ottawa (completing a 4,400 mile trip) to challenge the Silver Seven for the Stanley Cup. Extremely tired from their amazing voyage (which began on December 19, 1904, in the Yukon and ended on January 12, 1905), the Dawson City team did not get any chance to rest or practice and were beaten 9-2 in the opening game of the total-goals two-game series. McGee scored only one goal in the game, forcing one opposition player to suggest that he was less than impressive. It is unknown if McGee was aware of the comment, but in the second game of the series, he exploded with a 14-goal performance that has never been matched in Stanley Cup history.

The Ottawa club attacked from the opening faceoff, swarming Dawson City with a persistent onslaught that ended as a 23-2 slaughter. McGee scored eight consecutive goals at one point over an amazing nine minutes of play! It was widely reported that only the work of Dawson City netminder Albert Forrest (who at age 17 was the youngest player ever to compete in a Stanley Cup game) kept the game as close as it was. Just one month later, McGee scored the winning goal in a third and final game when his team fought off the Kenora Thistles to retain the Stanley Cup. McGee actually scored three times in each of the last two games—and he did so with a broken wrist!

The next season saw McGee score 28 times in just seven games and in the '06 playoffs, he was at his best again, scoring six goals over two games as Ottawa defeated Queen's University. But he was not finished there. McGee added nine more goals during a two-game series against a team from Smith Falls, Ontario. It marked the last time the Silver Seven held the Stanley Cup, because a team from Montreal would later outscore them 12-10 over two games to take the championship away. Reports, though, indicated that McGee played very well in the second match of the series. It would be the last game McGee would play.

Prior to the start of the 1907–08 season, the 24-year old McGee gave up hockey to take a government job which paid very well for the times. McGee had given everything to hockey—losing an eye and leaving with a variety of broken bones and scars as opponents zeroed in on him. One of his teammates on the great Ottawa teams, Frank Patrick (who is in the Hockey Hall of Fame as a builder), said of McGee, "He was even better than they say he was. He had everything—speed, stickhandling, scoring ability, and was a punishing checker. He was strongly built but beautifully proportioned and he had an almost animal rhythm." Such a great athlete as Frank McGee was not going to let the loss of an eye stop him from becoming one of hockey's first superstars!

Frank McGee joined the Canadian Army during World War I and was killed in action in France in 1916. He was elected to the Hall of Fame in 1945.

SIMON GAGNE
BORN: STE-FOY, QUEBEC
NHL SEASONS: 1999–2000 TO PRESENT
DEFINING MOMENTS: MAY 7 & 14, 2010

Many great hockey players, at some point in their careers, have to face serious injuries and still find a way to be productive. Simon Gagne is one such player who battled hard to get back into the lineup and did not let injuries stop him from helping his team. His determination to play helped his team pull off one of the greatest comebacks of the modern era.

Growing up in Ste-Foy, Quebec, allowed Gagne to play hockey at every turn. He was on skates at the age of two and was playing organized hockey by the time he was four. People marveled at his skating ability, much of it learned on the family's backyard rink. Gagne was mentored through minor hockey by his father, Pierre. The senior Gagne was a good minor pro player in Quebec, as was his father, Roger, a terrific player in the American Hockey League during the 1940s. As a third-generation hockey player, Gagne had both the background and the desire to play pro. He played in the prestigious Quebec Pee Wee tournament on two occasions, and his skills got him noticed to the point where he was selected to play in the Quebec Major Junior Hockey League for Beaufort.

His last two years of junior saw Gagne play for the Quebec Remparts, where he had a 30-goal, 69-point season in 1997–98. On the recommendation of former Flyer Simon Nolet (who was very familiar with the Gagne family), Philadelphia selected Gagne in the first round of the 1998 entry draft. Simon went back for one more year of junior and notched 50 goals and 120 points to lead the league in scoring. He made the jump to the Flyers for the 1999–2000 season and made the all-rookie team with 20 goals and 46 points. He followed that up with 27 markers the next year, and then in 2001–02 was outstanding with 33 goals and 66 points. He was also thrilled to be selected for the Canadian squad for the '02 Olympics in Salt Lake City, where he helped the country capture a gold medal for the first time in 50 years. Gagne had four points in six games during that tournament, and everyone remembers the newspaper front-page photo of him and Martin Brodeur celebrating the end of the gold medal game. Gagne was actually surprised to be selected for the team, but general manager Wayne Gretzky wanted him there.

However, for the two NHL seasons prior to the 2005–06 campaign, Simon Gagne had not produced to expectation. In 2002–03, he had only 9 goals and 27 points in an injury-shortened, 46-game season. He played 80 games in 2003–04, but scored only 24 times and totaled 45 points—good numbers for most players but not for the multi-talented Gagne, who should have been able to score 30 goals easily. He took the lockout year off completely and returned to find the new NHL very much to his liking—he potted a team-high 47 goals and 79 points (both career bests for Gagne). The swift 6', 190-pound left-winger was now exceeding expectations, and he had the good fortune to do it in a year when his contract was up for renewal.

Gagne's unselfish style of play had the Flyers contemplating giving him the team captaincy, but he felt a more senior player deserved the honor. He passed on it, but he was a strong performer in 2006–07 with 41 goals. The Flyers had high hopes for their young star, but a bad concussion reduced his 2007–08 season to just 25 games. This serious injury shut him down for the season and playoffs.

Gagne was very good during the next season; however, the following year saw a return of the injury bug. He was diagnosed with a double hernia in his groin, which eventually required surgery. He still managed to get into 58 games, scoring 17 times and accumulating 40 points. The Flyers barely snuck into the 2010 playoffs (by winning a shootout during the last game of the regular season) but were ready for the post-season. They knocked off New Jersey in five games, but once again, Gagne was injured—this time, two screws had to be surgically inserted into his right foot. He was able to return for the fourth game of the series against Boston—but the Flyers were already down 3-0 in games when they hosted the Bruins on May 7, 2010.

The game was tied 4-4 in overtime when Gagne got his first shift of the extra session. He then put the puck past Tuuka Rask in the Bruins net to send the over-19,000 Flyer fans home happy, at least for one night. "It's a good feeling," Gagne said. "I cannot ask for more (than) to be able to come back (and) to be able to score a big goal. It's fun to score goals but when you get those in overtime, it's the best feeling in the world. It's good to be able to win this game." Although the Flyers had new life thanks to Gagne's goal, nobody expected them to win the series. But exactly seven days later, on May 14, Philadelphia had a chance to pull off a miracle that only two other NHL teams had ever accomplished.

With the score tied 3-3 in the third, Gagne took control of the series by scoring a power-play goal to take a 4-3 lead. Gagne rifled a shot over the right shoulder of Rask for what turned out to be the game winner. The Flyers had won all four games Gagne appeared in during the Bruins series, and had come back from 3-0 in the last contest, played in Boston. "We could have quit," said Gagne, the first star of the game. "We got a couple of goals (three actually) to tie the game in the second period and after that, the game was right there for both teams. They took a penalty and we were able to score on the power-play." The Flyers knocked off Montreal in the next round to return to the Stanley Cup final for the first time since 1997. However, the Chicago Blackhawks ruined the dream ending by taking out the Flyers in six hard-fought games.

Gagne had scored nine times and totaled 12 points in the '10 playoffs for a team that really needed his offensive punch and leadership. For the last number of years, Gagne had battled through a variety of ailments and injuries to contribute to his team's success—and nothing was going to stop Gagne from contributing to a great moment in hockey history!

Simon Gagne was traded to the Tampa Bay Lightning prior to the start of the 2010–11 season, where he recorded 40 points in 63 games during the regular season. He added 12 points in 15 playoff games during the '11 post-season.

PAUL KARIYA

BORN: VANCOUVER, BRITISH COLUMBIA

NHL SEASONS: 1994–95 TO PRESENT

DEFINING MOMENT: JUNE 7, 2003

When hardrock defenseman Scott Stevens hit an opponent, the other guy was usually pretty lucky to get up. Philadelphia star Eric Lindros was one of these unfortunate ones who did not make it back from a Stevens hit—and Lindros was a large man. One guy who lived to tell the tale of a Stevens crunch was one of the smallest, yet most talented players in the game—Paul Kariya—who was determined not to let a bigger opponent stop him in his tracks.

It's hard to believe now, but Kariya was not the first player selected in his draft-eligible year of 1993. The Ottawa Senators had the top selection and wasted it on Alexandre Daigle. A better choice was made by Hartford, who scooped up huge defenseman Chris Pronger second overall. After Tampa took Chris Gratton, the Ducks selected Kariya with the fourth choice.

Kariya had made his reputation in the junior leagues of his native British Columbia (244 points in just 94 games) before attending the University of Maine. While playing in his first year with the Black Bears, Kariya racked up an impressive 25 goals and 75 assists in 39 games. His performance earned him the Hobey Baker Award as best U.S. collegiate player, making him the first freshman to win the highly coveted trophy. After playing for Canada's Olympic team in 1994 and helping the team win a silver medal, Kariya was ready for the NHL.

When he entered the league in 1994–95, Kariya displayed all

the talents necessary for a great career. A superb skater with a terrific sense of anticipation, Kariya also demonstrated a great shot that goalies had to respect. Kariya was always near the top of the list for shots on goal, and in 1998–99, he led all players with 429. But Kariya can do more than shoot, and he has the assist totals to prove it. In 1995–96, Kariya scored 50 goals and added 58 assists in just his first full NHL season. He came back with 44 goals and 99 points the next year to show he was for real. The following season was one to forget for young Kariya. First, he had a long contract dispute with the Ducks, then an ugly hit to the head kept him out of the Olympic Games.

The 1998–99 season was much better for Kariya, who played in all 82 contests and recorded 101 points (39 goals, 62 assists). He used a style of play that showed you do not have to take a penalty to be effective (Kariya has won two Lady Byng trophies, one in 1996 and one in 1997). Kariya also dedicated himself to the game and was willing to spend the time needed for conditioning. In 2001–02, the Ducks missed the playoffs for the fourth time in five years, and although he scored 32 goals, Kariya's assists slipped to 25, his lowest total for a full season. But although the Ducks were for sale, they brought in some help for their franchise player in 2002–03. Petr Sykora, Adam Oates, Sandis Ozolinsh, and Rob Niedermayer helped the Ducks increase their point total from 69 to 95. Kariya had only 25 goals, but his 56 assists ranked eighth in the NHL.

The Ducks, named after a Disney movie, wrote a script of their own by reaching the Stanley Cup finals, beating powerful teams like the Detroit Red Wings and the Dallas Stars along the way. Paul Kariya finally had that long NHL spring he had hoped for when the Ducks beat Minnesota in the Western Conference final and then took on the New Jersey Devils in the 2003 Stanley Cup finals. The Devils won their first two home games, but the Ducks battled back to take the next two, both in overtime. New Jersey won the fifth game 6-3 and had a chance to win their third championship in Anaheim on the night of June 7, 2003, a night that showed the hockey world that a top goal-scorer could also be tough as nails.

The Mighty Ducks were fired up in front of their hometown crowd and jumped out to a 3-0 lead on two goals by Steve Rucchin and one by Steve Thomas, with Kariya assisting on two of the first-period markers. However, the Devils scored early in the third to narrow the gap. Then Kariya was hit a devastating bodycheck by Stevens, a Devils defenseman who was always on patrol for a big hit. The blow knocked Kariya out glassy-eyed on his back. The Ducks star had just made a pass and was unaware when Stevens caught him with a blindside hit. Kariya's head hit the ice and he remained sprawled on the ice for sometime. Although he was somewhat wobbly, Kariya managed to skate off the ice. Few believed he would be back in this contest.

"I sensed that (Stevens) was there but I thought I had a bit more time than that," Kariya said of the non-penalized hit. "He's very patient with his hits and he times them right." Stevens was unrepentant and simply said, "You can't let your guard down. It's a physical game out there." Amazingly, Kariya shook off the hit and returned to the game in the same period. He was able to then blast a shot past Martin Brodeur in the Devils net at the 17:15 mark, giving the Mighty Ducks a 4-1 lead to take into the third period. "I was raring to get out there and play again," Kariya said afterward. "The doctors cleared me to go and I was back on the ice. It was nice to get an ovation from the crowd. I didn't expect anything but it was a nice lift." It was evident nothing was going to stop Kariya from helping his team get to the seventh game of the series. His goal was dramatic, and the crowd gave him another ovation when his bullet shot went into the Devils net. It was his sixth goal and twelfth point of the playoffs.

The Mighty Ducks won the sixth game 5-2 but lost the seventh 3-0 back in New Jersey. However, Kariya became the Anaheim all-time leader in assists (369) and points (669) before he left the team to play in Colorado the next year. He has also played for Nashville and St. Louis.

Paul Kariya has scored 402 goals and recorded 989 points in 989 career games. He did not play in the 2010–11 season while recovering from injuries.

SAKU KOIVU
BORN: TURKU, FINLAND
NHL SEASONS: 1995–96 TO PRESENT
DEFINING MOMENT: APRIL 2002

As Saku Koivu was looking forward to the start of the 2001–02 season, the Canadiens center suddenly felt very ill on the plane that was taking him from Finland to Canada for the start of training camp. Tests revealed that Koivu was suffering from non-Hodgkin's lymphoma, a form of cancer that was found in his abdominal area. Instead of wondering whether his team would make the playoffs for the first time in three years, Koivu was worrying about whether he would live, let alone whether he would ever play hockey again. Luckily, Koivu was in tremendous condition. Along with a positive spirit and competitive approach to everything he did, he was determined not to let this dreaded disease stop him.

The Canadiens had just won the Stanley Cup in 1993 and thought they had added another great player to their organization when they selected Koivu with their first pick (21st overall) of the

'93 Entry Draft. The 5'10", 178-pound Finnish-born center stayed in his homeland for two more years (winning a scoring title at the age of 20) before joining the Habs for the 1995–96 season. He was very impressive as an NHL rookie with a 20-goal, 45-point performance. For the next few seasons Koivu produced somewhere in the range of 45 to 55 points when healthy. Those numbers were good, but not superstar caliber as might have been expected from the talented centerman who was especially good at setting up plays. However, Koivu had many other attributes he brought to the team, including valuable leadership skills. The Canadiens had made many questionable moves since their last Cup win, but one of their better decisions was giving the team captaincy to Koivu. However, with the cancer diagnosis, there way no way of knowing if Koivu would ever come back.

Throughout the winter of '01–'02, Koivu took chemotherapy treatments. But he still showed up to most Montreal home games, promising teammates and fans that he would return soon. The Montreal club struggled through that entire year, but the Habs were on the verge of gaining a playoff spot when Koivu returned to action on the night of April 9, 2002, in a game against Ottawa. A win in this contest would assure a playoff spot for the Canadiens.

Montreal defeated the Ottawa Senators 4-3 that night and gained a playoff position as a result, but the real story of the contest was Koivu's return to action. As soon as the 21,273 Montreal fans in attendance saw Koivu back on the ice, he was greeted with a loud, boisterous standing ovation. "SA-KU, SA-KU," the fans chanted for the next eight minutes. Only the start of the national anthem calmed the crowd—for a few minutes.

Koivu's teammates were pumped by the return of their leader as well, and scored three times in the second period to take an insurmountable lead. Although he found himself on the losing end, Ottawa's Sami Salo, a fellow Finn, was pleased to see Koivu back in uniform. "I know if anybody can fight cancer, it's Saku. He's such a fighter. He was a national hero (in Finland) before. What do you think now? He's going to be more of a national hero, winning the fight against cancer. It's a great thing, especially for his family."

With Koivu in the lineup, the Canadiens opened the playoffs against arch-rival Boston, taking the first game of the series 5-2. Montreal got a hat trick from Donald Audette and Koivu notched three assists to get the series off to a good start for the Habs. Boston tied the series with a win on home ice, but the Canadiens were ready for their first game at home on April 23, 2002. The first period saw the teams exchange goals (Koivu earning an assist), but the Bruins scored twice in the second period to take a 3-1 lead into the third. The Habs vowed in their dressing room to play better in the final stanza and came out raring to go. Four straight goals gave Montreal a 5-2 win and a 2-1 series lead. In the third period onslaught, Koivu set up one goal and then scored the winner after he was moved back to his natural center position.

"It's a great feeling to come back like that and win the first playoff game in Montreal in four years," the 27-year-old Koivu said. "It was special tonight. I don't know what I thought when the puck went in because it all happened so fast. But it was great to score a winning goal in a game like this. The last time I scored here (in Montreal) was more than a year ago." The newspaper photos the next day showed an elated Koivu after scoring his goal, and it was easy to see he was showing some extra emotion for a special moment. Montreal went on to eliminate the heavily favored Bruins, but lost out to the Carolina Hurricanes in the next round. Koivu finished with 10 points in 12 playoff games and earned the admiration of all hockey fans with his inspiring comeback.

In 2002–03, Koivu had his best season in the NHL up till then with 71 points (21G, 50A). This was his first full campaign after being diagnosed with cancer. Two years later, he recorded 75 points for Montreal (including 53 assists) and stayed with the Habs until the end of the 2008–09 season. He then signed as a free agent with the Anaheim Ducks, where he is still a productive player. It seems nothing can stop the indestructible Saku Koivu!

Saku Koivu has scored 225 goals and 738 points in 938 career games played to date.

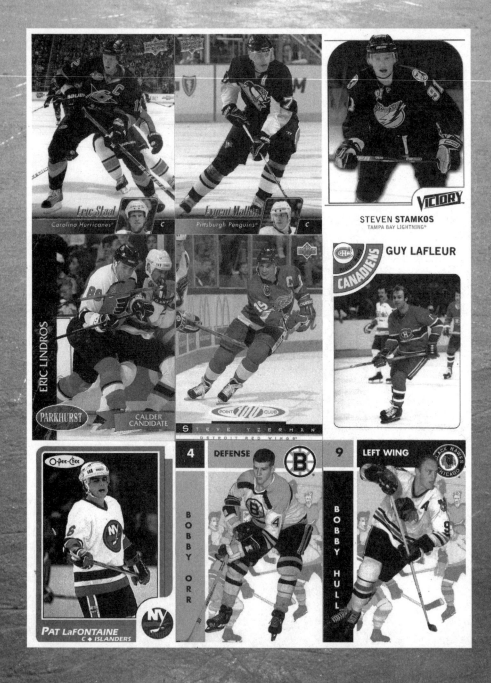

THRIVING UNDER PRESSURE

When a player gets picked at the top of the NHL Entry Draft (or was signed as a highly touted youngster before the Draft began in 1913), he is expected to do very well in the NHL. Many top players get used to high expectations at a young age, but it is nothing like what they face at the professional level. Many are expected to change the fortunes of an entire NHL team, while others are supposed to get the franchise started back in the right direction. It's a lot of pressure to deal with and, to be sure, there are those who cannot stand the heat too well. Others, however, learn to deal with it all, become great players, and fulfill their destinies. In this chapter we'll focus on the stories of those who made their mark, "Thriving Under Pressure."

Eric Lindros
Evgeni Malkin
Eric Staal
Steve Yzerman
Pat LaFontaine
Steve Stamkos
Bobby Orr ✓
Guy Lafleur
Bobby Hull
Gilbert Perreault

ERIC LINDROS
BORN: LONDON, ONTARIO
NHL SEASONS: 1992–93 TO 2006–07
DEFINING MOMENTS: MAY 23 & 25, 1997

Eric Lindros was tabbed as the "Next One" well before he was eligible for the NHL draft. Gifted with a big body and a wicked shot, Lindros filled the net at all levels of hockey. Opponents who got in his way were usually steamrolled, and soon, most observers were calling Lindros a linebacker on skates. He was never too shy about mixing it up, and he had the will to impose himself in any game at any moment. At age 15, for instance, he played for St. Michael's College near his home in Toronto and scored 24 goals in just 37 contests during the 1988–89 season. He then played for the famous Detroit Compuware team for part of the next season and racked up 23 goals in 14 games. He then moved on to play major junior hockey for the Oshawa Generals, notching 36 points in 25 contests and also helping the Generals win the Memorial Cup. Indeed, the young man was a force to reckon with.

Lindros knew that he was a dominating player, and that he was going to be highly sought after in the Draft. However, unlike most youngsters his age, Lindros was fully aware of his earning potential and sought to control where he played—not only in junior (he forced the Sault Ste. Marie Greyhounds to trade him to Oshawa), but also as a professional. All indications leading up to the 1990–91 season were that the Quebec Nordiques were going to do all they could to finish dead last overall one more time so they could select the precocious Lindros. By doing so, the Nordiques would have a star-studded lineup which would include Joe Sakic, Mats Sundin, and Owen Nolan, who were also first-round selections. But Lindros was not going to play along. He was very distrustful of the Nordiques ownership and felt the Quebec organization was more intent on losing than anything else. He also realized that his marketing potential would be extremely limited while playing in Quebec City. Lindros, his family, and his agent made it clear he would not report to the Nordiques if they selected him, but those warnings were ignored.

"I had been dreaming of draft day as long as I could remember but when it finally came, it left me feeling empty. I felt great satisfaction knowing that I had been the first player selected overall in the 1991 NHL Entry Draft. But at the same time I was upset that the first pick wasn't the happiest player—not even close. Knowing that things could never work out with the Quebec Nordiques took a lot of joy out of the day."

Lindros played the 1991–92 season in a sort of limbo (playing with the Generals as well as three different versions of Team Canada) because he refused to sign an NHL contract. When it looked like he was going to sit out another year, the Nordiques finally realized he was serious about not going to Quebec. He was finally dealt to the Philadelphia Flyers for six players and two first-round draft choices—a remarkable haul for a player who had yet to suit up in an NHL game. (The Nordiques did very well in acquiring so many assets, including Peter Forsberg—a star in his own right— and eventually used them all to win a couple of Stanley Cups, albeit in Denver, Colorado.)

If there had been pressure to perform on Lindros before the trade, the mountain of expectations had now grown even larger at the start of the 1992–93 season. Lindros did not disappoint. What made him stand out was his willingness to use his size to run over, if not crush, any opponent who stood in his way. His youthfulness and large frame made him look something of a man-child, but this player was ready to dominate. The 19-year-old, 6'4", 236-pound center played in only 65 games as a rookie but produced 41 goals and 75 points when he was healthy. By his third year, Lindros was MVP of the NHL and his fourth season saw him record a career-high 115 points. The Flyers slowly got better after his arrival, and even though they were never strong in net, they were a serious contender by the 1996–97 season.

Lindros played in only 52 games in '96–'97 but managed to record 79 points with the Flyers winning 45 games. They easily knocked off Pittsburgh and Buffalo in the opening two rounds of the playoffs but faced New York Rangers Mark Messier and Wayne Gretzky (two of Lindros's idols growing up) in the next round. With the Flyers up 2-1 in games, the teams faced each other once again on the night of May 23, 1997, at Madison Square Garden. A tied game was settled by Lindros, who scored a goal in the last minute to give his team a big win. The puck came out to Lindros at the face-off dot, and he whipped a back-hand drive into the top of the net with less than seven seconds to play. "We were lucky tonight," Lindros said later. "I think everybody in our dressing room knows we were lucky tonight. We know we have to play better."

Two nights later on May 25, 1997, the Flyers knocked the Rangers out of the playoffs with a 4-2 win on home ice. Lindros opened the scoring for Philadelphia and added an assist. His performance in the '97 post-season had many saying Lindros was now the best player in the game and that a torch had been passed from the likes of Messier and Gretzky to the new wunderkind. Lindros was not so anxious to accept the crown. "No, you've got to play in this league a number of years to be considered along those lines," he said. However, Messier said the combination of size, speed, and skill made Lindros special. "That's what sets him apart from anyone who's ever played this game," Messier said. "He had a great series right from the first game." Lindros, however, kept on point, warning his teammates that the journey was not yet over. "We've made it through three steps and it takes four to win it all. We're happy to get to the final but our mission is not accomplished yet," he said.

It turned out Lindros was right again as the Detroit Red Wings won the Stanley Cup in four straight games. Lindros had led all playoff scorers with 26 points in 19 games, but that was small consolation after the bad loss in the finals. Still, Lindros did deliver as the Flyers had hoped, with the team making it to the finals for the first time since 1987. In fact, it was the defining moment of Lindros's injury-plagued career when he lived up to the hype and took his team to the highest levels of the NHL.

Eric Lindros played in 760 career games recording 865 points (372 goals, 493 assists) with four NHL teams.

EVGENI MALKIN
BORN: MAGNITOGORSK, RUSSIA
NHL SEASONS: 2006–07 TO PRESENT
DEFINING MOMENT: 2009 PLAYOFFS

When the 2004 NHL Entry Draft was held at the RBC Center in Carolina, most agreed that Alexander Ovechkin was the prize catch. That's why the Washington Capitals happily grabbed the rights to the flashy left winger with their first overall selection. However, when the Pittsburgh Penguins took Russian-born Evgeni Malkin, a 6'3", 195-pound center, they were certain that he, too, would be a big star in the National Hockey League. Malkin's mother, Natalia, thought the same as well: "I knew when his dad brought him to the ice and put skates on him for the first time. At that moment, we both said to each other, 'He'll be a great player one day.' We saw it right away." It is not an easy situation when parents put that kind of pressure on a youngster, but Malkin would one day prove them right.

While Ovechkin joined the NHL for the 2005–06 and won the Calder Trophy as the best rookie, Malkin stayed at home and played one more year in his hometown of Magnitogorsk. He had 21 goals and 46 points in 47 games while playing for Magnitogorsk in 2005–06. It was not easy for Malkin to get over to the NHL, considering especially that he had signed on for an additional year in Russia (it was reported that he was under severe pressure to do so). However, he soon had a change of heart and found a way out of his homeland. He then hid out in Finland for five days while he waited to sign a deal worth just under $3 million with the Penguins. Malkin's Russian team was not very pleased with their 20-year-old star (they eventually tried to get the U.S. district courts in New York to rule that Malkin belonged to them, but the legal challenge failed). But once a travel visa was granted, Malkin was gone, and the Penguins could not wait to team this budding star with the recently drafted Sidney Crosby. Penguins management believed they now had the two best young players in the league, reminiscent of the days when Mario Lemieux and Jaromir Jagr had led them to two Stanley Cups in the 1990s.

Malkin's performance in the 2006–07 season certainly did not disappoint. He had 33 goals and 52 assists, which earned him the Calder Trophy. He showed an incredible athleticism as he ripped through the NHL in the early going of his rookie year (despite a shoulder injury he suffered in pre-season). Malkin can handle the puck with great ease and his skating skills include a burst of speed that he employs just at the right moment. Like many great players he can do almost anything at full speed and knows when he has to go to the net to make a play. However, Malkin's playoff performance in '07 was less than stellar. He looked bewildered as the need to succeed in the post-season eluded him totally (only four assists in five games). As a result, the Pittsburgh club bowed out meekly to the surging Ottawa Senators.

Malkin's disappointing performance in the playoff did not linger when the 2007–08 campaign began. Much more comfortable in his second season, he often played alongside superstar Sidney Crosby for the first half of the year. A bad ankle sprain forced Crosby out of the lineup, which allowed Malkin to return to his center ice position. He did not shrink from the challenge of playing without Crosby and produced 47 goals and 59 assists during the regular season. The slick center showed he could score goals in any variety of ways, and his drive to succeed was there for everyone to see. His ability to lead was also evident when Crosby was on the Penguins injured list. Malkin was nominated for the Hart Trophy that year, and even though he did not win the award, he had clearly shown he belonged in the NHL's upper echelon.

The Penguins were a better-prepared team for the '08 playoffs, in which they lost in the finals. Malkin was very solid with 22 points in 20 playoff games. However, it was during the 2009 playoffs that Malkin really shone. Team captain Crosby was terrific, but it was Malkin who won the Conn Smythe Trophy with a 36-point performance (and that came after leading the league with 113 points during the regular season!). The Cup returned to Pittsburgh that year, and Malkin showed that he had learned his lesson about playing when the pressure is the greatest. The Penguins would not have won without Malkin's enormous contribution in that Stanley Cup final.

The Penguins were down 2-0 in games to Detroit and had to find a way to win on the night they returned home. It was June 2, 2009. Malkin set up three Penguins goals that night, bringing his playoff point total to 33. Pittsburgh won 4-2. Now that they were back in the series, the fourth game took on even more importance, and Malkin responded with one goal and one assist in another 4-2 victory. The Penguins were down 2-1 during the contest but rallied to even the series and give them hope. Detroit roared back with a 5-0 in the fifth game, but the Penguins eked out a 2-1 win in the next game to force a seventh game.

Prior to the game, Malkin spoke about winning the Stanley Cup. "The Cup is all I want. I will give everything. One win, the Cup. I think about it a lot, especially in these last weeks. It's my dream." In a very close contest, the Penguins got two goals from Max Talbot to take the championship with a 2-1 win. The first goal was set up nicely by Malkin, giving him an incredible 36 points in the post-season. He took 24 shifts in this seventh game and led his team with three shots on goal (Talbot also took three shots) in just under 20 minutes of ice time. Malkin had earned the Smythe with one of the highest point totals in playoff history (only Wayne Gretzky and Mario Lemieux had ever recorded more in one play-off year). This series was a defining moment for the superstar, who responded perfectly to all the pressure and led his team to the coveted title.

Evgeni Malkin was the first modern-day player to score a goal in each of the first six games he played in the NHL. In 352 NHL games to date, Malkin has scored 158 goals and recorded 418 points. His first goal came against Martin Brodeur of the New Jersey Devils on October 18, 2006.

ERIC STAAL

BORN: THUNDER BAY, ONTARIO

NHL SEASONS: 2003–04 TO PRESENT

DEFINING MOMENT: 2005–06 SEASON & PLAYOFFS

To put it simply, Carolina Hurricanes center Eric Staal is a winner. In February 2010, Staal was part of the Canadian Olympic team (recording six points in seven games) that won the gold medal at the Vancouver games. He also won a Stanley Cup with the Hurricanes in 2006 (28 points in 25 games to lead all scorers), and a gold medal with Team Canada at the World Championships in 2007 (scoring 10 points in 10 games). Not many players have won the same three championships (others to have achieved this "triple crown" include Joe Sakic, Scott Niedermeyer, Chris Pronger, and Nicklas Lidstrom—all sure bets to be in the Hall of Fame one day). And to think he achieved all this by the ripe old age of 25! For Staal, it was quite an honour to be included with such elite players, but it should really be of no surprise to anyone who has followed his career.

Staal's skills were shaped at the development factory known as the Peterborough Petes of the OHL. He was there for three great seasons—in 2002–03, his final year with the junior team, Staal scored 39 goals and racked up 99 points in only 66 games. His name was bandied about as the potential number-one overall pick, but that honor went to Marc-Andre Fleury, who was selected by the Pittsburgh Penguins. But Staal did not have to wait too long at the 2003 draft, as the Hurricanes announced his name with the second selection. However, it was not a given that Staal would make the Carolina club on his first attempt, but he impressed enough to stay the entire season, scoring 11 goals and recording 31 points in 81 games. The lockout season of 2004–05 proved very beneficial to Staal, who played the entire year for the Lowell Monsters of the AHL. There he produced 77 points (including 51 assists) in 77 games. He was now better prepared for the NHL and responded with 45 goals and 100 points (the highest total on the Carolina club and the seventh-highest mark in the entire league) in just his second season. His good play earned him a spot on the NHL's second all-star team, but he was just getting warmed up for the playoffs. This would prove to be Staal's first chance to show he could dominate and deal with the pressures of the NHL's tough post-season marathon.

In the first round of the '06 post-season, the Hurricanes were matched up against the Montreal Canadiens and dropped the first two games at home in rather shocking fashion. The third game of the series was played on April 26, 2006, in Montreal, with the Hurricanes desperate for a win. A loss would put them down 3-0 in games, likely resulting in an elimination which would ruin a 52-win, 112-point regular season. Montreal had a 1-0 lead going into the third period, but team captain Rod Brind'Amour took advantage of a Montreal mistake and tied the game with less than 10 minutes to play. The game went into overtime when the Habs' Tomas Plekanec was called for a penalty. Montreal woes were compounded when Radek Bonk broke his stick while out to kill off the two-minute minor. The Hurricanes were able to pass the puck around more freely and finally, they were able to set up Staal for a blast as he crept in from the blueline. The shot eluded Montreal netminder Cristobal Huet, who did not even appear to see the high rising drive that blasted over his catching hand to give the Hurricanes the very important victory. Staal's teammates mobbed him along the boards as they celebrated the crucial turning point. "That's probably the biggest one I've scored," Staal said after the win. "I'll take it any way it comes." That Staal overtime winner sapped the energy from the Canadiens, and the Hurricanes won the next four contests to take the series in six games.

After beating Montreal, the Hurricanes easily ousted the New Jersey Devils in five, but they had to go through seven games before subduing the Buffalo Sabres in the Eastern Conference final. The surprising Edmonton Oilers met the Hurricanes in the Stanley Cup finals, and a 3-1 series lead was nearly lost, but Carolina won the seventh game on home ice to take the championship. Once again, Staal showed he could work in the spotlight and was the leading scorer for his team—this time in the finals—with eight points in seven games. "It was like your whole life, your entire hockey training was all balled into one moment," Staal would later comment on winning the Cup. "To see older guys raise the Cup over their heads was pretty special for me. I'm proud to have battled alongside them." Some of the veteran players Staal was referring to were Rod Brind'Amour, Glen Wesley, Bret Hedican, Ray Whitney, and Doug Weight—all first-time winners of the most coveted trophy in hockey.

As much as the veterans contributed, the efforts of youngsters like goalie Cam Ward (named winner of the Conn Smythe Trophy) and Staal were the deciding factor that gave Carolina their first Stanley Cup. Staal was now the face of the Hurricanes franchise, and he had proven to be one of the very best choices the club made when they drafted him so high in 2003. A player who thrives under great pressure (high draft choices always have the spotlight on them) is truly a valuable asset for any NHL team, which is why the Hurricanes wrapped up Staal with a long-term contract.

Eric Staal was named team captain of the Carolina Hurricanes during the 2009–10 season and continues to perform as one of the elite players in the NHL. He has recorded 504 points (226 goals and 278 assists) in 560 games to date.

STEVE YZERMAN
BORN: CRANBROOK, BRITISH COLUMBIA
NHL SEASONS: 1983–84 TO 2005–06
DEFINING MOMENT: 1997 PLAYOFFS

When you look back at the Hall of Fame career of Steve Yzerman, it would be easy to think the superstar had a pretty easy life in the NHL. After all, his great numbers give no other indication. However, if you look deeper, you'll find that the Detroit Red Wings did not really want to draft him. You might also find out that of the most successful coaches in hockey history would not have been too unhappy had the star center been moved to another team. Such slights only compounded the pressure already on the superstar. But, throughout it all, Yzerman thrived and picked up hockey's ultimate along the way.

Detroit was going to draft fourth overall in 1983. The team had its eye on American-born Pat LaFontaine who had once played junior hockey for Compuware, a team owned by Red Wings owner Mike Ilitch. LaFontaine had the look and style the Red Wings were hoping to use to rebuild and market their franchise, which, at that time, was in very bad shape. There was a big debate among hockey pundits as to who should go first overall at the '83 Entry Draft, but Minnesota ended all the speculation by taking Brian Lawton with the number one selection. The Hartford Whalers then took Sylvain Turgeon in the second slot. Red Wing general manager Jimmy Devellano never expected LaFontaine to last more than two picks, but now he was so close to Motown. However, the New York Islanders threw a wrench in Detroit's plans (many had thought they would select Andrew McBain) by taking LaFontaine third overall, leaving the Red Wings staff deflated. Ilitch even slumped a little in his chair. "The Detroit Red Wings are proud to take Steve Yzerman of the Peterborough Petes," Devellano said when it was time for his team to announce their selection. With the benefit of hindsight, Yzerman was the best player in the '83 draft, but no one was sure of that when the Red Wings took the slightly built (5'11", 185-pound) center.

If the Red Wings were at first disappointed with the selection of Yzerman, the player was not. In fact, Yzerman was more than happy to go to Detroit, where he knew he would get the chance to play in the NHL right away. "Detroit is a super club with a lot of class," Yzerman said. "They haven't forgotten the days when they were the best." He was also determined to make the critics one day say that the Red Wings got a great player with the fourth pick. With great pressure on his shoulders to produce, Yzerman made the team right after his first training camp and scored 39 times as a rookie to go along with 87 points. To prove it was no fluke, the sublimely talented pivot would record six consecutive seasons of 100 or more points, beginning with the 1987–88 campaign. He also scored 50 or more goals five times and truly became Detroit's heart and soul. However, as good as Yzerman performed, the Red Wings were not a very good team.

Detroit recovered in the early 1990s and Yzerman continued to produce high numbers, but playoff success was proving to be very elusive. After playoff defeats at the hands of Toronto and San Jose, the talk of Detroit trading their best player grew. When Scotty Bowman was brought into the Detroit organization, he let it be known that Yzerman could be a better player if he would pay attention to both ends of the ice. It was not pleasant for Yzerman to hear or accept Bowman's analysis of his play, and a trade seemed like a real possibility. Although he was nearly traded, the Red Wings never completed any of the proposed deals (one with Ottawa was almost done), and Bowman and the star center learned to live together. In 1995, the Red Wings made the finals for the first time since 1966 but were ousted in four straight games by the tight-checking New Jersey Devils.

After a disappointing 1996 post-season, the Wings were back in the finals in 1997. Before getting there, Detroit had to knock off the Colorado Avalanche, who were the defending champions. Detroit had defeated St. Louis and Anaheim in the first two rounds of the playoffs but lost the first game of the Western Conference final 2-1 in Denver. It was essential that Detroit even the series on the night of May 17, 1997, before going home for the next two games. Colorado was up 2-0 late in the second period, before Detroit got one back. An early power play in the third period saw Yzerman set up Sergei Fedorov to even the game, and then the Detroit captain scored a goal of his own to give his team the lead. Yzerman banked a shot off Patrick Roy's leg, and it trickled into the net for the winning goal. "I just tried to throw it at him," Yzerman said after the game. Roy believed he had made the save and gave Yzerman credit for making a "smart play." Detroit won the next two games at home and eventually won the series in six to put them back into the finals.

The first game of the '97 Stanley Cup finals was scheduled for May 31 in Philadelphia. The Red Wings did not want to get off to another bad start, and they opened the scoring with a short-handed goal before the game was seven minutes old. It was still anyone's game in the third period, with Detroit hanging on to a slim 3-2 lead. But just 56 seconds into the final frame, Yzerman scored on a shot from just inside the blueline to make it 4-2 and deflate the Flyers before their home fans. Yzerman was obviously happy to win the opener but was not yet "overly excited." "It's just getting under way and winning the first game is not an indication of the way this series will go," Yzerman elaborated. "We're just getting started." But the Flyers never recovered, and Detroit took their first

Stanley Cup since 1955 with a four-game sweep. Yzerman raised the silver trophy before a happy crowd at the Joe Louis Arena.

Yzerman would go on to win two more Stanley Cups (in 1998 and 2002) before retiring with 1,755 career points in 1,514 games. He lived up to all expectations and learned to thrive under the scrutiny of one of the most demanding hockey markets in the NHL. The Red Wings had indeed done very well to draft Steve Yzerman way back in 1983!

Steve Yzerman was elected to the Hall of Fame in 2009 and was named the general manager of the Tampa Bay Lightning starting with the 2010–11 season.

PAT LAFONTAINE
BORN: ST. LOUIS, MISSOURI
NHL SEASONS: 1983–84 TO 1997–98
DEFINING MOMENT: APRIL 18, 1987

When a team is considered a dynasty (and with four consecutive Stanley Cups to their credit, the New York Islanders certainly qualify), the club wants to do everything possible to keep it going. The Islanders were blessed to have a very high pick coming off their fourth straight title, and they were hoping the third overall pick in 1983 would help keep the good times rolling. It was a great deal of pressure to put on the shoulders of a talent like Pat LaFontaine, but he was ready for the challenge and did his best to keep his team in contention. By the time his career was over, LaFontaine not only thrived but also carved out a high-quality Hall of Fame career.

Even though LaFontaine was born in Missouri, his family moved to the more hockey-friendly Michigan when he was seven years old. Hockey was a part of his life ever since he could remember, and he would often hit the ice with his father and brother in outdoor and indoor settings. LaFontaine learned to skate very well because of all this practice. However, when he was just 12, he was told that he had exercise-induced asthma and that he should give up sports altogether. LaFontaine was not willing to accept that verdict, and he visited an allergist who found the real problem, which was then treated with shots. Soon, he was back in action, playing all the sports he possibly could. But it was quite obvious that he was a special hockey player.

When LaFontaine turned 16, he played for the Detroit Compuware team and posted incredible numbers, scoring 179 goals and 324 points in 79 games. It was assumed by many that LaFontaine would attend a U.S. college, but he opted instead to play major junior hockey in the province of Quebec. In 70 games with Verdun, he scored 104 goals and 320 points to propel his name among the best junior players for the 1982–83 season. The powerful New York Islanders had made a deal that secured a high draft, and they were thrilled to select LaFontaine. Rather than join the Islanders right away, the slick center decided to play for the American Olympic team (scoring 56 goals in 58 games prior to the Winter Games) and then added eight points in six contests during the tournament. The Americans did not win a gold medal, but LaFontaine immediately joined the Islanders and had 19 points in 15 games. He is best remembered as a rookie for his two goals (scored 35 seconds apart) against the Edmonton Oilers in the last game of the 1984 Stanley Cup finals. LaFontaine was starting to show that he could live up to the expectations of being a high first-round draft choice.

The veteran-laden Islanders were just starting to fade as a championship dynasty when LaFontaine came onto the team.

By just his fourth season, the 5'10" pivot scored 38 goals and 70 points in 80 games. However, the most memorable moment of his career came in the first round of the '87 playoffs when his overtime goal won the seventh game of the series versus Washington. The contest was played on April 18 and did not finish until well into April 19 , which was Easter Sunday. New York scored a late goal in the third period to even the score at 2-2. For a seventh game of a playoff series, it was a rather dull affair, but then the overtime began. The two teams traded one great chance after another, but nobody could bulge the twine. Bob Mason of the Capitals and Kelly Hrudey of the Islanders both provided spectacular netminding for more than 68 minutes of extra play.

After 8:47 of the fourth overtime period, the puck came back to LaFontaine at the Washington blueline. He spun and ripped a shot that rattled off the crossbar and landed in behind Mason, who then slumped to the ice knowing that all that effort was lost. With whatever energy he had left, LaFontaine leaped into the air as his teammates came out to mob him. It was two minutes short of 2 a.m. when he scored that winning goal. "That was a special feeling to win that Game 7 and be a part of some history as far as the National Hockey League goes," LaFontaine recalled. "I look at that goal and it was really a stepping stone in my career. Even today, wherever I go, people come up to me and start telling me where they were during the Easter Epic." The defining goal showed that LaFontaine could score in even the most pressure-packed situations. And for the next six years after that historic marker (it is now the tenth-longest overtime in NHL history), LaFontaine did not score less than 46 goals in any season; and two times, he had over 50.

LaFontaine had his best year as a Buffalo Sabre in 1992–93 when he recorded 148 points and was named to the NHL's second all-star team. Injuries (broken jaw, knee woes) started to become a problem for the star center, although he bounced back to score

40 goals and 91 points in 1995–96. He also played for the American team that won the first World Cup of Hockey Tournament.

Unfortunately, LaFontaine's career was never the same after he suffered a concussion in October 1996. It was a very scary time for the normally upbeat captain of the Sabres. It took a long time before he felt better or before he could perform simple tasks. He was later traded to the New York Rangers and recorded his 1,000th point (a great milestone for any player) at Madison Square Garden on January 22, 1998. To be sure, LaFontaine was a great player in the regular season, but he was also an exceptional playoff performer with 62 points in 69 playoff games. However, another concussion forced him to retire.

Not only did LaFontaine get elected to the Hall of Fame, the Sabres honored him further by retiring his number 16. "There are two things you never dream of happening when you play a sport, that is going into the Hall of Fame and the other is having your jersey retired," LaFontaine said later. "Having that thrill (of sweater retirement) and honour bestowed upon me ... is something I'll cherish forever."

Pat LaFontaine dealt with the pressures that go with being drafted high, the expectations of producing like a star, dealing with the role of team captain and with returning to play after serious injuries, all in a superb fashion that allowed him to carve out a great NHL career.

Pat Lafontaine finished his career with 1,013 points in 865 career games.

STEVEN STAMKOS
BORN: RICHMOND HILL, ONTARIO
NHL SEASONS: 2008–09 TO PRESENT
DEFINING MOMENT: APRIL 10, 2010

When a "non-traditional" hockey market gets to select first overall at the NHL Entry Draft, it automatically brings a great deal of attention to the player selected. In their brief existence, the Tampa Bay Lightning have selected first overall on three occasions. The first (in 1992) was defenseman Roman Hamrlik – a useful but unspectacular player. The second (in 1998) was center Vincent Lecavalier—who eventually became a superstar and led the team to their only Stanley Cup championship. The third time, the Lightning selected center Steven Stamkos (in 2008), and all that was expected of him was to lead the team back to respectability in very short order and perform just like Lecavalier—the best player in franchise history. For good measure, it was also hoped that Stamkos would help sell tickets to a shrinking fan base—heaping even more pressure on a young man still two years short of his 20th birthday.

Considering that Stamkos was the first pick overall, he got very little respect during his first NHL season. The Lightning had designed an entire marketing campaign based on his arrival in Tampa Bay, and he was looked upon as a new savior for a franchise that had become rather stagnant. The 2008–09 season began under coach Barry Melrose (who had not coached in the league since the 1990s), who was quite adamant that Stamkos was simply not strong enough to play in the NHL at the age of 18. Melrose lasted all of 16 games and was replaced with Rick Tocchet, a very accomplished player in his day. Tocchet took a different tack with the youngster and helped Stamkos with extra assistance off the ice, which included some conditioning work. Stamkos responded to his new coach by scoring 16 times in his last 25 games to finish the year with 23 goals and 23 assists—not bad for a first-year player, but not good enough for the Calder Trophy either. However, he did play for Canada at the World Championships and was tied for the tournament lead in goals with seven as the Canadiens took the silver medal.

Stamkos first got noticed when he played minor hockey and scored 105 goals, totaling 197 points with the Markham Waxers in 2005–06. He then joined the Sarnia Sting of the OHL for two seasons, recording 92 and 105 points respectively, before the Lightning selected him with the first pick of the '08 Entry Draft. His game is built around his great offensive instincts, combining good playmaking skills with a devastating shot that he can get on net from any angle. He is a smooth skater who can kick into high gear very quickly, especially when he sees a chance to lead the attack. Being able to work alongside a veteran like Martin St. Louis has been invaluable to a player like Stamkos, and having tough wingers like Ryan Malone and the unpredictable Steve Downie has helped him adjust to the NHL.

The 6'1", 196-pound Stamkos knew he needed to get better prepared physically for his second season and spent the summer of 2009 training with former NHL star Gary Roberts, a man known for being a fanatic about physical fitness. Roberts (who played briefly with Stamkos in his last NHL season) designed a special program for Stamkos. The main idea was to emphasize strength development without reducing Stamkos's speed on the ice. To accomplish this, Stamkos was pulling 100-pound sleds, running sprints, and completing balancing exercises designed to give him a strong set of core muscles. Stamkos was put through this regimen six days a week, and it all paid off once the 2009–10 season got underway. The goals came pretty regularly for Stamkos during the season, many of them with the extra man as he led the entire league in power-play goals with 24.

There were just two games left in the '09–'10 regular season when the Lightning hosted the Florida Panthers on April 10. Stamkos needed two markers to hit the defining 50 mark, and he was also trying to stay ahead of Sidney Crosby for the league lead in goal scoring. Just 4:11 into the first period, with the Lightning on a power play, Stamkos took a cross-ice feed just inside the top of the faceoff circle. He blasted a slap shot that went straight into the Florida net for his 49th of the season. At the 5:28 mark of the second, Stamkos took a pass just inside the Panthers zone and let a wrist shot go past Florida netminder Scott Clemmensen for his 50th goal of the season. The hometown crowd showed their appreciation, and his teammates took time to congratulate the red-faced Stamkos who was just 20 years and two months old when he hit one of hockey's great milestones. To top off his great night, he scored the winning goal in the shootout to give his team a 4-3 win.

After the game, Stamkos was at a loss for words. "I can't even explain what I feel. Sheer joy, happiness. Just seeing the guys come and jump all over me and to share it with my teammates that have really been there since day one and that have helped me and pushed me to be the player I am. They really helped me get that goal." It was especially nice for Stamkos to have his father in the stands, watching. They would later pose for photos with the puck from the 50th goal.

One night later in the final regular season game, Stamkos scored his 51st goal of the season (into an empty net) to put him into a tie with Sidney Crosby for most goals. If anyone thought Stamkos could not deal with the pressure of being the first overall selection and the new star of the Tampa Bay franchise, they were now silent.

Steven Stamkos shared the Rocket Richard Trophy (most goals

in the regular season) with Sidney Crosby for the 2009–10 campaign. During the 2010–11 season, Stamkos scored 45 goals and then had 13 points in 18 playoff games as the Lightning made it to the Eastern Conference Final.

BOBBY ORR
BORN: PARRY SOUND, ONTARIO
NHL SEASONS: 1966–67 TO 1978–79
DEFINING MOMENT: MAY 10, 1970

The Boston Bruins organization went on a scouting trip in the spring of 1960, in a desperate search for new hockey talent. They had been tipped about a couple of youngsters playing bantam hockey for a team from Parry Sound, Ontario, and were anxious to see these two boys play in a tournament in Gananoque, Ontario. The Boston scouts scattered themselves over the entire arena so they could all get different points of view. When they gathered together to discuss what they had seen in the first period, nobody spoke of the two players they had been told to watch. Instead, they all agreed a 5'2", 110-pound defenseman wearing sweater number 2 was the most outstanding player. Who is he, they inquired. Soon, they were told his name was Orr, Bobby Orr, and he was just 12 years old. The next question was whether the team from Parry Sound was sponsored by any of the other five NHL teams. The answer was no and the chase to secure the most talented player for the last-place Bruins was on at full throttle.

Once word of Orr's exploits reached the other clubs, they also came calling for the young defenseman. Toronto, Montreal, Detroit, and Chicago all showed interest, but Boston scout Wren Blair was the most persistent. The Bruins were a last-place club and needed to find a new messiah to lead them out of the wilderness. Orr's parents were rightfully protective of their son but trusted Blair, and he was agreeable to their terms. At the very tender age of 14, Orr was playing major junior hockey for the Oshawa Generals of the OHA, commuting from his home to the working-class town every weekend. Orr showed he could play with older boys (21 points in 34 games), and the next season saw him in Oshawa full time. In 193 career games with the Generals, Orr recorded 280 points (107 were goals), shattering all the league records for defensemen along the way. In 1965–66, the Generals were in the Memorial Cup tournament, with Orr recording 36 points in 12 games! Only a groin injury prevented him from leading his team to the championship, and the junior club from Edmonton was able to take advantage of his absence to take the trophy.

As Orr was set to turn professional as an 18-year old, the expectations for him had already become enormous. "He's a much better junior player than (Hall of Fame defenseman) Doug Harvey was," Blair said. "I'd say he's as good a prospect as Bobby Hull (Chicago's superstar at the time) was when he left junior ranks and went with the Black Hawks at the age of 18." If that was not enough pressure, he would have to face headlines like "Future Greatness Ticket Hung on Oshawa's Orr" and "Boston's Future Looks Brighter with Orr." Luckily, Orr tended to stay away from all the media attention and hype, keeping a level head to go with his natural shyness. "I make mistakes out on the ice," Orr said during his last year of junior. "I feel sometimes that I have to live up to all that publicity and when I don't the fans get on me." As for joining Boston, Orr was positive about going to a basement-dwelling team. "I want to play for the Bruins. They're building for the future and they have the makings of a good club. I want to be there when they do make it." Orr could not have been more accurate.

His first two seasons (starting in 1966–67) were shortened because of a knee injury, but Orr and the Bruins rapidly improved. By his third year, he had 64 points (21G, 43A) in 67 games and had become the most dominating player in the game. The 1969–70 season saw Orr lead the entire league in points (120) and he won virtually all the major awards (including best defenseman and most valuable player in the league). The Bruins had been getting better in the playoffs, and in the 1970 post-season, they easily defeated New York and Chicago to make it to the Stanley Cup finals.

The Bruins were up 3-0 in games with the fourth contest scheduled for the Boston Garden on the hot, steamy afternoon of May 10. The St. Louis Blues were really no match for the Bruins, but on this day, they were not going down without a fight. They forced the game into overtime with a 3-3 tie. The Bruins stormed out for the extra session and got the puck deep in the Blues end. Sensing the moment was at hand, Orr charged in from the blueline as teammate Derek Sanderson had the puck behind the St. Louis net. A perfect pass to the hard-charging defenseman right in front of the net resulted in a quick, deadly, accurate shot by Orr that Blues netminder Glenn Hall had no chance to stop. The Bruin savior leaped into the air as he tripped over the stick of St. Louis defenseman Noel Picard. He looked like Superman completing a mission. When he landed on the ice, Orr had fulfilled his destiny, and the Bruins were champions for the first time in 29 years!

"I never thought there could be such a day. This is what every kid dreams of, scoring the winning goal in a Stanley Cup overtime final. Wow. I can't find words to express what I feel," Orr said in the Bruins dressing room. Orr really didn't have to say anything; the smile on his face said it all, and his great play throughout the playoffs was rewarded with the Conn Smythe Trophy. He was now a 21-year-old man who had grown to 6' and 190 pounds. Yet, in many ways, he was not all that much different from the youngster the Bruins had spotted nine years earlier. However, Orr had now dealt with everyone's expectations and excelled beyond everyone's wildest dreams.

Bobby Orr won the Norris Trophy as the NHL's best defenseman a total of eight times and was elected to the Hall of Fame in 1979.

GUY LAFLEUR
BORN: THURSO, QUEBEC
NHL SEASONS: 1971–72 TO 1990–91
DEFINING MOMENT: MAY 10, 1979

When captain Jean Beliveau retired on June 9, 1971, after a long and illustrious career, the Montreal Canadiens could have been in some trouble, even though they were coming off a surprising Stanley Cup win the previous spring. However, on June 10, just one day after Beliveau's announcement, the Habs selected junior scoring sensation Guy Lafleur with the first pick of the 1971 Amateur Draft. Montreal general manager Sam Pollock (perhaps the best hockey manager of all time) had secured the first pick overall through some very crafty wheeling and dealing. The fact that hockey's newest superstar was a French-Canadian was just as pleasing for the Habs, who now had their legacy passed on from Maurice Richard and Beliveau to Lafleur. There was some talk that the Canadiens might consider taking Marcel Dionne (another French superstar) instead of Lafleur, but the slick right winger had better size (6', 190 pounds) and a flair for the dramatic that no one else could match.

Although it seemed kind of ridiculous that the Stanley Cup champions were getting the best junior available, there was also the belief that Lafleur was always meant to wear the red, white, and blue of hockey's most successful team. A gifted goal scorer with speed to burn, Lafleur was known for flying down the wing and pounding pucks past opposing goalies. He had his first 50-goal season when he was just 17 and playing for the Quebec Aces of the QJHL. He then spent two seasons with the Quebec Remparts, scoring 233 goals in just 118 games. In his final year of junior, he took his team all the way to the Memorial Cup championship, and in the process, edged out Dionne (who played junior in the OHL) for the trophy. Winning a major championship to cap off a great junior career only seemed to heighten the expectations for the blond star. Pollock had some fun at the draft by calling a timeout when he was called upon to make the first pick, but soon stated that the Canadiens were taking Lafleur, as if there had ever been any doubt. The headlines the next day said that Lafleur was expected to replace the legendary Beliveau, who had only won ten Stanley Cups!

It was not easy for Lafleur when he first joined the Canadiens at the start of the 1971–72 season. He scored 29 goals as a rookie, but that did not seem enough for a player who had scored as much as he had previously. A 28-goal season followed next (along with his first Cup win in 1973), but a 21-goal effort in his third year had many wondering if he was going to be a big bust. However, Lafleur decided to ditch his helmet (there was no rule about wearing one at the time), and for some reason, that seemed to loosen him up. For the next six seasons, "the Flower" scored 50 or more goals each year. He also led the league in points for three consecutive years. He was a terror for other teams to deal with as he powered down the wing at breakneck speeds. With Lafleur, the Habs built another dynasty (with nine Hall of Fame players and one coach on the roster) and had no problems winning Cups in 1976, 1977, and 1978. Lafleur was outstanding in each of those years. However in the spring of 1979, the Boston Bruins presented a challenge that threatened Montreal's chances of four straight titles.

Montreal had been favored to oust Boston as they had in '77 and '78, but the Bruins tied the semi-final series at three with a win on home ice. The seventh and deciding game of the series was played on May 10, 1979, at the Montreal Forum. The Bruins played an outstanding game and were up 3-1 going into the final period. Montreal coach Scotty Bowman decided that if he was going to lose, it was going to be with his best players on the ice for most of the final stanza. Lafleur knew he was being challenged, and he was also closely checked by Don Marcotte of the Bruins, one of the best defensive players in the entire league. Nevertheless, Lafleur set up two goals (one by Mark Napier and the other by Guy Lapointe) as Montreal tied the game. Then Boston scored to go up 4-3 with under four minutes to go.

A shocking penalty for too many men on the ice to Boston gave the Habs one more chance to tie the contest. Center Jacques Lemaire took the puck down the wing and then dropped it back to Lafleur, who hammered a shot just inside the post on the far side of the net. Bruins goalie Gilles Gilbert had no chance to stop the laser beam of a shot which evened the score with just 1:54 to play. Montreal then won it in overtime and would go on to take the Cup again for the fourth consecutive time.

"I don't ever remember playing that much in a game," Lafleur said later. "But what difference does it make? We had to do anything possible to beat a team that just wouldn't give up. We had several players who seemed to be on the ice all night. I wasn't the only one who worked a little overtime. Sure, we were concerned heading into the third period behind by two goals because the Bruins were checking quite well. We couldn't think of saving anyone for the next series. We just had to go out and try to save this series."

Thanks to the efforts of Lafleur, the series was indeed saved, but his performance should not have surprised anyone since he had been dealing with the pressure to score big goals for many years. At the most important moment, Lafleur had come through, meeting expectations and dealing with the pressures placed on all true superstars.

Guy Lafleur scored 518 goals as a Montreal Canadien and was elected to the Hall of Fame in 1988.

BOBBY HULL
BORN: POINTE ANNE, ONTARIO
NHL SEASONS: 1957–58 TO 1979–80
DEFINING MOMENT: MARCH 12, 1966

Robert Marvin "Bobby" Hull first learned to skate with the help of two sisters before he turned three years of age. A gift of Christmas skates got the toddler out on the ice, and a few hours later, he was navigating across the frozen Bay of Quinte by himself. He also took to the game of hockey and would get up early on many a cold winter morning to practice his skills. His father, Robert Sr., had been a pretty good hockey player, and he spent some time teaching his young son the finer points of the game—albeit in a sometimes-harsh fashion. Bobby also played plenty of shinny, a game that can only be played successfully if you had learned to control the puck against players of all ages. Bobby had to wait until he was 10 years old to play any organized hockey in his area. But that had little fall-out because he just loved to carry the puck while he played center and that certainly got him noticed early. By the time he was about 12, Hull was playing bantam hockey in Belleville, Ontario, where a scout from the Chicago Blackhawks happened upon a game.

"Who is the chubby kid with the puck all the time?" Bob Wilson inquired. The scout was told that the boy's name was Bobby Hull. Wilson quickly made sure Hull's name was put on Chicago's list, which would give him some time to get the family to sign the appropriate forms that would make him a Blackhawk. It took some convincing (especially resistant was Bobby's mother, who did not want to see her son leave home at such a young age), but Wilson soon had what he believed to be a future superstar secured for the Chicago squad. Hull could out-skate just about anybody he played against, his puck handling skills were already well developed, and his physique was promising much more power and speed to come (he would grow to be 5'10" and a very sturdy 195 pounds). "It was strictly luck that I spotted him," Wilson recounted. "The kid was so outstanding any man in this business would have spotted him if he had been there first. I look at 10,000 kids in a year but you see a boy like Hull once in lifetime."

Wilson told the media in Belleville that Hull would play junior hockey at 16 years of age, and by the time he was 18, the handsome blond would be in the National Hockey League. By the age of 23, Wilson further predicted, Hull would be a star. While such bold predictions put heaps of pressure on Hull, Wilson turned out to be exactly right. It was, however, not quite as easy as it all sounds. Hull really only excelled in his second season of junior hockey (when he scored 33 goals for St. Catharines of the OHA), and in his first two years in the NHL, he scored 13 and 18 goals respectively. However, Hull was always a quick learner, and he soon discovered that others could carry the puck and feed him passes. He also adjusted to playing on the left wing, where it was believed he would be most effective. In just his third year with Chicago, Hull potted 39 goals to lead the entire NHL. The next season (the 1961–62 campaign) saw him score 50 goals (an incredible number achieved by only two other players at that point—Maurice Richard and Bernie Geoffrion) when he was just 23 years of age!

The Blackhawks had been rebuilt just as Hull arrived in the Windy City, with Glenn Hall, Pierre Pilote, Bill Hay, Stan Mikita, and Elmer Vasko forming a young nucleus that won the Stanley Cup in 1961. But it was Hull's scoring prowess that made the Blackhawks a feared team. Goaltenders all over the league worried about facing a Hull blast (once timed at 118 miles per hour) and coaches even assigned specific players to check Hull, telling them not worry about anyone else. The pressure on Hull to score every night soon became enormous, but in 1965–66, nothing was going to stop him from breaking the record for most goals in one season. He scored his 50th of the year on March 2, 1966, and then went into a scoring slump for the next four games. On the night of March 12, 1966, Hull hoped to make history in front of the hometown fans on a Saturday night.

The game against the New York Rangers was already into the third period before Hull was able to unleash his famous slap shot at opposing netminder Cesare Maniago. The Blackhawks were on a power play when Hull took the puck into the Rangers end with his standard rush up the ice. He pulled up at the blueline and waited as the New York defenders backed up to defend their net. Hull was now right in the middle of the ice. He then wound up with a low, hard shot which got past a slightly distracted Maniago. Finally, goal number 51 and a new NHL record! The Chicago Stadium exploded with fans littering the ice with everything they could get their hands on, especially hats. It took a full seven minutes to start the game after Hull's rousing ovation.

"The Ranger defenders backed in and I moved 10 feet over their blueline," Hull said of his record-breaking marker after the game. "I moved the puck out in front for the slap shot. I got it out too far and didn't get real good wood on the thing. I think I must have caught it with the heel of the stick. I'll admit I've taken better shots," a clearly relieved Hull continued. "There's the physical pressure but it's the mental strain of an entire year that kills you when you're going for a record." The "Golden Jet" would finish the year with an incredible 54 goals.

In all, Hull led the NHL in goals on seven occasions, proving that he could deal with all that was thrown at him and still become one of the greatest players in the history of the league—and the greatest Blackhawk of all time.

Bobby Hull scored 610 career goals in the NHL and was elected to the Hall of Fame in 1983.

GILBERT PERREAULT

BORN: VICTORIAVILLE, QUEBEC

NHL SEASONS: 1970–71 TO 1986–87

DEFINING MOMENTS: OCTOBER 10, 1974 & MAY 7, 1975

As a youngster growing up in Quebec, Gilbert Perreault admired the skill and style of the legendary Jean Beliveau, captain of the Montreal Canadiens. Perreault watched Beliveau practice and emulated his moves when the youngster played hockey for the Montreal Junior Canadiens in the late 1960s. In his last two seasons of junior, Perreault recorded 97 and 121 points respectively, leading his team to the Memorial Cup in back-to-back seasons. By the time his junior career was over, Perreault was the consensus best player available for the June draft in 1970. In all honesty, he would have loved to have been selected by the Montreal Canadiens who were about to see Beliveau retire. However, the 1970–71 season was to be the first for the Buffalo Sabres and the Vancouver Canucks, and one of these new franchises would have the opportunity to select Perreault first overall.

George "Punch" Imlach was in charge of Buffalo, and he had every intention of drafting the best player available. Imlach knew lots about building winning teams (he put together teams that won four Stanley Cups in Toronto during the 1960s), and Perreault was clearly his man. A spin of a wheel would determine who would get the first choice. The Sabres had the numbers from eight and above, while Vancouver had the numbers from one to seven. The wheel spun and NHL president Clarence Campbell said it landed on the number one, meaning the Canucks had the first choice. But

Imlach quickly jumped up from the Sabres table and pointed out that the wheel had stopped at number 11. Campbell confirmed it and the Sabres took Perreault with the first pick of the '70 Entry Draft. Perreault said he wanted to play in Montreal but conceded that Buffalo would give him a chance to play right away. "In Buffalo I'll get a chance to play regularly, which maybe I would not get in Montreal. So maybe it is wise the way it works out." Wearing number 11, Perreault had the weight of an entire franchise on his shoulders as he went to the first-ever Sabres training camp. He would not let the team down, and the Sabres quickly became a sporting presence on the western New York landscape.

Buffalo had little in terms of talent, but they were going to build around Perreault, who got off to a good start, leading the team in scoring in his rookie year with 72 points in 78 games played. From game one, Perreault was one of the most exciting players in the NHL. Opposing defenders would shake at the sight of the slick Sabre whose moves could take him through a whole team, if necessary.

The highlight of his first season came on the night of March 12, 1971, when he scored his 35th goal of the season versus the St. Louis Blues. Perreault was able to find a puck in a scramble in front of the St. Louis net, and he slammed home a shot from about eight feet out in the second period of Buffalo's 5-3 win. His marker broke the rookie record for most goals in a season, held by Nels Stewart. Perreault would then add three more goals before the season ended. "This is a big thrill for me," Perreault said after the game. "And I am happy to get the record-breaker in Buffalo for our fans. I have been treated very well by all the people here and I am happy."

By the start of the 1974–75 season, the Sabres had built a team that was aiming for the best record in the league. All the players (with the exception of goalie Roger Crozier) from the first season were gone, and Perreault just knew this year could be special. It started on the night of October 10, 1974, when the Sabres whipped the Boston Bruins 9-5 on home ice. Perreault scored three times and had assists on two others. Perreault's good friend and linemate Richard Martin also scored twice in the contest. Perreault, Martin, and right winger Rene Robert formed one of the greatest forward lines in league history. They were dubbed "the French Connection." Perreault's great speed led the very skilled trio to many goals, and when he came down the ice with his mouth open, opposing defenseman scrambled to keep up with his great moves. When he wasn't scoring goals, Perreault could dish the puck to the hard-shooting Martin or the lightning-quick Robert. In fact, the line would lead the Sabres to 113 points during the regular season.

The 24-year old Perreault had 96 points in just 68 games during that regular season. The team was now ready for the playoffs. The Sabres easily eliminated the Chicago Blackhawks in the first round and then took on the Montreal Canadiens in the second round. The Habs had also recorded 113 points during the year, but Buffalo had home ice advantage. The teams split the first four games with the fifth set for Buffalo on the night of May 7, 1975. The game went into overtime tied at 4-4. Then the Sabres got a faceoff in the Montreal end. Perreault beat Montreal's Jacques Lemaire on the draw and got the puck quickly over to Robert, who bested Ken Dryden for the winning goal. It was a great moment of redemption for Perreault, who had been checked effectively by Lemaire all series long. He bristled at the suggestion that Lemaire was getting the better of him and his line. "Our line is shadowed all year," Perreault said while Sabres coach Floyd Smith added, "If Perreault can't beat him (Lemaire), then nobody can." The Sabres then went to Montreal and closed out the series with a 4-3 win, earning a spot in the Stanley Cup finals after just five years of existence.

The Sabres lost the Cup to Philadelphia in six difficult games. Perreault would never make it back to the finals in his illustrious career. The splendid center played his entire career in Buffalo—a fitting conclusion for a man who made the Sabres franchise something special from the first day he was drafted. It is not a stretch to say the Sabres might not even exist if not for the efforts of their best ever player.

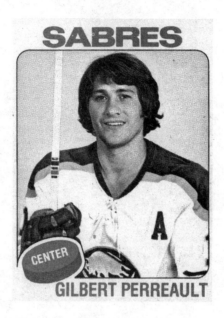

Gilbert Perreault would play in 1,191 career games, scoring 512 goals, and recording 1,326 points. He was elected to the Hall of Fame in 1990.

PERSEVERANCE

Hockey players often have to work through great adversity to make it to the NHL. Family problems, personal and financial issues, uneven opportunities, bad teams, performance problems—there are many obstacles. Talented athletes have to persevere and believe in themselves. Many could have easily quit and given up on their dreams, but those who endured—those who stuck it out, often against great odds—achieved great moments in their careers. In this chapter, we'll look at the stories of the following players who showed great "Perseverance":

Bobby Ryan
Steve Downie
Gordon "Red" Berenson
Johnny Bower
Bobby Clarke
Johnny Bucyk
Dave Andreychuk
Lanny McDonald ✓
Dan Cleary
Glen Metropolit
Patrick Kane

BOBBY RYAN
BORN: CHERRY HILL, NEW JERSEY
NHL SEASONS: 2007–08 TO PRESENT
DEFINING MOMENT: JANUARY 8, 2009

It is something of a miracle that Bobby Ryan is playing hockey at all, given what happened to his family when he was just 10 years old. After returning home from a Philadelphia Flyers hockey game in 1997, the native of Cherry Hill, New Jersey went to sleep. His next memory is being at his grandfather's house and not knowing how and why he got there. His father, Bob Stevenson, a successful executive in the insurance industry, had come home in a drunken state and gone looking for his wife Melody, who he suspected was taking drugs. Stevenson was a one-time boxer and the damage he inflicted on his wife during his alcohol-induced rage was considerable. It got him charged with attempted murder, among other offenses. Amazingly, his wife forgave Stevenson. They reconciled and planned to drop the charges, but state prosecutors were not nearly so sympathetic.

While waiting for his case to be heard, Stevenson jumped bail and left the state of New Jersey. He went to California, changed his surname to Ryan and was later joined by his wife and son (who also changed his surname to Ryan). A good hockey program was found for the youngster so he could continue his hockey development near Los Angeles. It was working out for the family under their new identities (the mother did not change her married name) but authorities eventually caught the senior Ryan in 2000 and returned him to New Jersey, where he was sentenced to a five-year prison term.

An only child, Bobby Ryan was told in very strict terms to always use his new surname (the father took it from the movie *Saving Private Ryan*) and to say nothing about what happened in New Jersey. Strong, sincere, and very determined, Ryan continued to play hockey (including a stay in Michigan) and eventually made his way to Owen Sound to play major junior hockey. He spent summers with his mom and would visit his father in Camden, New Jersey, where he was incarcerated. The elder Ryan has many regrets about how his actions affected his family but is comfortable in saying that his being a fugitive for a period was helpful to his son, even though the entire episode was sure to leave scars on Bobby. If anything affected him, Ryan hid it very well and did not hesitate to tell the entire story by the time he was about to be drafted, because he realized that sooner or later it would all come out anyway.

The 6'2", 205-pound right winger was taken by the Anaheim Ducks just after the Pittsburgh Penguins selected Sidney Crosby first overall at the 2005 NHL Entry Draft. Ryan was returned to junior, where he played two great seasons for the Owen Sound Attack of the OHL, recording 74 goals and 197 points in 122 games. At 20 years of age, it seemed Ryan was a sure bet to make the Ducks in 2007–08; instead, he had to play in the minors (49 points in 48 games) because of salary-cap issues with the big team. His professional performance left no doubt he was ready for the NHL. Ryan had finally arrived.

In his first full season, Ryan scored an impressive 31 goals (finishing second in the Calder Trophy race for top rookie) in the 2008–09 campaign. But the night that showed he was really a big-league player happened on January 8, 2009, when the Ducks were visiting the Los Angeles Kings.

Anaheim fell behind early by a 3-0 count, but late in the second period, Ryan scored a power-play goal when he took a pass along the goal line and quickly swept past the Kings netminder. Just 16 seconds into the third, he poked a rebound in the Kings net for his second of the night. At the 1:35 mark of the final stanza, Ryan took the puck down the left wing, spun around a Kings defender while still controlling the puck and then put it around a sprawling Jonathan Quick in the Kings net to score a highlight reel goal! Ryan had also completed a "natural hat trick," and scored his three tallies in just 2:21 of play. It set a team record for fastest three goals and was the quickest mark for a U.S.-born player in NHL history. After the game, Ryan spoke of how he wanted "to continue to play well and stay in the NHL. Everything is a mystery to me right now." However, it seemed Ryan had figured things out just fine and told reporters he would send a souvenir of this game to his mother.

Ryan has a very quick release and uses his bulk very well. If he improves his skating a little, the sky is the limit for this young man who has already amazed everyone with his ability to overcome great odds and be a star in the NHL.

Bobby Ryan has scored 105 goals in 250 career games to date. He scored one of the most spectacular goals in playoff history when beat two Nashville defenders and the goalie during the 2011 post-season.

STEVE DOWNIE

BORN: NEWMARKET, ONTARIO

NHL SEASONS: 2007–08 TO PRESENT

DEFINING MOMENT: FEBRUARY 9, 2010

Steve Downie is only 24 years of age, but he has already experienced a lifetime of ups, downs, and tragedy. It all began when he was almost nine and on the way to an early-morning practice. His father, John, was driving when the vehicle suddenly hit an icy patch and skittered out of control. The Jeep-type vehicle went into a ditch, hitting a couple of trees, and a utility pole crashed through the windshield, striking John on the top of the head. Steve was rescued from the crash with cuts and bruises. For 20 minutes, workers tried their best to free his father. Horrifyingly, the boy saw his father pass away at the scene. The tragedy meant that his mother had to raise Steve and his brother on her own. If that was not enough for a youngster to deal with, Downie lost some of his hearing about four years later when the bones around his eardrums began to harden. Through it all, Downie was still able to focus on hockey and was eventually selected in the first round of the NHL Entry Draft by the Philadelphia Flyers in 2005.

Downie did have the great numbers in his junior career to really justify a first-round selection, but his demeanor left much to be desired. He played in three Ontario cities (Windsor, Peterborough, and Kitchener) and could be counted on for 20-plus goals a season—and for causing a heap of trouble. His first incident came in Windsor when he had a vicious fight with a Spitfire teammate in practice. Later, just as he made his NHL debut with the Flyers, he was suspended for 20 games after launching himself during a pre-season game at Dean McAmmond of the Ottawa Senators in a reckless and dangerous manner. The Flyers had to be wondering what kind of player they had drafted, so when a chance presented itself, they traded the 6-foot, 200-pound right winger away in a deal that saw Philadelphia acquire defenseman Matt Carle. Downie finished the 2008–09 season with 23 games played for the Lightning (scoring three goals) and another 23 contests with the Tampa Bay farm team in Norfolk (25 points and 107 penalty minutes). But he was not getting the message about his behavior, and took another 20-game banishment when he was ruled to have deliberately slashed an AHL official with his stick.

However, the next year was different. Rick Tocchet was the head coach of the Lightning for the entire 2009–10 season, and he was able to get a good amount of production from Downie by calming the wild winger at just the right moments. Tocchet played a game similar to Downie's when he was in the NHL and could sense when Downie might be in danger of losing his now-famous temper. Although he still racked up 208 penalty minutes in '09–'10, Downie managed to score an unexpected 23 goals for a team that needed its youngsters to start playing effectively. It naturally helped when he got put on a line with star center Steven Stamkos and veteran Martin St. Louis, but it is also true that both those players benefitted from having Downie do a great deal of the dirty work to get them more free ice. Since he is not a very large player, Downie relies on his great inner drive to compete at the NHL level. He can work very well along the boards and will go at any defenseman fearlessly. Downie can make a clever pass or let go a good shot, but it seems his best work is done in front of the opposing net when his surprisingly soft hands get him a share of goals.

Despite the tragedy he suffered as a child and the suspensions he absorbed as he went up the hockey ranks, Downie persevered and started to make a viable contribution to his team. The night that best sums up his efforts occurred on home ice against the

Boston Bruins on February 9, 2010. The Bruins stormed out to a 5-0 lead in the contest and it looked like it would be an easy victory. However, St. Louis scored twice to give the Lightning a little life and then Downie scored twice himself (the first time he ever scored two goals in one game) to get Tampa Bay within one. His first goal was a nice tip-in from in front of the net when he redirected a Victor Hedman shot from the point. The second also came from hanging around the opposition goal where he took two swipes at a rebound before finding the back of the net past Tuukka Rask. The Lightning tried valiantly to tie the game, but the clock ran out.

"I definitely thought we battled hard," Downie said after the game. "We were down 5-0 at home and to come back and make it a game showed some determination. It's something to build on. It shows that we're not a team that gives up. We were battling right until the end of the game..." These comments are really indicative of Downie's own life more than anything else, and how he has persevered through great adversity. Although he has a long way to go, Downie has made incredible strides for someone who was once thought to be such a troubled young man.

Prior to the start of the 2010–11 season, Tampa Bay general manager Steve Yzerman rewarded Downie with a new two-year contract. "We are pleased to get Steve under contract," Yzerman stated. "We look forward to him building on the success he had last season and becoming an even bigger part of the team." Downie has recorded 96 points (including 41 goals) in 197 career games to date.

GORDON "RED" BERENSON
BORN: REGINA, SASKATCHEWAN
NHL SEASONS: 1960–61 TO 1977–78
DEFINING MOMENT: NOVEMBER 7, 1968

Gordon "Red" Berenson had played a number of years in the NHL, but his career was essentially going nowhere. He came into the league in an unusual manner in 1961 after playing U.S. college hockey at the University of Michigan. The native of Saskatchewan had played some junior hockey with the Regina Pats (where he was considered one of the best juniors in all of Canada) and then played for the Belleville McFarlands who won the World Hockey Championships. He earned All-American honors at Michigan, scoring 43 goals in his final season as a Wolverine, and then signed with the Montreal Canadiens. However, the 6'1", 190-pound Berenson did little to justify the buildup that came with his joining the fabled hockey club.

Berenson scored a grand total of 23 goals in 136 games and only two more in 26 playoff games. Although he was with Montreal when they won the Stanley Cup in 1965, the team got tired of waiting for him to develop, so they sent Berenson to the New York Rangers in June 1966. The Rangers were not nearly as deep as the Canadiens, so it was thought Berenson would benefit from more ice time on Broadway. But he did not score a goal in 30 games for New York in 1966–67 (he missed most of the year with a broken jaw) and managed just one assist in four playoff contests. He considered quitting, but loved the game and decided to give it another try. The next year, the center iceman scored only twice in 19 games before he was traded to the expansion St. Louis Blues in November 1967. He contemplated not going, but realized it was his last chance to produce at the NHL level. St. Louis coach Scotty Bowman gave him a chance to play regularly and Berenson started to show the skills that everyone had assumed he had in abundance. He was a master at controlling the puck and showed more than one flashy move when he was on the attack. He finished the year with 22 goals in 55 games, and by the end of the '67–'68 season, the slick pivot was considered the first star of the NHL's new West Division, which consisted of six new expansion teams.

However, it was on the night of November 7, 1968, that Berenson exceeded all expectations, scoring six goals in one game against the Philadelphia Flyers. At 16:42 of the first period he took the puck in his own end and got around Flyers defenseman Ed Van Impe to beat goalie Doug Favell with a high flip shot over the sprawling goaltender. He then scored four times in the second period to give him five on the night. On the second goal, he outraced Flyer defender Joe Watson to a loose puck before firing a shot into the right side of the net past a startled Favell. Berenson's next two goals came just 33 seconds apart and were both set up by teammate Camille Henry. Berenson grabbed the puck after his third tally as a souvenir of his first NHL hat trick, before adding one more before the second frame was over. One more in the third gave him his six on the night, equaling an NHL record. After the game, which the Blues won 8-0, Berenson marveled that none of his goals were of the fluke variety. "What I liked about it is that they were all clean-cut goals, right out of the textbook. Not one rebound."

Berenson would score 35 goals in 1968–69 and record 82 points in 76 games with the Blues, who made it to the Stanley Cup finals for the second year in a row. He scored 33 goals the following year, and although the Blues lost in the finals again, Berenson's playoff totals with St. Louis would show 29 points (19 of them goals) in 46 games over his first three seasons with the team. In all, Berenson would score 261 goals and notch 658 points in 987 games played before his career ended.

Berenson's fine performance proved that players could have a successful NHL career even if they took the college route to get there. Since that time, many college-trained players have made it to the NHL, and in some way they should all thank Berenson for persevering and paving the way.

Gordon "Red" Berenson was selected for Team Canada in 1972 for the historic Summit Series. He appeared in two games and recorded one assist. He would later coach for three seasons, posting a 100-72-32 record between 1979 and 1982. In 1984, Berenson returned to his old alma mater—the University of Michigan—where he has been head coach of the hockey team ever since.

JOHNNY BOWER
BORN: PRINCE ALBERT, SASKATCHEWAN
NHL SEASONS: 1953–54 TO 1969–70
DEFINING MOMENT: 1964 STANLEY CUP PLAYOFFS

Goaltender Johnny Bower was already 33 years old when the Toronto Maple Leafs decided they wanted him for their 1958–59 rebuilding project. Leafs scout Bob Davidson was watching Bower closely during that season, one in which Bower was once again starring for the Cleveland Barons of the American Hockey League.

Bower had already played in the NHL for the New York Rangers in the early- and mid-Fifties, but they had sent him down to the minors despite a fine performance in the 1953–54 season. (Bower had played in all 70 games for New York that season, winning 29 games and recording five shutouts.) However, the Rangers decided to replace him with Lorne "Gump" Worsley, which relegated Bower to the minor leagues.

Bower made the most of this situation, playing for Providence, Cleveland, and Vancouver (of the Western Hockey League). He had won championships and a plethora of individual awards in the minors, all of which started to make the NHL seem like a distant memory. It's easy to understand why Bower might not have wanted to leave the comfort of a secure job in Cleveland, but Toronto drafted his rights in June 1958 and told the netminder he had no choice but to go back to the big league. Bower, who was earning a $10 bonus for any shutout he earned as a Baron, asked the Maple Leafs for $10,000 a year. Toronto offered a two-year deal.

The Leafs really wanted Bower for just a couple of years to give them a veteran presence in net. The idea appealed to Bower, who decided to give it one more try, but he made it clear that if he did not make the Leafs, he would be heading back to Cleveland. He shared netminding duties with Ed Chadwick to start the 1958–59 season but soon found himself the number one goalie. The Toronto club had many young players on the rise and made the playoffs with a miracle finish to end the '58–'59 campaign. The Leafs made it all the way to the finals in '59 and then again after the 1959–60 season, although they lost the Stanley Cup both times to the mighty Montreal Canadiens. By then, Bower had not only established himself as the Leafs' top netminder, but as one of the best in the entire NHL. In April 1962, the Leafs won the first of three straight Stanley Cups (and the first in 11 years), and Bower fulfilled his boyhood dream of lifting the fabled trophy.

In the 1963 playoffs, the Leafs were such a strong team that they only needed 10 games to take the Cup for the second year in a row. But in the 1964 playoffs, the Leafs really needed the 40-year-old Bower to be as good as he ever was to beat Montreal and Detroit. The first-place Canadiens, led by snipers such as Jean Beliveau, Bernie Geoffrion, Bobby Rousseau, and Gilles Tremblay, were a formidable opponent. The Habs took a 3-2 series lead and many were pointing the finger of blame at Bower for the Leafs' inadequate play. However, Bower responded with a 3-0 shutout in the sixth game, forcing the teams back to Montreal for the seventh. It took a magnificent effort from Bower and a hat trick from Dave Keon to turn the Habs back 3-1. Montreal did not score their lone goal until the third period and pressed for the equalizer throughout the final stanza, but the 40-year-old Bower turned back all their drives until the Leafs put one into the empty net to secure the win. Earlier in the series, many thought Bower was all but finished, but he gave up only one goal over the final two games to get the Leafs back to the finals.

It was much the same against Detroit (led by the incomparable Gordie Howe and a group of veteran Red Wings like Alex Delvecchio, Marcel Pronovost, and Bill Gadsby) in the finals. Bower had to backstop the Leafs to wins in the final two games to clinch a third straight championship. The final game was very tight until the third period with the Leafs up 1-0. Bower kept the Red Wings off the board, and then the Leafs poured in three in the final frame to win the seventh game 4-0. Bower was interviewed on television after the game and thanked Leaf fans for their support. "I'd like to thank the people of Toronto for having so much patience with us," Bower said. "I know we did have a few bad games. It certainly is wonderful to win the Stanley Cup and I certainly give a lot of credit to the Detroit Red Wings who played so well. The city of Toronto deserves the Stanley Cup more than anybody else!" Bower put everything in terms of the team, but it seemed he was thanking the Maple Leaf fans for not turning on him when their club struggled.

Toronto coach and general manager Punch Imlach often referred to Bower as the greatest athlete he had ever seen. By the time his NHL career was over, Bower had won four Cups (he won his final championship in 1967) and the Vezina Trophy two times (he shared one Vezina with Terry Sawchuk). His great career would be recognized when he was elected to the Hockey Hall of Fame. None of this would have happened had Bower not shown the dedication needed to play professional hockey—a career that can be difficult even at the best of times.

Johnny Bower, known as "The China Wall," was elected to the Hockey Hall of Fame in 1976. He spent 13 years in the minors and 11 in the NHL. In 1970, he retired from the game. He was 45.

BOBBY CLARKE
BORN: FLIN FLON, MANITOBA
NHL SEASONS: 1969–70 TO 1983–84
DEFINING MOMENT: MAY 9, 1974

Bobby Clarke had such determination that he was not going to let a serious disease get in his way. When Clarke was 14, he was told he had juvenile diabetes. This news could have destroyed the dreams of many young boys, but not Clarke, who only thought about being a hockey player. He had no fear for his life, but he was extremely concerned about his hockey career. Clarke had no interest in school and his father, Cliff, worried that his son would end up in the mines like he had. Quitting school at a young age did not seem like a good idea, but Clarke wanted to totally dedicate himself to hockey. After all the tests were done and the appropriate medication was decided upon, Clarke knew there was no looking back. Doctors told him he could continue playing hockey—which he likely would have done anyway. No disease such as diabetes was going to hold him back.

When he turned 17, Clarke tried out for the junior A team in Flin Flon. His coach, Patty Ginnell, noted that Clarke was not very big—in fact he was quite thin and wore glasses. But as soon as Clarke showed what he could do on the ice, Ginnell was no longer concerned. He would lead the Western Hockey League in points for two consecutive seasons (168 in 1967–68 and 186 in 1968–69) and score 102 goals over that same time span. It was thought that Clarke would be a high pick in the 1969 Amateur Draft, but most NHL teams were scared away by the diabetes issue. Philadelphia scout Gerry Melnyk, however, was a believer and insisted the Flyers take him. Melnyk staked his reputation on Clarke becoming an NHL player, which convinced general manager Bud Poile that he should select the rugged center in the second round (although a doctor was consulted before Philadelphia announced Clarke's name). It was not a selection the Flyers would ever regret.

Many believed Clarke would have to start off in the minors, but he made the Flyers on the first try, scoring 15 goals and 46 points as a rookie. His goal totals were impressive—27, 35, 37 and 35 over his next four seasons. The 1972–73 season saw him record 104 points and the Philadelphia club started to become a force in the NHL. Clarke oozed leadership and his style on ice was infectious. He was constantly in motion and it seemed that his sheer will would always rule the day for the Flyers. He was soon named team captain of a squad that liked to play the game very physically and would follow their leader with no questions asked. Clarke had filled out to 5'10" and 185 pounds, but he left the toughness to a group of players whose sole purpose seemed to be to protect their leader. Good goaltending, strong defense, intimidation, and timely goals were the strengths of the Flyers teams of the 1970s. By 1974, the Philadelphia club made it to the Stanley Cup finals, where they faced an experienced Boston Bruins team led by the incomparable Bobby Orr.

The Bruins took the first game of the series with a late goal in the third, forcing the Flyers to make sure they won the second game on May 9. However, the hometown Bruins went up 2-0 in that first period. But then Clarke went to work, getting the Flyers on the board early in the second. Boston kept the lead until the last minute of the game when Clarke picked up an errant Bruins clearing attempt and set up Moose Dupont for a shot that tied the game, sending the contest into overtime.

Goalie Bernie Parent was outstanding for the Flyers early in the extra session, turning away great scoring chances by the Bruins. As tension mounted, Philadelphia coach Fred Shero sent Clarke, Bill Flett, and tough guy Dave Schultz out for a shift and they worked the puck in the Boston end. Clarke got free for a backhand drive that was stopped, but goalie Gilles Gilbert gave up a rebound that Clarke buried in the net. Clarke leapt into the air and was mobbed by his teammates. His three-point night had his team back in the race for the Cup. After the game, Clarke remarked, "This changes everything around. Now they have to win in our building. We won by working the same way we always win."

The Flyers eventually won the championship in six games, taking the last contest 1-0 on home ice (the Bruins never did win a contest on the road) before a wild Philadelphia crowd that pressed onto the ice surface for the celebration. One year later, the Flyers repeated as champions and Clarke's toothless grin was very much in evidence. His gummy smirk directed at goalie Bernie Parent after the second Stanley Cup win in Buffalo became an iconic image in the annuals of playoff history. The tireless star had shown the hockey world that nothing was impossible and that any obstacle could be overcome if you really wanted it bad enough.

Bobby Clarke was elected to the Hockey Hall of Fame in 1987.

JOHNNY BUCYK
BORN: EDMONTON, ALBERTA
NHL SEASONS: 1955–56 TO 1977–78
DEFINING MOMENT: MAY 3, 1970

For many years, it seemed like left winger Johnny Bucyk was always in the wrong place at the wrong time. The burly left winger (6', 215 pounds) was always a productive player, but often he was on such poor teams that his will to stay in the game had to be challenged. He began his NHL career with the Detroit Red Wings just after they won their second straight Stanley Cup. Bucyk played in only 38 games in 1955–56, scoring just one goal. He added another tally in the playoffs, but the Red Wings lost in the finals to the Montreal Canadiens. The 1956–57 season saw Bucyk score 10 goals and total 21 points in 66 games, but he was by his own admission a "spot player," which meant he never got a regular shift. But the summer of 1957 brought a major change to Bucyk's career when he was dealt to the Boston Bruins. It was a major deal, given that goalie great Terry Sawchuk was going back to Detroit, but Bucyk hoped the change of teams would mean more ice time.

The 22-year-old Bucyk was actually pleased with the deal because it reunited him with Bronco Horvath and Vic Stasiuk, two former Edmonton Flyers (WHL) teammates and fellow Ukrainians. They formed the "Uke Line" for the Bruins with each player scoring over 20 goals in 1957–58. Boston made it the finals, but lost to a mighty Montreal squad led by Jean Beliveau, Doug Harvey, and Maurice Richard in six games. The first year in Boston had been generally a good one for Bucyk, and he was happy when coach Lynn Patrick told him, "John, you're going to be with the Bruins for a long while to come." But the next season saw the Boston squad upset by a surging Toronto club in seven games in the semi-finals, and then what Bucyk called the "dark days of defeat" settled in over him and the Bruins.

From 1959–60 to 1966–67, the Bruins missed the playoffs every year. Bucyk was the Bruins' best and most consistent player through these difficult times (never scoring less than 18, and notching 27 twice in that timeframe). He was named captain of the team for the '66–'67 season but found that role too demanding, so the Bruins decided to go with three alternate captains instead (with Bucyk getting one of the "A"s on his sweater). But the most significant thing that happened was the emergence of Bobby Orr (starting in '66–'67 as an 18-year old) and the trade that brought Phil Esposito to the Bruins (starting the 1967–68 campaign). Bucyk was soon a 30-goal scorer, and would score 51 in his best season.

Suddenly the Bruins were no longer pushovers, but a dominating force by the end of the '67–'68 season. It took until the 1969–70 campaign, but the Bruins made it all the way to the finals after beating two tough teams in New York and Chicago during the first two rounds of the playoffs. Just a few days shy of his 35th birthday, Bucyk was ready as the St. Louis Blues provided the opposition in the finals. "I was really up for the St. Louis series because I had waited so many years, dreamed so many times of being on a Stanley Cup–winning team. During the regular season, I didn't score a goal against the Blues. I guess they had my number." The Stanley Cup final was a different story, starting with the opening game on May 3, 1970.

Bucyk opened the scoring in the first contest with a shot from about 25 feet out that beat Jacques Plante with less than a minute to play in the first. The Blues tied the game early in the second, but Bucyk scored his seventh goal of the post-season to give Boston the lead again. It was a typical Bucyk goal, as he parked himself at the side of the Blues net and buried a pass from teammate Johnny McKenzie. Bucyk scored his third goal of the game in the third when he put home a rebound. The Bruins then cruised to a 6-1 victory. "When they (the Blues) shadow Bobby (Orr), it takes one of their forwards out of the game as far as I am concerned," Bucyk said about the St. Louis strategy of assigning Jimmy Roberts to watch Orr's every move.

The Bruins were never seriously threatened by the Blues, but the fourth game proved to be more difficult than the others. The Blues actually led 3-2 in the third, but Bucyk (standing right beside the net again) scored to send the game into overtime. Bucyk felt that goal was the most important of his career because he wanted to clinch the championship on home ice. If Bucyk had not scored the equalizer, one of the most historic goals in NHL history might not have happened. Just 40 seconds into overtime, Orr pinched in from the right, setting up a give-and-go with Derek Sanderson. After Orr scored, he flew through the air, only to be mobbed by teammates seconds later. He finally had his Stanley Cup and he accepted the trophy on behalf of his teammates. It was Boston's first title in 29 years. Bucyk took the trophy around the ice and held the Cup high so that all the fans could see it.

Bucyk and the Bruins won another Stanley Cup in 1972 and he persevered long enough to play in 1,540 games and record 1,369 points. He holds the Boston team record for most seasons played (21) and most career goals (545).

Johnny Bucyk was elected to the Hall of Fame in 1981, and his number 9 was retired by Boston in 1978.

DAVE ANDREYCHUK
BORN: HAMILTON, ONTARIO
NHL SEASONS: 1982–83 TO 2005–06
DEFINING MOMENT: 2004 STANLEY CUP FINALS

When the Tampa Bay Lightning made it to the Stanley Cup finals for the first time in team history, captain Dave Andreychuk knew it was going to be his last chance to win a championship. Despite a 22-year career, the big left winger (at 6'4", 220 pounds) had never made it to the finals before. He had had his first good opportunity with Toronto, but fell one game short in 1993. Another chance slipped away when he played for the Colorado Avalanche in 2000. However, the Lighting were one the best teams in hockey during the 2003–04 season. They eliminated the New York Islanders and the Montreal Canadiens in the first two rounds of the post-season. It then took Tampa Bay seven games to defeat the Philadelphia Flyers (led by stellar forwards like Mark Recchi, John LeClair and Simon Gagne) in the Eastern Conference final. The moment was not lost on Andreychuk.

"Obviously, you dream about this day and for it to happen. You don't know how you're going to feel. I don't really feel relief. I feel excitement more than anything else," the 40-year old said after the Lightning eliminated the Flyers. "Our job is not done yet. We feel this is another step. We have to be focused," Andreychuk continued, sounding every bit like a team captain. Teammate Fred Modin also made note of Andreychuk's first appearance in the finals. "It's great to see him get a chance at the Cup," he said.

The Lightning faced off against the Calgary Flames in the final.

And winning the Cup for Andreychuk may have given the Lightning a little edge over their opponents. However, Calgary was hot in the playoffs, and led by the likes of Jarome Iginla, Martin Gelinas and Craig Conroy, would take the first game 4-1.

There was no way the Lightning wanted to go to Calgary down two games, and they came out fast to open the scoring. It was still a one-goal game going into the third period. Then Andreychuk set up Brad Richards to make it 2-0; then Tampa Bay defenseman Dan Boyle scored to make it 3-0. Andreychuk helped set up the fourth Lightning goal by Martin St. Louis, and from then on Tampa Bay cruised to a 4-1 victory. However, the Flames would win their first home game 3-0, putting the pressure right back on the Lightning to even the series. And that's what they did.

On May 31, the Lightning managed to eke out a 1-0 win to even the series once again. Tampa netminder Nikolai Khabibulin made 29 saves, while Brad Richards scored the only goal of the contest. The Flames were down two men and the Lightning managed to work the puck to Andreychuk, who found Richards open at the point. The pass allowed Richards to find the far side of the Calgary net at 3:48 of the first period. "It was ugly," said Tampa coach John Tortorella, "but we found a way." In the biggest games of the playoffs, Andreychuk had also found a way with assists on very important goals. The Lightning were hopeful returning to home ice, but the equally resilient Flames surprised everyone with a 3-2 overtime win to go up 3-2 in the series. Calgary now had a chance to win the Cup on home ice. Was Andreychuk about to see another shot at the Cup disappear?

It was a very close contest in the sixth game, but a St. Louis tally in double overtime forced a seventh and deciding game in Tampa Bay on the night of June 7, 2004. Andreychuk had played in his share of game sevens, appearing in nine such contests and winning four of them. On this night, Andreychuk played 21 stellar minutes and took a team-high 32 shifts as the Lightning took advantage of his experience. The Lightning managed a 2-1 win with Andreychuk the deciding force behind the victory—this time for hockey's ultimate prize.

"Dave Andreychuk, come get the Stanley Cup," were the words of NHL commissioner Gary Bettman as the silver trophy was brought to center ice. After the game, Andreychuk revealed he had a chance late in the season to be traded to a team that had better chances to win the Cup. "I didn't want to go anywhere," he told the Tampa Bay management. "I am going to savor this moment with my teammates and family. This, obviously, is the pinnacle. It's what we all play for. It took a while for me to get here," Andrey-chuk said. When asked what he was thinking when he first lifted the Cup, he joked, "Not falling, first of all, not dropping it."

Given Andreychuk's long wait, there was no doubt the Cup was in good hands!

Dave Andreychuk played one more season before retiring with 640 goals, 698 assists and 1,338 points in 1,639 career games.

LANNY MCDONALD
BORN: HANNA, ALBERTA
NHL SEASONS: 1973–74 TO 1988–89
DEFINING MOMENT: MAY 25, 1989

There are many reasons why the Toronto Maple Leafs have not won a Stanley Cup since 1967, not the least of which is the number of poor trades they have made. However, none of these trades had a more devastating effect on the fortunes of the team than the dealing away of heart-and-soul right winger, Lanny McDonald. After a stellar junior career with Medicine Hat (112 goals in 138 games), the hard-shooting McDonald was chosen fourth overall by the Leafs in 1973. He got off to a very slow start (17 goals in his rookie year) but as the Leafs added more talent to their roster (young players like Darryl Sittler, Borje Salming, Ian Turnbull, and Mike Palmateer), McDonald's goal scoring started to improve. By his third campaign he scored 37 times and then added seasons of 46, 47 and 43 goals, making him one of the best left wingers in the league. He also scored one of the Leafs' most memorable overtime winning goals in the 1978 playoffs.

But then the Leafs hired Punch Imlach back to run the team he had once led to four Stanley Cups—and the general manager was bent on causing chaos for the Leafs. In one of many deals that rocked the foundation of the team, McDonald was foolishly traded to the Colorado Rockies on December 29, 1979. Other Leaf stars to leave the team afterward included the likes of Palmateer, Dave "Tiger" Williams, Turnbull, and Sittler.

McDonald was shocked that he was no longer a Maple Leaf. "I couldn't believe what had just happened. My dreams had just been shattered. No one grows up wanting to play for the Colorado Rockies," he said. If McDonald appeared bitter and angry, that reaction paled in comparison to how Leaf fans felt. A group protested outside Maple Leaf Gardens prior to the next Leafs game, but it was to no avail—Imlach wanted to show who was boss, and dealing the popular McDonald was one way he could flex his authoritative muscle.

McDonald played in Colorado for the next three years and produced at his usual high level, despite being on one of the worst teams in the league. However, the Rockies were going nowhere fast and figured they could trade their best forward for two players. McDonald therefore found himself on the move again—this time to his home province of Alberta. The Calgary Flames sent Bob MacMillan and Don Lever to Colorado to complete the transaction.

At first McDonald reacted like he did when the Leafs dealt him—he did not want to go. But playing for the Flames was a great opportunity to compete for a good team again. McDonald would also thrive playing in a Canadian city where hockey was important. In 1982–83, he scored a whopping 66 goals (the second highest total in the entire league that year, next to Wayne Gretzky), and in 1985–86, he helped take the Calgary club to their first-ever appearance in the Stanley Cup finals. The '85–'86 campaign was McDonald's last great regular season (71 points in 80 games) and he was a strong force in the playoffs with 18 points (including 11 goals) in 21 games. But the Flames had used so much energy in defeating the Gretzky- and Messier-led Edmonton Oilers in an earlier round that they had little left for the finals against Montreal. They were defeated in just five games and McDonald was inconsolable, believing his last chance at a Stanley Cup was gone. He was almost right.

The next two seasons fell well below average for McDonald and he was virtually sure the 1988–89 season would be his last. He only appeared in 51 games that year, but he did manage to score his 500th career goal and record his 1,000th point—both significant NHL milestones. But the Flames did have a powerful team that year, and in the '89 post-season, they defeated Vancouver, Los Angeles, and Chicago to reach the finals for the second time. And again, the Canadiens provided the opposition. The deeper Calgary club pushed the series to 3-2 in games with the 6th contest scheduled for the Montreal Forum. It was the night of May 25, 1989.

McDonald had played in only 13 playoff games (no goals), but Calgary coach Terry Crisp, perhaps playing a hunch, told him to dress for this one. McDonald had scored his first career goal back in 1973 at the Forum, so maybe playing in comfortable surroundings would result in one more big goal for the man with the mustache.

The game was tied 1-1 when McDonald joined a Calgary rush into the Montreal end. A perfect pass by Joe Nieuwendyk landed on McDonald's stick and he made no mistake, putting a shot over the shoulder of Montreal netminder Patrick Roy. The Flames never relinquished the lead, winning the contest 4-2 to take their first-ever Stanley Cup.

The smile on McDonald's face said it all as he accepted the Cup along with co-captains Jim Peplinski and Tim Hunter. The Flames had become the first team other than the Canadiens to win the Cup on Forum ice. With former Montreal stars like Jean Beliveau and Henri Richard looking on, McDonald and the rest of the Flames gathered around to accept the trophy from league president John Ziegler. "I think you appreciate it a heck of a lot more after 16 years than you do after one or two," the 36-year-old McDonald said of the win and of the end of his long NHL career. He also said that winning the Cup was, "the most peaceful feeling I've experienced in hockey. There is just no feeling like it. It's something I wish a person could describe to people outside, how much hard work it takes for 25 guys to put it all together."

McDonald had persevered long enough to experience the ultimate in hockey, and to have his name inscribed on the Stanley Cup was an honor he richly deserved.

Lanny McDonald was elected to the Hall of Fame in 1992.

DAN CLEARY

BORN: CARBONEAR, NEWFOUNDLAND
NHL SEASONS: 1997–98 TO PRESENT
DEFINING MOMENT: MAY 24, 2008

Not many National Hockey League players come from Newfoundland. Of those who do, one of the most successful is Dan Cleary, a native of Carbonear (a town on the Avalon Peninsula) and a player who nearly lost his chance for stardom.

Cleary began his hockey dream by moving to Ontario to play for the Junior A Kingston Voyageurs when he was just 15. "I didn't have any idea what to expect," Cleary said of leaving his home and moving to eastern Canada. "Just seeing all of the people, the cars and the buildings was just completely different. But for me personally...the opportunity was in Ontario." Cleary went on to play major junior hockey for the Belleville Bulls of the OHL (scoring a hat trick in his very first game) where he recorded an impressive 323 points over four seasons. His best year came in 1995–96 when he recorded 115 points in 64 games. His good play got him noticed by NHL scouts and in 1997, he was taken 13th overall by the Chicago Blackhawks during the Entry Draft. It looked like fast-skating Cleary had the world by the tail, poised as he was for a good NHL career.

However, Cleary was not mentally or physically ready for the rigors of big-league hockey. He had little discipline, a poor work ethic, and an immature approach to a hockey career that looked so promising for such a gifted offensive player. After a mere 41 games with Chicago, Cleary was dealt away to the Edmonton Oilers where he played for four unremarkable years. The Oilers would also give up on the troubled 6', 205-pound right winger, buying out his contract and making Cleary a free agent. He signed a one-year deal with Phoenix but was let go after a 6-goal, 17-point season in the Arizona desert. Once again a free agent, Cleary did his best to stay positive, but he felt desperate and very uncertain about his future. "Every day was a long day," he recalled. "Phoenix didn't qualify me and I was really worried and nervous. My wife (Jalena) and I just stayed positive. I know down deep inside we were both thinking about (his future in the NHL) but we never spoke about it." Cleary also realized he had to make changes and started to take off-ice training seriously. It seemed to work and in September 2005, he accepted a tryout offer from the Detroit Red Wings despite a better offer from the Maple Leafs—a team with less talent and more opportunity. "I just had a feeling about Detroit. I told my agent to call them and see if they would give me a tryout and they did," Cleary said later. Picking Detroit would prove to be a great choice, a clear sign Cleary was indeed getting more mature.

Cleary did not have a great season in 2005–06 but he did start to establish himself as a key role player and as a defensive forward for the Red Wings. In his second season in Motown, Cleary notched 20 goals and added 20 assists for 40 points in 71 games. He notched 42 points in 2007–08 and had a memorable playoff, appearing in 22 post-season games while scoring a very important goal in the first game of the Stanley Cup finals. Detroit had eliminated Nashville, Colorado, and Dallas to make it the finals after racking up 54 wins and 115 points during the regular season. The finals opened in Detroit on the night of May 24, 2008, and the

Red Wings faced the young and talented Pittsburgh Penguins for the championship.

The game was scoreless until the Red Wings potted one in the second period to take a 1-0 lead. Mikael Samuelsson then scored his second of the night to make it 2-0 for Detroit, but then Nicklas Lidstrom was called for an interference penalty. Cleary was out trying to kill off the last part of the penalty when teammate Brad Stuart fired a puck down the ice from a faceoff just outside the Detroit blueline. Cleary took off like a rocket, trying to outrace a Pittsburgh defender for the loose puck. Cleary's determination to get there first forced Pittsburgh goaltender Marc-Andre Fleury to try and play the puck—but he was not able to do so. The black disk ended up on Cleary's stick. He quickly let go a shot that went over Fleury's shoulder and into the Pittsburgh net, ending any hopes of a Penguins comeback. It was the first goal Cleary had ever scored in a Stanley Cup final game—and he was also named third star of the contest. Detroit's 4-0 win put the Red Wings in the driver's seat, where they would take the Cup in six games.

"Ever since I've come to Detroit, a lot of good things have happened. It's certainly been home for me. They certainly showed faith in me," Cleary said later. Perhaps Detroit coach Mike Babcock summarized Cleary's role with Detroit best when he said, "He was a dynamic player as a 16-year old. It just happened too quick for him and he wasn't able to handle it emotionally. He bounced around. We happened to get him at the right time. He came in with the right attitude and started working." Babcock might have also added that Cleary showed that he had matured—he had overcome the doubts swirling about him and come out a winner. The hard-working Cleary was signed to a new five-year deal in 2008 that will see the Red Wings pay him a total of $14 million. In 417 career regular-season games as a Red Wing to date, Cleary has produced 217 points.

Dan Cleary is the first Newfoundland-born player to have his name engraved on the Stanley Cup.

GLEN METROPOLIT
BORN: TORONTO, ONTARIO
NHL SEASONS: 1999–2000 TO 2009–10
DEFINING MOMENT: DECEMBER 5, 2007

Glen Metropolit did not grow up in one of the better neighborhoods in Toronto. The area was Regent Park, a drug-infested part of the city where Metropolit lived with his single mother and two siblings (he did not know his biological father and his stepfather eventually left as well) in a housing project. There were unsavory characters around the area and trouble around every corner. When his mother lost her job, Metropolit and his brother Troy were shunted off to a variety of foster homes, since the basic necessities could no longer be provided at home. One Christmas saw the brothers sleeping on mats on a gym floor and their gift was a set of gloves and a hat provided by a local church. At one point, the brothers were even separated and placed in different homes.

Despite the bad situation, Metropolit never held anything against his mother, Linda Lafferty. "She's the best mom you could have. She'd give me her last dollar to go to a hockey game. She has the biggest heart of anybody I've ever seen." Luckily for Glen, he had many friends who mostly focused on hockey. Otherwise he would have likely ended up in jail. His brother Troy played some hockey with Glen but took another road once the interest in hockey waned. Troy has since been in prison for many years.

Hockey became an outlet for Metropolit, a sport that kept him away from all the trouble at home and in the streets. He did his best to stay at the local rink as much as he could and would only go home when the lights were turned out. "Hockey was his world," recalled his mother. "Watching hockey. Playing hockey. He'd be sitting watching TV and playing with a hockey stick and a ball. Everything was hockey."

When he turned 16, an uncle (Neil Karrandjas) took an interest in Metropolit, which turned out to be the most important thing that happened in his life. "He was the uncle who had the good job and he'd take care of me, give me hockey sticks if I needed them," Metropolit recalled years later. "He got me on the straight and narrow. I could have been out doing other stuff but I'd be out skating with him and all his buddies." The practice paid off. In 1993–94, he played junior hockey in Richmond Hill, just north of the city, where he recorded 100 points in just 49 games. Still, sensing that he might get into trouble in Toronto, the youngster moved to British Columbia for one year, posting a 117-point season with the Vernon Vipers.

His good play got him noticed (but not drafted into the NHL): he played the next four years in the lower minor leagues, in cities like Nashville, Atlanta, Pensacola, and Quebec City. After an 81-point season with Grand Rapids of the IHL, the Washington Capitals signed the 5'11", 195-pound center as a free agent. He scored six goals and recorded 19 points in 30 games for the Capitals in 1999–2000, but was more often in the minors than in the big league. However, in 2003, he had the honor of playing for Team Canada at the World Hockey Championships. He then decided to play in Europe for three years and his 63-point season in 2005–06 for a Swiss league team landed him another free-agent deal with the Atlanta Thrashers. His time was due, and on the night of December 5, 2007, all that perseverance paid dividends as the hometown kid, with many friends and family in attendance, faced off against the Leafs at the Air Canada Centre in Toronto.

The game was not going very well for the Thrashers, who found themselves down 2-0 after two periods of play. However, a power-play opportunity early in the third gave the Atlanta side another chance to get into the game. Defenseman Greg De Vries let a shot go from the point and Metropolit, standing in a good position in front of the Leaf net, tipped the puck past netminder Andrew Raycroft to get the Thrashers on the board. Less then four minutes later, Metropolit sent a pass across to Slava Kozlov, who put it past Raycroft to tie the game. Then Metropolit bumped Alex Steen off the puck behind the Leafs net and fed a pass to Kozlov, who put it away for a 3-2 Atlanta lead. The Thrashers went on to win 5-2 and Metropolit was the talk of the game (he was also named second star of the contest). "Metro was the difference," said Atlanta coach Bob Hartley. "He skated very well and opened it up for us. It's nice to see. He's been working very hard. We gave him a chance and he took advantage of it. We figured he'd come in and give us big goals, and that's what he's doing." The Thrashers liked Metropolit's speed and skill level when they scouted him in Europe and their investment was paying off.

The Atlanta player noted who was in the crowd that night. "Everyone came out of the woodwork here," Metropolit said after the game. "Kids from high school were up there. I saw faces. It was so rewarding getting a goal. It was special. Everyone lives vicariously through me." They all applauded when he came out for the three-star selection. Since that game against the Leafs, Metropolit was on a variety of NHL teams (including St. Louis, Boston, Philadelphia, and Montreal) before returning to Europe for the 2010–11 season.

Metropolit best summarizes his road to success by understanding it's those who persevere that ultimately achieve no matter what the circumstance. "It's so important for kids to know they can make it out of a bad situation if they keep on chasing their dreams. I just held on to that all the time. Don't let anyone belittle you or tell you you're not good enough. Keep working and stick to your confidence and you can achieve whatever you want." Quite the achievement—and quite the refreshing outlook—for a kid who could have taken a different route in life if not for hockey.

Glen Metropolit's eight-year NHL career may be at an end, but in 407 career games he posted a respectable 159 points.

PATRICK KANE
BORN: BUFFALO, NEW YORK
NHL SEASONS: 2007–08 TO PRESENT
DEFINING MOMENT: JUNE 9, 2010

When hockey players talk about how they made it to the NHL, you most often hear about the pivotal role their parents played in getting them to the highest level of the sport. Patrick Kane is no exception, but his story is the modern tale about just how much parents have to sacrifice to see their sons achieve the greatest accomplishment of all—winning the Stanley Cup.

A native of Buffalo, New York, Kane began his hockey career playing in the house leagues close to home and attending Sabres games with his family whenever he could. Patrick Sr. and his wife Donna soon came to realize that their son had a great deal of talent, and dedicated time and money to developing Patrick's skills. He worked hard, often attending summer-long hockey camps. In fact, his father recalled one year where Patrick "played more than 300 games and scored more than 1,000 goals. Patrick could tell you that out of 365 days a year, he would be on the ice for about 350 days."

When he was just 14, Kane had become too good for the local teams he was playing on, so the decision was made to get him better competition in the Detroit area. Patrick was homesick and unhappy to be away from home at such a young age; the Kanes made sure they attended as many games as possible, no matter what the driving might be or the cost of lodgings, which sometimes involved the entire family. The father was able to join his son on many occasions because he ran a Jeep dealership and as the boss, he could set his own work schedule. Eventually the business had to be sold (it was no longer profitable when the cost of gas rose to ridiculous levels); at the same time, the cost of hockey continued to rise. Fortunately, the U.S. national development program finally took Kane at the age of 16, just when it looked like they were going to ignore his prodigious talent. He could score at roughly a goal-per-game pace, but he would remain unknown until he played one year for the London Knights of the OHL.

Kane scored 58 goals and added 83 assists for the Knights during the 2006–07 season, and added another 31 points in the playoffs. The Blackhawks then selected him with their first choice in the 2007 NHL Entry Draft. It was thought that Chicago general manager Dale Tallon was going to select James van Riemsdyk, or maybe Kyle Turris, but Kane was the man the Blackhawks thought had the most offensive potential. When his name was announced, Kane turned to his father, embraced him, and said, "Dad, we did it." Kane was given a three-year entry-level deal that assured him of $875,000 per year and more if he hit certain bonuses over the last two seasons of the contract. In December 2009, Kane signed a contract extension totaling $31 million. All the sacrifices made by Kane and his family (a conservative estimate of $200,000, by their accounting) had paid off handsomely because of the great persistence of both Patrick and his parents.

In his first year with Chicago, Kane took the Calder Trophy as the NHL's best rookie when he scored 21 goals and totaled 72 points in 82 games. The improving Blackhawks saw their young sniper up his goal total to 25 the next year (2008–09), when the team made it to the Western Conference final for the first time in many years. Kane's first playoff appearance saw him record 14 points in 16 post-season games, but the Detroit Red Wings were far too experienced for the Blackhawks, who went down in five games.

The 2009–10 season was a special one for Kane. First he helped Team USA win a silver medal at the 2010 Winter Olympics in Vancouver. He then scored his 30 goals and 58 assists to lead the Blackhawks in team scoring with 88 points—matching his sweater number. Kane was also generally outstanding in the playoffs (10G, 18A) but was criticized for a lack of offense in the finals versus Philadelphia. However, his total of four goals and five assists in the last series indicated that the slowly maturing Kane was still pretty effective. His greatest moment came on the night of June 10, 2010, when the Blackhawks had a chance to end their 49-year Stanley Cup drought right in Philadelphia.

The series between Chicago and Philadelphia was tied at two games each until the Blackhawks took the lead with a 7-4 win at home ice, putting them one win away from the championship. The Flyers, however, were not going to go down easily on home ice, pushing the final game into overtime tied at 3-3. Early in the extra frame, Kane took a pass from teammate Brian Campbell and steamed past Philadelphia defenseman Kimmo Timonen. The Blackhawk 5'10", 178-pound winger was at such a poor angle that a shot on goal did not appear to be a good play. However, top goal scorers know there is always a chance if a shot is put on net. Kane let go a quick snap shot, which went past Flyers netminder Michael Leighton.

It was not a shot that should have gone in. For a moment the arena was frozen as Kane celebrated wildly, since he had just scored the Stanley Cup–winning goal. Even his Chicago teammates did not know how to react, but it became evident very quickly that the puck did indeed get past Leighton, where it rested under the padding that surrounds the bottom of the net. The Philadelphia crowd was silenced, sad at the thought that their team's incredible playoff run was over.

Kane and his teammates whooped and hollered as the Blackhawks captured their first Cup in nearly 50 years. For Kane, it was not only a great moment of triumph, but also a time of vindication—scoring a goal when it mattered most. Kane's overtime Stanley Cup–winning tally—while not as beautiful as some others—will keep his name forever prominent when most important goals in hockey history are discussed. "I just took a quick shot to the far side of the net and it went through (the goalie's legs). It was just like the Olympic goal (Sidney) Crosby scored. This is something unbelievable to be a part of. I mean, we won the Stanley Cup. To score the winning goal in the Stanley Cup finals—it was unbelievable."

At just 21 years of age during the 2009–10 season, Kane still realized how much had gone into making him an NHL player. He seemed truly appreciative, saying, "How could I not be lucky? I'm very lucky, very fortunate for what happened to me throughout my life and my career. And it all starts with your parents. If I had the same talent and two different parents, I'm not sure I would be in this situation." It seems that making it to the NHL is a matter of perseverance, not only from the player, but from the entire family as well.

Patrick Kane has recorded 303 points in 317 games played to date for the Chicago Blackhawks.

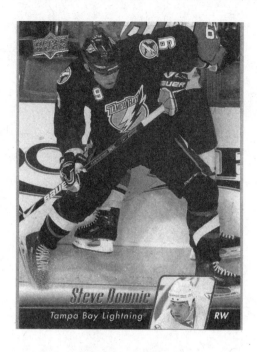

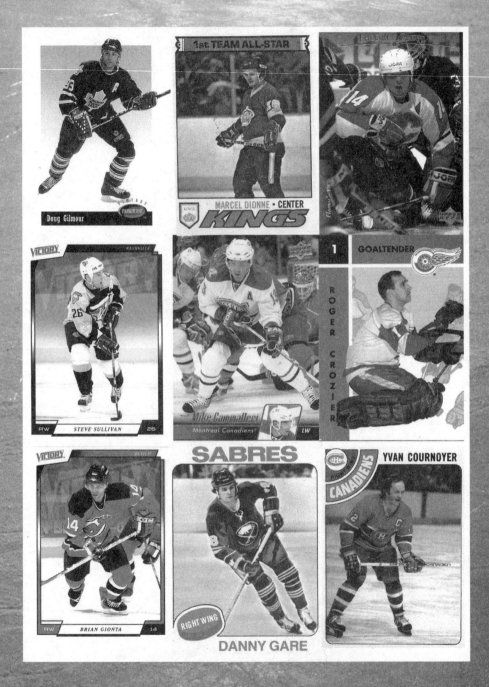

Doug Gilmour

1st TEAM ALL-STAR

MARCEL DIONNE • CENTER
KINGS

GOALTENDER

ROGER CROZIER

STEVE SULLIVAN

Mike Cammalleri
Montreal Canadiens

SABRES

CANADIENS

YVAN COURNOYER

BRIAN GIONTA

RIGHT WING

DANNY GARE

TOO SMALL

How many hockey players have heard it before: "Sure he's good, but he's too small." Too many players, coaches and managers have listened to that cliché, despite the fact that year after year it is proven wrong by a new group of small-in-stature stars. It has been shown many times over that the smallest players can make the biggest contributions. This chapter tells the stories of the following players who were deemed "Too Small":

Marcel Dionne
Roger Crozier
Dave Keon
Danny Gare
Theo Fleury ✓
Yvan Cournoyer
Doug Gilmour
Steve Sullivan
Brian Gionta
Mike Cammalleri

MARCEL DIONNE
BORN: DRUMMONDVILLE, QUEBEC
NHL SEASONS: 1971–72 TO 1988–89
DEFINING MOMENT: 1979–80 SEASON

It was thought that Marcel Dionne would grow up to be a large man like his father, Gilbert, who stood 6'2" and was once a lumberjack. But it never happened. Nevertheless, Dionne more than learned to thrive in hockey even at 5'8" and 185 pounds. He might not have looked like a hockey player, but his scoring prowess could not be ignored.

Hockey, however, has its belief systems, which meant that the diminutive Dionne would always be questioned and doubts about his ability to play in the NHL would never go away. But Dionne did not let that stop him. He never let his size become an issue. In fact, Dionne was always a great player on every team he was ever on, despite what critics were saying about him.

Dionne would say about others who did not believe in him, "They're not satisfied unless you're the perfect physical specimen, so they criticize your body. You make the best of what you got. It's not easy for guys of our stature. The terrible thing about it is that they forget there are a lot of young kids that have dreams. It's okay if they criticize me but what they don't realize is the number of people out there in the same boat." For these young players, Dionne was a great role model because he let his play on the ice do all the talking.

After a stellar junior career with the St. Catharines Blackhawks of the OHA, Dionne was selected second overall by the Detroit Red Wings during the 1971 Entry Draft. Guy Lafleur, also a Quebec native, was taken first by Montreal that same year, leaving Dionne as something of an afterthought. Everyone expected Lafleur to take the NHL by storm, but it was Dionne who produced greater numbers in his first three years. As a rookie he scored 28 goals and added 49 assists for 77 points in 78 games played. Dionne quickly showed that he was more than good enough to play in the NHL and that size was not going to affect his ability to create offense. Still, he recognized he had to play a certain style of game to be successful. "I'm no Phil Esposito," he said, referring to the Bruins large star center. "There's no way I'm going to stand there in front of the net. I've taken a lot of ribbing about my size but I'm smart enough not to start swinging whenever someone calls me a name." Dionne was even better in his second year, notching 90 points (including 40 goals), and by his fourth season, he had recorded 121 points – all for a brutal Detroit team.

The fact is Dionne never warmed up to Detroit management or coaching and was openly outspoken about the fact that the Red Wings could only ice a handful of legitimate NHL-quality players such as Nick Libbett, Mickey Redmond, Danny Grant, and Gary Bergman. So when the Los Angeles Kings offered $300,000 a season, Dionne jumped at the opportunity to go out to the West Coast and leave the Red Wings behind. Unfortunately, the Kings were never really that much better than the Red Wings. They usually floundered at the bottom of the league, but that did not stop Dionne from being one of the greatest stars in the game. He maintained his quick, shifty demeanor and his touch around the net would only get better in Los Angeles. He would score 50 or more goals and record 100 or more points six times while with the Kings. Eventually, he was teamed with wingers Dave Taylor and Charlie Simmer, forming a trio that became known as the "Triple Crown Line." The line was a constant scoring threat to any opposing team.

In 1979–80, Dionne really rose to the occasion and showed that he could lead the NHL in scoring despite playing on a rather average team. He led the "Triple Crown Line" to a great year as he recorded a league-best 137 points, while Simmer scored a league-high 56 goals (tied with two others) and Taylor totaled 90 points. Dionne was actually tied in points with a rookie named Wayne Gretzky but was awarded the Art Ross Trophy on the basis of having scored more goals (53 to Gretzky's 51). Dionne nearly lost the points lead as Gretzky notched three points in his final game of the season versus Colorado. It had been a season-long chase for Gretzky, and now it looked like he was in a good position to win the scoring title. However, Dionne responded with two assists in the last game of the year on two goals by Simmer, despite having Vancouver Canucks defensive forward Jerry Butler assigned to check him. Butler had shut down Gretzky two games earlier, but he could not hold off the stocky Kings center. It was the only time Dionne would lead the NHL in points as Gretzky and Mario Lemieux dominated the scoring race for the next 16 years.

Dionne was very gracious when he spoke of Gretzky, the NHL's rising star. "If he wins the scoring title, he'll deserve it," Dionne said prior to the final week of the season. "The kid is great. I had a big lead (a 26-point bulge at the halfway point of the '79–'80 campaign) but he's come on. Make no mistake, he's nobody's fluke." Dionne also observed that if healthy, the Oilers were primed to win the Stanley Cup in a few years—a very accurate prediction, as it turned out.

While there were no championships for Dionne, he did finish his illustrious career with the New York Rangers, playing two years on Broadway. His time in the NHL ended with 731 goals (fourth all-time) and 1,771 points (fifth all-time) in 1,384 games played. Not bad for a player many believed to be too small to ever post such numbers in the NHL!

Marcel Dionne was elected to the Hockey Hall of Fame in 1992.

ROGER CROZIER

BORN: BRACEBRIDGE, ONTARIO

NHL SEASONS: 1963–64 TO 1975–76

DEFINING MOMENT: 1964–65 SEASON

Sometimes, being small in stature is not such a bad thing. Award-winning goaltender Roger Crozier is one of the best examples of this fact. As he began hockey in his hometown of Bracebridge, Ontario, Crozier was not the least bit interested in playing as a goalie. He hated whenever it was his turn to go in net during road hockey games. Instead, Crozier preferred to play forward because he was a good skater with a canny ability to handle the puck.

When he turned seven years old, Crozier became eligible to play minor hockey, but it was difficult for him to compete because of his small size. He started out playing center but was up against boys who were taller and much more aggressive. In just his third game, he was knocked down hard to the ice and sat out the rest of the game. His coach then suggested he give goaltending a try. The idea appealed to Crozier even though he had no experience wearing all the goalie equipment. At first, he had difficulty maneuvering in the large pads and was clumsy with the large goalie stick. As a result, he began to think he might be too small to play any position in hockey. But soon, he started to adapt to the netminding position and his athletic nature took over. Crozier felt much better when he won his first game (by a 5-2 score) and the coach was pleased with his play in net. He quickly became one of the best goalies in the area and scouts started to notice that Crozier's acrobatic style was quite effective.

Crozier's confidence soared when he was given a trophy as the best goalie at his level of play; he soon found that he could play with older boys. He kept working on becoming a better goalie by learning how to position himself. His parents bought him some new equipment as a reward for playing so well. Still young, Roger would hear on occasion that he was too small and that he flopped on the ice too much. Such talk only served to motivate Crozier, who backstopped his team to a bantam-age championship. By the time he was 17, Crozier was asked to try out for the Chicago Blackhawks junior team in St. Catharines. He made the team, but once again doubt began to creep into his mind about his size and his ability to play at such a high level. Luckily, he was allowed to go home for a couple of days to think things over, and he returned with a more confident attitude. After a slow start, Crozier felt more comfortable being away from home and posted a 25-19-4 record over the regular season. The St. Catharines club was on fire and would win the Memorial Cup in 1960, with Crozier winning eight of 14 games in the last two rounds of the tournament to decide the championship.

The young netminder was not sure he could play pro hockey. Nevertheless, he left school to concentrate full-time on the game. His marriage at age 19 gave him even more incentive to become a pro goalie. However, the Chicago organization did not like his performance in the minors and traded his rights to Detroit in the summer of 1963. "Nobody asked me. Nobody told me. They just traded me like an old car," Crozier lamented to his wife, Arlene, about the deal. "Now we'll have to move to a new city where we don't know anybody. We don't even know where I'll be sent." It turned out he played most of the 1963–64 season with Pittsburgh of the AHL, and he won 30 games. He was even promoted to the big team when regular netminder Terry Sawchuk was injured, and posted a 5-6-4 record in 15 games. In the playoffs, Crozier was in net the night the Red Wings eliminated the Blackhawks in the semi-finals.

During the summer of 1964, the Red Wings lost Sawchuk's rights to the Toronto Maple Leafs and gave the starter's job to Crozier. Everyone seemed to think Detroit general manager Sid Abel had gambled and lost (critics included Gordie Howe, Detroit's best player, who felt the team erred in not keeping Sawchuk). One of the best goalies in the league, Jacques Plante, also thought Crozier would never replace Sawchuk. But the Red Wings liked what they had seen of Cozier. And by the time the 1964–65 season was over, the critics had all been quieted.

Now that he had the number one netminding job to himself, the acrobatic goalie showed he was worthy of the role. The 22-year-old Crozier got off to a great start in '64–'65 by allowing only 11 goals in his first four starts (he would play in all 70 league games). He sparkled against the New York Rangers during a 1-0 victory (making 19 saves) and then earned another shutout (making 26 stops) with a 4-0 win over Boston early in the season (he would lead the league in shutouts with six). As the season came to a close, Crozier beat the Maple Leafs 4-1 on the last Saturday night of the year and registered his league-best 40th win of the year. Asked after the game about how easy it was to play the position of goaltender, Crozier said, "Oh, sure. It's a snap. First your brain snaps. Then your nerve snaps." He nearly won the Vezina Trophy (given at that time to the goalie(s) on a team who allowed the fewest goals), but lost it on the last night of the season when the Leafs beat him for four goals. Crozier's outstanding play was rewarded with the Calder trophy (best rookie), and he was also named to the NHL's first all-star team!

Even though the Red Wings were upset in the first round of the playoffs in '65, Crozier took his team all the way to the finals in 1966 and was named winner of the Conn Smythe Trophy, despite the fact that Detroit lost to Montreal. In two short years, the smallish Crozier (listed at 5'8" and 165 pounds) had overcome self-doubts, severe injuries (a broken jaw on more than one occasion), and the critics who said he would not be up to the job of becoming an NHL star. And to think it all began because he was too small!

Since the 1999–2000 season, the Roger Crozier Saving Grace Award has been given to the goaltender (who has played a minimum of 25 games) who finishes with the best save percentage. The award honors the memory of Roger Crozier, who passed away at the age of 53 after battling cancer.

DAVE KEON
BORN: NORANDA, QUEBEC
NHL SEASONS: 1960–61 TO 1981–82
DEFINING MOMENT: APRIL 18, 1963

The Toronto Maple Leafs were not really quite sure what they had in center Dave Keon when the 20-year-old came to training camp in September 1960. The Leafs had recruited the youngster out of Noranda, Quebec, and it paid off when the smooth-skating Keon attended St. Michael's College in Toronto. He posted very impressive numbers (170 points in 142 games) while playing junior A, but the Leafs management were not so sure he could do the same in the NHL. Keon was not especially strong in pre-season games and it looked like he was heading to the minors. However Bert Olmstead, a senior player on the Leafs at the time, convinced coach and general manager George "Punch" Imlach to keep Keon with the big team. Olmstead was convinced the smallish Keon would get knocked around in the minors where the officiating was not as good as in the NHL. The Leafs had been hoping the 5'9" Keon would fill out a little more (he was listed at 165 pounds). Nevertheless, they shared Olmstead's concern, and kept him in Toronto. It was not a move they would regret.

Keon never did fill out much, but could he ever skate! His energy level seemed boundless. The Leafs were on the verge of great things and Keon's arrival gave the team three top centers (Red Kelly and Bob Pulford being the others). The new Leafs rookie scored 20 goals and totaled 45 points, a performance that earned him the Calder Trophy as the best first-year player in 1960–61. During his second year, Keon scored 26 times and added 35 assists to earn him a spot on the NHL's second all-star team. He was also named winner of the Lady Byng Trophy (gentlemanly play). The Leafs also took the Stanley Cup for the first time in 11 years when they beat defending champions Chicago Blackhawks in the finals.

The concern the Leafs had over Keon's small stature never materialized. His superb skating skills made him difficult to catch, and he had been well trained at St. Mike's on how to play defensive hockey, especially for a man of his size. Whatever he lacked in size, Keon more than made up for by being one of the smartest players in the league. He used his speed to great effectiveness (he was a superb penalty killer) and that allowed him to play a very efficient and clean game. He also had a great knack for playing his best during the most important games—especially in the playoffs.

There is no better example of this than his performance on April 18, 1963. The Leafs were hoping to clinch their second straight Stanley Cup on home ice. They were up 3-1 in games and wanted to close out the Detroit Red Wings in the fifth game of the series. Detroit was not likely going to challenge this Toronto team, which had finished in first place during the 1962–63 season, but the Leafs did not want to take any chances of going back to Motown. The game was scoreless until Keon was sent in on a breakaway when the Leafs were short-handed. He made no mistake as he beat Terry Sawchuk in the Red Wings net. Detroit tied the game in the second period, and it looked like the game was going into overtime, but late in the third period, the Leafs' Eddie Shack tipped in a shot from the blueline to give Toronto a 2-1 lead.

Detroit pressed for the equalizer and the Leafs took a late penalty to make things tense for the Toronto fans in attendance. However, Keon came to the rescue as his long shot down the ice found the back of Detroit's empty net with just five seconds to play. It was Keon's second short-handed tally of the night, making him the first player to score two such goals in a single playoff game in NHL history.

"Sure I was shooting at the net on the last shot but if I missed I was not going to be sad," Keon stated as the Leafs celebrated in their dressing room. He also paid tribute to the Red Wings. "They're tougher than Montreal (the Canadiens had been ousted in the semi-final by the Leafs in five games). Canadiens are all offence. (The Red) Wings check after they score. And that wears you down."

Nothing, it seemed, could wear Keon down as the Leafs won four Stanley Cups with him on their team. He would go on to be one the greatest and most complete players in the long history of the team, and one of the best two-way players ever to play in the NHL. Few might have thought that was possible back in 1960 when they were not sure a smaller player could survive in a big man's game.

Dave Keon is still the only Maple Leaf to win the Conn Smythe Trophy (in 1967) as the best player in the playoffs (as of 2011). Keon was elected to the Hall of Fame in 1986.

DANNY GARE
BORN: NELSON, BRITISH COLUMBIA
NHL SEASONS: 1974–75 TO 1986–87
DEFINING MOMENT: APRIL 27, 1975

The National Hockey League of the 1970s was a very violent place to play the game. The Philadelphia Flyers brawled their way to the top of the league, and soon, many other teams were looking for big, strong forwards who were not afraid to fight. Teams used intimidation to the fullest, and a game against the "Broad Street Bullies" was sure to produce a game summary sheet filled with penalties. The rules were often poorly enforced, and many smaller players were forced out of the game because they could not handle the heavy slugging that permeated many NHL games during this era.

When right winger Danny Gare was developing his hockey skills as a young boy in Nelson, British Columbia, his chances of becoming an NHL player were, therefore, probably quite remote. However, his father, Ernie, was a very good coach, and he frankly told his son he would have to be able to handle himself in any scrap he might get involved in on the ice. Young Danny (who would only grow to 5'9" and 175 pounds) learned his lessons well. "He (Ernie Gare) taught me how to box at a young age," Danny Gare recalled. "He said, 'You're small, you have to be strong.' I used to work out a lot with weights. He said, 'You've got to learn how to fight because it's a big man's game and it's a tough game.' And he was (a) pretty tough customer when he played. I used to watch him and I knew he was talking out of experience. So, I used to box and hit the speed-bag quite a bit."

Gare left B.C. to play junior hockey in Alberta with the Calgary

Centennials and in 183 career games, he recorded 242 points (123 were goals). He also racked up 360 penalty minutes and his feisty play got him noticed by the Buffalo Sabres, who early in their history had an impressive record at the draft. The Sabres chose Gare 29th overall in the 1974 draft and hoped the 20-year-old would develop over time. The Sabres did not have to wait long, as Gare earned a spot on the team in his first attempt. He impressed by fighting heavyweight Dave Schultz of the Flyers in his first pre-season game, proving he was not going to be pushed around despite his size. In his very first regular season game, Gare scored just 18 seconds into the game against the Bruins. "You dream of doing something like that when you're a kid: playing in an NHL game, scoring a goal right away," Gare recounted years later. It was the second-fastest goal by a rookie in his first NHL game. Gare would go on to score a total of 31 goals as a rookie, and the Sabres were one of the top three teams in the NHL with 113 points during the regular season (Montreal and Philadelphia also racked up 113 points each). As impressive as his regular season was, Gare was just as good in the playoffs with one game in particular being his defining moment.

Buffalo had easily eliminated the Chicago Blackhawks in the first round of the playoffs but were now up against the mighty Montreal Canadiens, whose lineup included Jacques Lemaire, Guy Lafleur, Larry Robinson, and Ken Dryden. The Sabres had home ice advantage and wanted to get off on the right foot. It was the afternoon of April 27, 1975, and the Sabres well knew Montreal's illustrious playoff history. A goal early in the third period gave the hometown side a 5-4 lead that they nursed late into the game. There was less than a minute to go, and Gare was out with linemates Don Luce and Craig Ramsey to finish off the Canadiens. Gare was in good position in his own end when a pass attempt hit his stick and deflected past Buffalo goalie Roger Crozier. Gare's gaffe allowed Montreal to tie the game 5-5, and the deflated crowd wondered whether the young Sabres could bounce back in overtime.

But Sabres fans had nothing to worry about as Gare's line took to the ice. A faceoff in Buffalo's end led to a three-on-two breakout by the Buffalo trio. Ramsey crossed the blueline and Montreal defenseman Larry Robinson tried to body the puck carrier, but not before a pass landed on Gare's stick as he was steaming down the wing. Gare fought off the back-checking Henri Richard of the Habs and snapped a shot past Ken Dryden in the Montreal net. Gare slid into the boards and was mobbed by his teammates as the crowd went wild. "I always like to hang wide on the wing," Gare said afterwards, "so that guys like Ramsey have room to feed me. It was a perfect pass...and aimed between Dryden's legs. There it went and as I fell to the ice relief whizzed through my mind." Gare was thrilled to have gone from goat to hero and given his team a very important victory. The Sabres beat Montreal in six games before losing in the finals to Philadelphia.

Gare would go on to score 50 goals in 1975–76 and then tie (with two others) for the league lead with 56 tallies in 1979–80. After a 46-goal effort in 1980–81, he was traded to Detroit. Two of his four seasons as a Red Wing were very good and Gare finished his career in Edmonton, where he played alongside Wayne Gretzky for part of the 1986–87 season—a year that saw the Oilers win the Stanley Cup. "There's not too many players that I got a chance to grow up and idolize and then got a chance to play with. But I had that pleasure with Danny Gare," Gretzky said. The Great One's kind words are a testament to Gare's fine career which proved that a small player can have a big impact!

Danny Gare was elected to the British Columbia Hockey Hall of Fame and his number 18 has been retired by the Buffalo Sabres. He was captain of both the Sabres (1977 to 1981) and the Red Wings (1982 to 1986).

THEO FLEURY
BORN: OXBOW, SASKATCHEWAN
NHL SEASONS: 1988–89 TO 2002–03
DEFINING MOMENT: APRIL 14, 1991

Theo Fleury recognized the situation he faced when he was about 14 years of age. "The other guys were huge," he recalled about his development in minor hockey. "You'd have guys six-foot-something, 200 pounds. And I was five-foot-something and 135 pounds, soaking wet with rocks in my pocket—and rocks in my head, too. I guess people talked a lot about that (his lack of size). I never thought of them as bigger than me. I blocked it out. What's their size got to do with me? I wish I had a dollar for every time someone has said I'm too small to play. A small player has to prove he *can* play. Big ones have to prove they *can't*. Big guys get the benefit of the doubt."

When Cliff Fletcher was general manager of the Flames, he was known for liking big hockey players. When the team was in Atlanta between 1972 and 1980, the one most noticeable trait of the club he put together from scratch was their enormous size. Many were real strapping lads at least six feet tall. The Flames made the playoffs in just their second year and were always a difficult team to play against. However, there are exceptions to every rule, and a quality general manager like Fletcher knows there is a place for the highly skilled, smaller player. During the 1987 Entry Draft, a Calgary scout named Ian McKenzie insisted the Flames take Fleury with the 166th overall choice. Though the Flames had taken seven players before selecting Fleury, many of the scouts at the Flames table were upset that Fletcher had caved in to McKenzie's persistence. But outside of Stephane Matteau, none of those selected before the 5'6" Fleury had had any impact on the Flames (most did not even make it to the NHL).

When a high-producing junior like Fleury gets selected so low in the draft, there are two points which should be noted. First, good scouts really earn their pay focusing on higher round picks that turn out to be excellent players; and second, the hockey world still thinks size matters above all else! That said, not many people knew the real Theo Fleury. He put in endless hours practicing the finer points of the game. He was small but tenacious and would not back down from larger players. His size was a constant issue, met with skepticism at all levels, and his boyish looks only added more doubt about his ability to play in the toughest junior and professional hockey leagues. Fleury, however, made up for the size concerns by continuously playing at a high energy level. He was in perpetual motion, forcing the larger lads to keep up.

Even McKenzie was not completely sure and had to convince himself that Fleury could be a legitimate NHL prospect. "I'd seen him all the time in major junior. Maybe forty times. And every time I would say to myself, 'What a great player. Too bad he's too small.'" But then McKenzie realized he might be missing the very essence of what made Fleury a terrific prospect. "He ends up doing something spectacular (everytime he plays) and everyone talks about him like he's six-foot-two. The kid's a big league player." Fleury had put up the necessary numbers in junior hockey to get noticed (472 points in 274 career games over four seasons) but only McKenzie was willing to put his reputation on the line.

From the moment he arrived at his first Flames training camp, Fleury challenged everyone on the ice. Many figured that if he survived, he just might be an NHL player one day. Theo was indeed short compared to most of the other players. But he was not small, nor did he play that way. In fact, he would eventually fill out to a sturdy 182 pounds. He drove many of his own teammates crazy, but he did get noticed. Calgary coach Terry Crisp noted, "There is no quit in Theo Fleury."

The Flames indeed liked what they saw but sent Fleury to their American Hockey League team in Salt Lake City. In 40 games during the 1988–89 season, Fleury recorded 74 points. He then got promoted to the big team, where he promptly registered 34 points in 36 NHL games. To top off his amazing first season as a professional, Fleury added 11 points in the playoffs as the Flames won their first-ever Stanley Cup! He had certainly proved he belonged in the big league.

Fleury scored 31 goals in his first full NHL season and then 51 in 1990–91 when he led the Flames in scoring. He also played with a great deal of emotion, which often landed him in the penalty box, but at other times, it was exactly what he needed to compete. The 1991 playoffs was one such instance where Fleury rose to the occasion and proved every naysayer wrong.

The Flames hooked up with their Alberta rivals and defending Stanley Cup champions, the Edmonton Oilers, in the first round of the playoffs. It was an old-fashioned best-of-seven series that was not decided until overtime of the seventh contest. It was a rough-and-tumble match-up, with hitting the likes of which the NHL has rarely seen. Emotions were riding high. The Flames would eventually lose the series, but it was the sixth game in which Fleury really displayed his best.

The Flames were down 3-2 in games when they traveled back to Edmonton for the sixth contest on April 14, 1991. The game went into overtime tied at 1-1, at which point Oilers captain Mark Messier turned the puck over to the ever-tenacious Fleury near center ice. The mighty little Flames dynamo grabbed the loose puck and sped in alone on Edmonton netminder Grant Fuhr. Fleury made no mistake and buried a shot past Fuhr to secure a 2-1 Flames win and force a seventh game back in Calgary. It may have been the most significant goal of Fleury's career, and his celebration was one for the ages. His slide all over the ice—complete with pump action and euphoric, big, gap-toothed smile—eventually landed him back in the Calgary end before his teammates could catch up to him. It was a celebration that no one would ever forget. In one of the most important games of the year, Fleury had once again proved that even the smallest player can rise to the greatest heights on the biggest occasions.

Theo Fleury's story is even more amazing considering he suffered physical abuse inflicted by a junior hockey coach. He would go on to record 1,088 points (455 were goals) in 1,084 career games.

YVAN COURNOYER
BORN: DRUMMONDVILLE, QUEBEC
NHL SEASONS: 1963–64 TO 1978–79
DEFINING MOMENT: 1973 PLAYOFFS

When Yvan Cournoyer was set to join the Montreal Canadiens, they had a roster full of smallish players. Bobby Rousseau, Claude Larose, Andre Boudrias, and Bill Hicke were all well under the six-foot mark. The Habs were not sure if they had room for another such player, but his great speed and shot bought Cournoyer extra consideration and eventually he won over his teammates, coaches, and fans right across Canada with his exciting brand of hockey.

When Cournoyer was 15, he stood a mere 5'3". In fact, he was the smallest player for the Lachine Maroons, a Quebec junior team. Nevertheless, he dreamed of one day playing for the Montreal Canadiens. Just two years later, he scored 37 goals in 42 games for the Maroons and caught the eye of the Canadiens scouting staff. He played major junior hockey between the ages of 18 and 20 and was a prolific goal scorer (115 goals in 124 games) with the Montreal Jr. Canadiens. The small man was actually Montreal's best junior prospect when the Habs called him up for a five-game trial during the 1963–64 season. Cournoyer promptly scored four times. By this point, Cournoyer had grown to 5'7" and weighed somewhere around 160 pounds (he would fill out to a sturdy 178 as time passed), but questions about his size would not go away.

Montreal coach Toe Blake always wanted his team to be a good defensive club, but checking was simply not Cournoyer's game early in his career. As a result, he often found himself on the bench, called upon only when the Canadiens had a power-play opportunity or when the coach wanted a change of pace. Still, he had a good hand in helping the team regain the Stanley Cup in 1965 (he scored an important goal in the seventh game of the finals versus Chicago), and by the 1965–66 season, he was playing on a more regular basis, scoring 18 goals in 65 games. He scored 25 in 1966–67, but Montreal lost the Cup to Toronto in the playoffs. Cournoyer was still not seen as a great player, but he kept improving by posting 60 points (28 were goals) in 1967–68. At this point, Blake would admit this about his speedy right winger, "The guy is small, alright, but very solidly built. He has broad shoulders and wrists and terrific leg muscles. He's no lighter or smaller than Henri Richard was when he broke into the NHL. And he's more ruggedly put together than some of the other good little men in this league—Dave Keon (of Toronto) for example."

Blake developed Cournoyer slowly and was rewarded in 1968–69 when the man they called "the Roadrunner" scored 43 times. Cournoyer had finally learned his defensive responsibilities well enough to earn the coach's respect, and he learned that his skating and terrific shot were going to give him the edge he needed to really excel at the NHL level. He was challenged physically (by the likes of Boston's Glen Sather and New York's Brad Park) and while he was never going to be a fighter, Cournoyer did show he was not going to back down or be intimidated. The next four seasons saw him score 27, 37, 47, and 40 goals, establishing himself as a consistent and respected player. He was selected to play for Team Canada during the historic Summit Series of 1972 (recording five points in eight games), but his best individual performance was yet to come.

The 1972–73 season saw Cournoyer enjoy one of his best years (40 goals, 39 assists), helping the Canadiens to a league-best 52 wins and 120 points. The Habs were anxious to reclaim the Stanley Cup after losing it a year earlier and romped through the first two rounds of the playoffs with series wins over Buffalo and a tough Philadelphia Flyers team. Cournoyer had already recorded 13 points in 11 playoff games, but he saved his very best for the finals against Chicago.

It looked like the Habs were going to take the series in five games, but they lost a wild 8-7 game at home in the fifth contest to send the teams back to Chicago on the night of May 10, 1973. The game was tied 4-4 going into the third period (Cournoyer had set up Montreal's fourth goal by Frank Mahovlich) when a Blackhawks defenseman had a word for Cournoyer as the final period was about to start. "Hey Shorty, what do you plan to do when you grow up?" inquired the 6'3", 220-pound Jerry Korab. "I'm not sure. Score goals I guess," retorted Cournoyer. Like his shot, Cournoyer was deadly accurate with his prediction.

Perhaps Korab was feeling smug because the Blackhawks had held Cournoyer (who had scored five goals and added four assists in the series so far) in check for most of the night. No matter. The period started and 10 minutes in, Montreal's Jacques Lemaire took a shot that came off the glass behind the Chicago net. The puck bounced out in front of the goal, and Cournoyer, with his exceptional hand-eye coordination, knocked the puck right in mid-air and put it past a startled Tony Esposito in the Blackhawks net. It was Cournoyer's 15th goal of the playoffs. For good measure, he helped set up teammate Marc Tardif for the insurance goal in the 6-4 Habs win. It was his 25th point of the post-season, the most of any player.

Cournoyer's great play landed him the Conn Smythe Trophy and a new car. "It's nice I won the Smythe and the car. I wasn't even aware of all that," he said modestly after the game (as he marveled at how well his 37-year-old teammate Henri Richard had played as well). "They were hitting me a lot tonight but that was OK. Some nights you need a few body checks to wake you up," Cournoyer added. Chicago forward John Marks said of Cournoyer, "Just when you think you have him tied up, he disappears on you."

There was no more doubting Cournoyer's ability to play in a big man's game, and he would go on to score 428 goals and 863 points in 968 games to cap off a brilliant Hall of Fame career.

Yvan Cournoyer won a total of nine Stanley Cups, and he played out the last of his career in 1978 as team captain.

DOUG GILMOUR
BORN: KINGSTON, ONTARIO
NHL SEASONS: 1983–84 TO 2002–03
DEFINING MOMENT: 1993 PLAYOFFS

Everyone who plays hockey has always had heroes while growing up. No matter what position you play or how big or small you might be, there are always certain players who capture your attention. When Doug Gilmour was growing up in Kingston, Ontario, he had two favorite hockey teams—the Maple Leafs and the Bruins. He liked Leafs defensemen such as Tim Horton, Bob Baun, and Jim McKenney, but he also admired Bobby Orr of the Boston team. "Bobby Orr was the Wayne Gretzky of the times," Gilmour recalled. "I was a defenseman until I hit junior hockey then I changed to centre. You always try to pattern yourself after a player who played the same position." Gilmour also admired his older brother, David, who was 13 years his senior and a teammate of Toronto's future star Darryl Sittler when the two played junior in London, Ontario. And although Don Gilmour never pushed his younger son to play hockey, he impressed upon Doug that he should play hard *every* time he hit the ice.

Gilmour was a blueliner as he moved up in minor hockey, but when he was 16 years old, he was cut from a junior B team 15 games into the 1979–80 season. A coach named Larry Mavety decided to take a chance on Gilmour for a Tier II team in Belleville, Ontario, and Gilmour responded with 23 points in 25 games. The next season, he attended the training camp of the Cornwall Royals. He was 5'9" and just 145 pounds and determined not to let his lack of size deter him in any way. He was moved to the center position and quickly responded with 35 points in the 51 games played. He also helped the Royals win the Memorial Cup in 1981, scoring the winning goal in the last game. Gilmour then recorded 119 points in 1981–82, but NHL scouts felt he was too small to be effective at the pro level. So they passed on him at the Entry Draft. Gilmour came back and recorded 177 points in 1982–83, but that only got him drafted 134th overall by the St. Louis Blues. Gilmour was sent to play in Europe before the Blues, initially reluctant to sign him, relented and finally gave him a contract.

It was thought that Gilmour might be an effective defensive player, but he was no slouch on the attack. He scored over 20 goals in each of his first three seasons and then scored 42 times in 1986–87 and totaled 105 points. Soon, all opponents had to be wary of Gilmour on the attack as he produced over 80 or more points over each of the next five seasons. He was traded to Calgary in 1988 in a multi-player swap and promptly helped the Flames win the Stanley Cup (scoring the Cup-winning goal in the Montreal Forum) in 1989. A contract dispute with the Flames forced another trade—this time to the Toronto Maple Leafs, who were nowhere near as strong as the Flames when Gilmour arrived on January 2, 1992, as part of a 10-player deal.

If Gilmour was known as an effective player prior to his arrival in Toronto, he soon became a league superstar. Virtually overnight, the small but ever-feisty Gilmour made the Leafs a contending team. With coaching and player changes fully implemented, the Leafs were on the hunt for the Cup by the middle of the 1992–93 season. Gilmour promised Leafs fans that the team was going to do something special in the '93 playoffs—and he kept his word. His game 7 performance (one goal and three assists in a 4-3 Leaf overtime win) against Detroit pushed the Leafs ahead to the second round. His overtime-winning goal against St. Louis was a classic and it got the Leafs off on the right foot in the second round.

The Blues were a stubborn team, but Toronto prevailed in seven games, putting them into the Western Conference final against Wayne Gretzky and the Los Angeles Kings.

The series opened on the night of May 17 with the teams tied 1-1 going into the third period. Then Doug Gilmour took over the game. First he put a hit on Kings defenseman Alexei Zhitnik that sent the Los Angeles player toppling upside down to the ice. Then he set up teammate Glenn Anderson for the go-ahead goal with a pretty pass. Gilmour added a goal of his own to make it 3-1 when Kings goalie Kelly Hrudey failed to control a loose puck. Gilmour also set up teammate Bill Berg when he stole the puck in the Kings end to make it a 4-1 Leafs lead. The Kings were none too pleased that Gilmour had done them in with three third-period points (equaling a Leaf playoff record). Tough defenseman Marty McSorley then took a vicious run at the Toronto star, leaving him face down on the ice. The Kings were clearly going after the best Leafs player and were trying to send a message despite the one-sided game. But to no avail.

After the game, the Leafs and Kings both felt Gilmour's play was the difference in the contest. "Gilmour was great, just great," said Toronto coach Pat Burns. "Dougie goes back to pick up his checks and finishes them (scoring chances) at the other end." Gretzky also acknowledged Gilmour's impact on the game. "Gilmour played well in the third period and when that happens, the people around him gain confidence." Despite winning the first game, the Leafs lost the series in seven games with Gretzky raising his level of play to put a dagger in the hearts of long-suffering Leaf fans. In 393 career games as a Maple Leaf, Gilmour recorded 452 points and became a mega star during the second half of his career. He would play for four other NHL teams before his career ended. But Gilmour was at his best when he played in Toronto, especially in the 1993 playoffs.

The key to success for Gilmour was that he never worried too much about what people said regarding his size. "Throughout my life, if somebody said I was too small, that just meant I wanted to beat them that much more to prove somebody wrong. I've always looked at it (such) that I never thought I was small. I know I am but you never think of it that way when you put your equipment on. You just go out and play like you're the same as everybody else." Inspiring words from one of the game's most dynamic players.

Doug Gilmour set a Toronto team record with 127 points in 1992–93. He finished his career with 1,414 points (including 450 goals) in 1,474 career games. He will likely be voted to the Hall of Fame in the near future.

STEVE SULLIVAN
BORN: TIMMINS, ONTARIO
NHL SEASONS: 1995–96 TO PRESENT
DEFINING MOMENT: APRIL 10, 1999

When the New Jersey Devils selected center Steve Sullivan 233rd overall during the 1994 Entry Draft, it was not with the expectation that the 5'8", 161-pound player would ever make it to the NHL. Sure, he had been a prolific scorer (66 goals and 121 points in 1995–96) while playing junior in his hometown of Timmins, Ontario. And sure, he had posted good numbers (113 points in 1993–94) in Sault Ste. Marie for two seasons of major junior. Nevertheless, he was still thought to be too small for the professional ranks. However, he did make the Albany River Rats (the Devils farm team in the AHL) and earned a first team all-star selection for his play during the 1995–96 season, in which he had 75 points in just 53 games. His play with the River Rats got him into 16 regular season games for the Devils in '95–'96 (he scored a goal in his first-ever NHL game), and he produced a respectable nine points. He also scored three goals in four playoff games to finish out the year. The smallish, crafty center with good wheels was beginning to show he could play with the bigger boys.

Sullivan started the next season dividing his time between Albany and the big league team but then a trade took place that would change his career. The Toronto Maple Leafs were forced to trade Doug Gilmour when their star center would not sign a new contract. The Devils were very interested and offered up defenseman Jason Smith, prospect Alyn McCauley, and Sullivan to Toronto to complete the deal. The Leafs were not a very good team in 1996–97 and gave Sullivan a little more ice time than he was getting in New Jersey. He responded with 16 points in 21 games to finish the season. The next year saw Sullivan play in 63 games, but he was able to score only 10 goals and total just 28 points for the mediocre squad.

However, the next season saw Pat Quinn take over as coach of the Maple Leafs and he stressed offensive play. At first, the Leafs were not sure about bringing Sullivan back, especially considering that Quinn loved big players. Sullivan was neither aggressive nor tall, two attributes that would not endear him to the new Leafs mentor. However, when the Leafs could not find anyone else to bring into the lineup, Sullivan was given another opportunity, and he made the most of it. In 63 games played in 1998–99, Sullivan hit the magic 20-goal mark for the first time in his career, and he added another 20 assists for a very respectable 40-point year.

Sullivan's shining night of the season came late in the year when the Florida Panthers came in to play the Leafs in Toronto. It was April 10, 1999. Sullivan showed Leafs fans that the team had more talent at center than just captain Mats Sundin, a man who stood 6'5" tall and weighed 230 pounds. The first period saw the Leafs score two goals. That proved to be just the beginning of a long night for the Panthers. Sullivan scored twice in the third period to give the Leafs a commanding 4-0 lead. His first goal came after he stole the puck from a Florida defenseman and made a wrap-around attempt that went past Panthers netminder Sean Burke. His second goal was a clean breakaway—he deked Burke before putting a shot into the net for his 18th of the season.

Toronto scored twice more in the third to give them a 7-1 lead, but Sullivan was not done yet. On a Leaf power play, he tapped in a shot for his 19th goal of the year and, with less than four minutes to play, Sullivan scored his 20th goal of the season and fourth of the game when he stuffed a puck past Kirk McLean (who had replaced Burke during the second period). "I've never scored four before. Heck, I've never scored three. I just felt great every time I had the puck and I always seemed to be in the right spot," Sullivan said after his great performance. "It (this game) builds our confidence. We played our game and scored some goals. We want to make sure we hit the playoffs clicking on all cylinders."

The Leafs were not even supposed to make the playoffs in 1999, but thanks to surprising performances by players like Sullivan, Toronto won 45 games and recorded 97 points. They knocked off Philadelphia and Pittsburgh in the first two rounds before bowing out to the Buffalo Sabres in the Eastern Conference final. Sullivan contributed six points in 13 playoff games and his future as a Leaf seemed secure.

However, Sullivan was rather upset he was not in the Leafs line-up every game to start the next season (only one point in seven games) and asked for a trade. Quinn, never a big fan of small players, decided to put the upset Sullivan on waivers, and Chicago picked him up for nothing. That decision cost the Maple Leafs a good hockey player. Sullivan got more ice time with the Blackhawks and scored 22, 34, 21, and 26 goals over the next four years.

Contract issues forced Chicago to trade Sullivan to Nashville where he has continued to excel when healthy. He scored a career-best 31 goals in 2005–06 for the Predators, ending all debate about whether this small player could survive in the game. Sometimes, all a smaller player needs is a chance to show what he can do.

A serious back injury forced Steve Sullivan to miss more than an entire year starting in 2006, but he came back and was awarded the Masterton Trophy for his sportsmanship, perseverance, and dedication to hockey.

BRIAN GIONTA
BORN: ROCHESTER, NEW YORK
NHL SEASONS: 2001–02 TO PRESENT
DEFINING MOMENT: FEBRUARY 1, 2011

The entire Gionta family of Rochester, New York, is pretty small. Sam Gionta, the father, is just 5'4", while mother Penny is just at the 5-foot mark. Their children, all boys—Joe, Stephen, and Brian—are each listed at 5'7", but there is more to measure with the Giontas than just height.

Center Brian Gionta has always heard that he is way too small for professional hockey, but he has proved skeptics wrong year after year. Given the way the game is played now with stricter rule enforcement, there is no reason why the stocky, 173-pound Gionta cannot have a very long and productive NHL career.

Gionta never believed anything would come easy for him, but he was very willing to work hard because he had confidence in his abilities. Growing up, he worked in his father's hardware store and learned to play hockey in his spare time. He first began playing locally, scoring 52 goals and 89 points in just 28 games with the Rochester Jr. Americans in 1994–95. His fine play got him a placement in the Metro Toronto Junior League with the Niagara Scenic for the next two seasons. He scored 104 total goals. He then attended Boston College for the next four years where he helped the Eagles make the "Frozen Four" each of those seasons. In his final season, he had 33 goals and 54 points, earning the title of Hockey East Player of the Year. He also learned what it takes to be successful when his team won the NCAA championship in 2001.

The New Jersey Devils selected Gionta with their third choice of the 1998 draft (82nd overall) and let him develop in college hockey. The Devils had always done well drafting U.S. college players and Gionta was no exception. Like many Devil players, Gionta also played in the AHL for Albany but was a regular with the big team by the 2002–03 season when he played in 58 games (scoring 12 goals). He was also a member of the Devils Stanley Cup–winning team in '03 (one goal and nine points in 24 playoff games). He had a 48-goal, 89-point season in 2005–06 and then settled into being a 20-plus goal scorer every year with an average of 45 to 60 points. The Devils had a good player, but when Gionta became a free agent after the 2008–09 season, they were reluctant to give him a large contract. Instead, they let him become a free agent, and the Montreal Canadiens were there to scoop him up with a five-year, $25-million contract.

Gionta responded to his new surroundings with a 28-goal year in 2009–10 with Montreal making it to the third round of the playoffs—their best showing in years (Gionta contributed 15 points in 19 playoff games). The Habs were very impressed with Gionta's work ethic and determination and gave him a special role before the start of the 2010–11 campaign. There was plenty of speculation as to which player was going to be named the next captain (the team did not have any player in that role in '09–'10), and there were a number of candidates to consider. The team settled on Gionta; he was given the prestigious honor just before the new season began. "It's pretty special," said the 31-year-old who became only the second American-born player to get the "C" stitched on his Habs jersey (Chris Chelios was the other). "It's an honour no matter what but for sure it's a big honour to be asked in Montreal. There are so many guys before you. There is so much history in the organization. To be a part of that is a huge thing," Gionta added. Montreal coach Jacques Martin had this to say about his new captain. "Brian leads a lot by example, how he practices and how he handles himself on the ice as well as off the ice. It was fairly obvious to the organization and to his teammates, that he is our leader in our dressing room and that's why he is wearing the 'C.'"

Proof of the coach's words came on the night of February 1, 2011, when the Canadiens were down 2-0 to the hometown Washington Capitals after just one period of play. It was the kind of game a visiting team could easily write off as out of reach, but Gionta was having none of that and led his team back into the contest. He broke in on the Washington goal on a 2-on-1 rush. He kept the puck and drilled home a shot to get the Habs back into the game before the 10-minute mark of the second. Then he stole the puck from a Caps defenseman and went in alone to tie the game with a wrist shot for his 18th goal of the year. There was no scoring in the third period or in overtime, which meant the game was going to a shoot-out. Gionta put on some impressive moves on his opportunity and was the only player to score in the shoot-out, to give Montreal the win. "It's tough in this league to get chances that are wide open, where you're not forced or pressured," Gionta said after the game about all his goals. "To have that kind of time, it makes all the difference." Gionta was perhaps being a little modest because his slick moves froze the Washington goaltender on each goal he scored this night. As his coach had accurately predicted, Gionta showed he was every bit the leader Montreal needed.

His being named captain of the illustrious Canadiens shows that even the smallest players such as Brian Gionta can rise to the occasion and successfully fulfill the highest roles in the game.

Brian Gionta has 404 points (including 209 goals) in 616 career games to date.

MIKE CAMMALLERI
BORN: RICHMOND HILL, ONTARIO
NHL SEASONS: 2002–03 TO PRESENT
DEFINING MOMENT: 2010 PLAYOFFS

Mike Cammalleri has always been a very focused individual. Watch before a game and you will see him sitting on the bench preparing for the contest by visualizing a shot on goal while taking a pretend swing at a puck. He has always been the type who, if he put his mind to something, would accomplish his task without fail. Although he has never been large in stature (he is generously listed at 5'9" and 182 pounds in the *NHL Guide and Record Book*), Cammalleri understood that he had to develop whatever skills he needed to make it in big-league hockey. For example, he would practice his shot in the basement of his home, firing puck after puck until it was time to practice another skill. Developing his shot was a key cause of his rise through the hockey ranks, so it was time well spent and a strong indicator of his single-minded approach to getting where he wanted to go.

A native of Richmond Hill, Ontario, Cammalleri was involved in many sports growing up, including softball, track, and soccer. He showed great athleticism in each sport. However, hockey was where he excelled the most, and he played on many great teams as he went through the minor hockey system in and around the Toronto area (including playing for the renowned Toronto Red Wings). Cammalleri was often the captain of most teams he played on, but he always emphasized team play over individual glory. Many tournaments saw Cammalleri-led teams do very well, but it was usually his wingers who would get named MVP—a strong indication that Cammalleri made others better.

Cammalleri's family also believed in education, so he took accelerated courses when he played Tier II hockey for the Bramalea Blues of the OPJHL. He hoped that would make him ready to attend an American college. He scored 67 goals and 191 points in 87 games over two seasons for the Blues, and that got him into the University of Michigan. After a couple of years at Michigan, he was selected 49th overall by the Los Angeles Kings in 2001. He did not turn pro until the 2002–03 season when the Kings assigned him to their farm team, the Manchester Monarchs of the AHL. His final year in Manchester saw him record 109 points (46G, 63A) in just 79 games played. He did play in 59 games (recording 23 points) for the parent Los Angeles club but was not a fulltime King until the 2005–06 campaign. He proved he belonged in the big league by scoring 26 times and then added seasons of 34 and 19 goals scored. Fearing they would not be able to sign him to a new contract, the Kings dealt Cammalleri to Calgary in June 2008, and he scored a career-high 39 goals in his one and only year as a Flame.

Montreal was looking to completely retool their team for the 2009–10 season and made Cammalleri the centerpiece of their new team. He loved the idea of playing for the historic franchise and liked that his new linemates would include ex–New Jersey Devil players Scott Gomez and Brian Gionta. "It excites me to play in Montreal. There's a passion for the sport there that you only find in select places. It's an electric feeling to play here night after night," Cammalleri said about Montreal after signing a six-year deal worth $30 million.

The Canadiens first-line trio had no size but plenty of gumption, and only a serious ankle injury kept Cammalleri from adding to his impressive totals of 26 goals and 24 assists. Montreal struggled to make the playoffs, but they secured a spot during their last regular season game and then had to face the first-place Washington Capitals as their reward. The Capitals jumped out to a 3-1 series lead, but the Canadiens still believed they could win. After staving off elimination with a 2-1 win right in Washington, the Habs returned home to face the Caps in the sixth game of the series on April 26, 2010, in another must-win situation.

The game would provide Cammalleri with a golden opportunity to show he could still focus on the task at hand and be a star player for his team. Montreal netminder Jaroslav Halak was brilliant facing 53 shots on the night, but it was Cammalleri who scored two first-period goals to get Montreal off on the right track. His first goal, a wrist shot from the face-off circle, came on a Montreal power-play just 7:30 into the contest. Less than two minutes later, he scored his second of the contest and the fifth of the series to give the Habs a 2-0 lead. Montreal, backed by great netminding, took the contest 4-1 and forced a game seven showdown in Washington two nights later. Montreal would eke out a surprising 2-1 win that night, pulling off another playoff upset that has long been the tradition of the storied Canadiens organization.

The Canadiens were not done yet. The Pittsburgh Penguins were also expected to roll over the Habs, but Montreal was ready for Sidney Crosby and Evgeni Malkin. The teams split the first four games of the series, but the Pens won the fifth to take the lead.

Montreal would not quit and won the sixth game 4-3 at home, setting up another game seven situation for the night of May 12, 2010. Montreal scored just 32 seconds into the final game and gradually built up a 4-0 lead before a stunned Pittsburgh crowd.

Cammalleri scored his 12th goal of the playoffs to make it 3-0 at 3:32 of the second period—making it very difficult for the Penguins to come back. "I don't claim we're a great team. I don't claim we're perfect and I don't claim that everything we do is on purpose. I think we're just finding ways to win," Cammalleri said after the game. It was also the last game ever played at the Mellon Arena ("the Igloo"), a fact not lost on the Montreal star. "We've been talking about it a lot. That's a cool piece of history for us," Cammalleri commented about the historic final game.

Through all of the 2010 post-season, it was the superb goal-scoring efforts of Cammalleri (notching 13 goals, becoming the first Canadiens player to score that many playoff goals since Jacques Lemaire in 1979) that got Montreal through to the third round. He totaled 19 points in 19 games and displayed an uncanny ability to get himself open to shoot—and when he fired, it was usually on net and past a startled netminder. His performance showed that he was not just a good, small-sized, regular season player, but that Cammalleri could score big goals when it mattered most.

Mike Cammalleri has recorded 384 points (including 177 goals) in 496 career games.

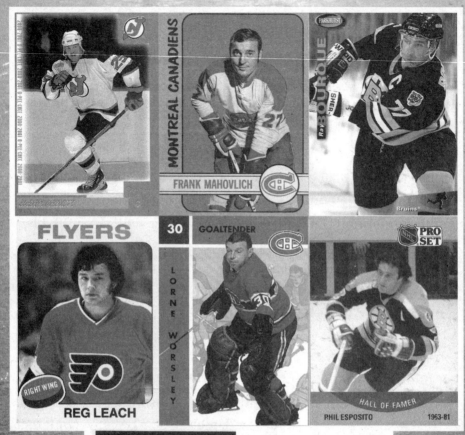

MONTREAL CANADIENS

FRANK MAHOVLICH

RAY BOURQUE

Bruins

FLYERS

RIGHT WING

REG LEACH

30 GOALTENDER

LORNE WORSLEY

NHL PRO SET

HALL OF FAMER

PHIL ESPOSITO 1963-81

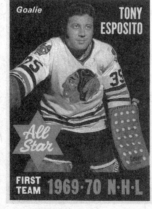

Goalie TONY ESPOSITO

ALL Star

FIRST TEAM 1969-70 N·H·L

VICTORY

JOE THORNTON
C · 19

TRADED AWAY

For many players, getting traded is a shocking event—especially the first time it happens. There is a feeling of rejection and hurt that takes time to get over. But in the end, there are really two ways players react to a trade—they withdraw while struggling to fit into a new team or they become rejuvenated and play better than ever. Of course, there are those veteran players who ask to be dealt in the hopes that it will give them a fresh start, and some deals give upcoming players a chance to show they belong in the NHL. In fact, more than one player has achieved his greatest moment after a trade, making the deal a life-changing moment. In this chapter the stories of those who were "Traded Away" will focus on the following players:

Phil Esposito
Frank Mahovlich
Joe Thornton
Gump Worsley
Jason Arnott
Tony Esposito
Eddie Giacomin
Reggie Leach
Raymond Bourque ✓

PHIL ESPOSITO
BORN: SAULT STE. MARIE, ONTARIO
NHL SEASONS: 1963–64 TO 1980–81
DEFINING MOMENT: 1972 CANADA-RUSSIA SERIES

There are some trades that are so one-sided they are never forgotten—by fans, teams, players, and the media alike. One such deal involved Phil Esposito who was still an emerging player for the Chicago Blackhawks at the end of the 1966–67 season. The Hawks had finished on top of the league in '66–'67 but had a poor playoff when management deemed it necessary to make changes. In a hastily put together deal, Chicago sent Esposito to the Bruins. It was a deal that hurt the Blackhawks, a transaction that created a monster in Boston. The deal also gave Esposito the confidence he needed to become a leader in his own right, now that he had escaped the shadow of Bobby Hull and Stan Mikita.

Esposito played his first professional hockey games in his hometown of Sault Ste. Marie, Ontario, in the Eastern Hockey League (EPHL). He thought he was going to stay there for a little while but Chicago, who owned his playing rights, moved the entire team out of the Soo (where he worked in the steel mills in the summer) to St. Louis for the start of the 1962–63 season. The move did not seem to bother the lanky 6'1", 195-pound center as he racked up an impressive 90 points (including 54 assists) in just 71 games. He played 43 games for the Braves in 1963–64 and had an amazing 80 points before he was called up to the big-league Chicago club. It was the last time Esposito played in the minors.

Esposito's first full NHL season saw him score 23 times and add 32 assists in 1964–65. The Blackhawks made it to the Stanley Cup finals that year only to lose to the Montreal Canadiens in seven games. Esposito upped his goal total to 27 the following year, but this time Chicago was out in the first round of the playoffs. The 1966–67 campaign saw Esposito extend his point total to 61 (21 goals, 40 assists) as he thrived as the pivot on a line with the high-scoring Hull and checking winger Chico Maki. Chicago finished in first place for the first time in team history and it looked like they were in good position to win the Stanley Cup. However, the veteran-laden Toronto Maple Leafs had other ideas and upset the Hawks (a team they trailed by 17 points in the regular season) in six games. Esposito had no goals and no assists and admitted that Peter Stemkowski and Bob Pulford of the Leafs had done a good job of shutting him down in the post-season.

When news of his post-season trade to Boston reached the outspoken Esposito, he told Chicago management that they would mess up a good team that could win for years. His prophecy turned out to be correct. Coach Billy Reay and general manager Tommy Ivan did not appreciate Esposito speaking his mind and no longer wanted anything to do with him. On May 15, 1967, Esposito was traded to the Boston Bruins, a perennial basement dweller. "I was in shock. I was no longer a Blackhawk. I was a Boston Bruin. You don't think that you're ever going to be traded," Esposito said years later. Hull told Esposito at the time of the deal, "Go to Boston, play good hockey and show these jerks what a mistake they made." Esposito took his former teammate's advice to heart and turned the deal into one of the greatest in NHL history.

The Bruins gave up little (Pit Martin, Gilles Marotte, and goalie Jack Norris) to add Esposito, Ken Hodge, and Fred Stanfield to a team rebuilding around the greatest player in hockey history— Bobby Orr. They started to roll and Esposito not only led the NHL in points in 1968–69 (126), he also helped the Bruins become Cup champions in 1970 and 1972. Esposito also became one of the most prolific point producers in NHL history with a total of six seasons of 100 or more points in Beantown. Although Chicago did make it to the finals in 1971 and 1973, they were never winners, and no player on the Blackhawks produced to the level of Esposito.

Esposito was great in the NHL (winning the Art Ross Trophy four times and taking the Hart Trophy twice) but his greatest moment came during the 1972 Canada-Russia Series. With Bobby Hull (ruled ineligible) and Bobby Orr (injured) out for this series, Esposito was in the spotlight, and he played superbly for the entire eight games against the Soviets. It all started in the first game of the series when he scored the opening goal just 30 seconds in. It ended when he assisted on Paul Henderson's dramatic winner with 34 seconds to play in the last contest to give Canada a 4-3-1 edge in games.

The final game in Moscow saw Esposito deliver what was one of the greatest performances in hockey history. Esposito scored the opening goal for Canada to tie the game 1-1. He also helped his team defensively by going behind goalie Ken Dryden to stop a sure Soviet goal with the Russians already leading the game 4-3. Down 5-3 to start the third, Esposito scored early to make it 5-4 and then assisted Yvan Cournoyer to tie the game 5-5. He refused to leave the ice as the game was coming to a close and was able to whack a loose puck at the Russian goal, which Henderson eventually put away to give the Canadians a thrilling, pressure-pucked come-from-behind victory.

"Looking back, it was one hell of a series," Esposito said years later. "It was the toughest thing I ever had to in my life as a hockey player. The mental anguish we all went through was overwhelming. And I was never able to play at that level again. From that moment on, for me as a player, it was all downhill."

Esposito could never hope to match the high he achieved in September of 1972, but he was still an impactful player with the

Bruins, and later with the New York Rangers for a number of years. He finished with 717 goals and 1,590 points in 1,282 career games.

As Esposito racked up points, awards, and championships, all the Chicago Blackhawks could do was watch and wonder why they traded away a true superstar.

Phil Esposito was elected to the Hockey Hall of Fame in 1984.

FRANK MAHOVLICH
BORN: TIMMINS, ONTARIO
NHL SEASONS: 1956–57 TO 1973–74
DEFINING MOMENT: 1971 STANLEY CUP PLAYOFFS

When Frank Mahovlich was first traded, it came as something of a relief for the superstar left winger. For more than 10 seasons he had been the best player on the Toronto Maple Leafs, the team that recruited him out of northern Ontario. Despite four Stanley Cup titles and 296 goals for the Leafs, a rocky relationship with coach Punch Imlach always made life rather difficult for the man known as "The Big M." It was hoped that the trade to the Red Wings in March 1968 would revive his career, and it did. In his first three seasons with Detroit, Mahovlich scored 94 goals in 163 games (including a 49-goal campaign in 1968–69). "It was like lifting a big load from my shoulders when I left the Leafs," Mahovlich said in trying to account for his success in the Motor City. He also enjoyed playing alongside veteran superstars like Gordie Howe and Alex Delvecchio.

But the Red Wings got off to a terrible start in 1970–71 and decided to make some major changes—including the trading of Mahovlich to the Montreal Canadiens, despite his 14 goals and 32 points in 35 games played that year. At the time of the trade, Montreal general manager Sam Pollock (one of the shrewdest dealers in NHL history) said the transaction was a "once-in-a-lifetime deal. I never made a deal like that before. I never will again." Montreal gave up three players (Mickey Redmond, Guy Charron, and Bill Collins) to obtain the 6', 205-pound Mahovlich, and they never regretted the move. But when the trade was completed in February 1971, many wondered if the once-fleet-footed Mahovlich was still a dominating hockey player.

Montreal had a very turbulent season in '70–'71, coming off a year when the usually mighty Habs had shockingly missed the playoffs. Mahovlich, however, immediately started producing in Montreal, scoring 17 times and totaling 41 points in 38 games to finish the regular season. He also liked the fact that he was now teammates with his younger brother Peter, who had joined the Habs in an earlier trade.

However the Canadiens could only muster a third-place finish and faced the very tough Boston Bruins in the first round of the playoffs. Boston, led by league MVP Bobby Orr, was strongly favored to oust the Canadiens, but the Montreal side had other ideas. The decision to use then-unknown Ken Dryden in net seemed to distract the Boston club, which had scored a league-leading 399 goals (including a league-leading 76 tallies from Phil Esposito) during the season. The next biggest surprise was the performance of Mahovlich who recaptured the post-season glory he had enjoyed with the Maple Leafs in the Sixties.

The Canadiens scored more goals than expected and forced the Bruins to a seventh-game showdown in Boston. The Bruins opened the scoring in the last contest, but Mahovlich scored quickly to tie the game 1-1. Another Mahovlich goal (his seventh of the series) early in the third gave the Habs a 3-1 lead and they hung on to win 4-2. It was one of the biggest upsets in hockey history as the 57-14-7 Bruins were knocked off by a team that had finished 24 points behind them in the regular season standings.

After beating Minnesota in the next round, the Habs had to play Chicago—the best team in the NHL's Western Division—in the Stanley Cup final. Bobby Hull (44 goals) and Dennis Hull (40 goals) paced the Chicago attack along with Stan Mikita, Jim Pappin, and Pat Stapleton. It was a close series with the Blackhawks taking a 3-2 series lead. Montreal had to win at home to force another Game 7, but it did not look good for the Canadiens when Chicago had a 3-2 lead going into the third period. But then, "The Big M" (who had missed a penalty shot earlier in the first period) went to work.

First he tied the game with his 14th goal of the playoffs at 5:18 of the final frame, rapping home a pass from Jean Beliveau. Then, less than three minutes later with his team short-handed, he took advantage of a Bobby Hull turnover to set up his brother Peter for the winning goal (with his 27th point of the post-season) to give Montreal a 4-3 victory. Mahovlich described setting up the winning goal: "Pete went after the puck and it went to the boards. I went after it and everybody came at me. So I passed it over to Pete." A come-from-behind, 3-2 win in Chicago two nights later gave Montreal another Stanley Cup championship.

The surprising Montreal club had many heroes in the spring of 1971, but none bigger than Frank Mahovlich who made the most of his trade to the Canadiens. He would also add another Cup with Montreal in 1973, giving him six titles over his illustrious career.

Frank Mahovlich finished with 533 goals and 1,103 career points. He was elected to the Hockey Hall of Fame in 1981.

JOE THORNTON

BORN: LONDON, ONTARIO

NHL SEASONS: 1997–98 TO PRESENT

DEFINING MOMENT: APRIL 15, 2006

Joe Thornton was selected first overall by the Boston Bruins in the 1997 Entry Draft, but everything did not go so smoothly for the big center (6'4", 235 pounds) when he first made the NHL team. Rather than sending him back to junior, the Bruins kept Thornton on the big-league roster, but he rarely played, dressing for just 55 games and scoring only seven times. Pat Burns was coaching the Bruins at the time, and he clearly felt Thornton was not ready for major ice time as a rookie. Thornton played in 81 games the following season and scored 16 times, but the next season saw "Jumbo Joe" score 23 times and total 60 points in 81 games as he started to prove why he was drafted first overall.

By the 2002–03 campaign, Thornton had become a 101-point player (36 goals and 65 assists that year, good for third place in the scoring race), and he was also named to the NHL's second all-star team. In the season before the lockout, Thornton's point total dropped to 73. The Bruins simply wanted more out of their star. When played resumed in 2005–06, Thornton was still producing at a better-than-a-point-a-game pace (33 points in 23 games), but Boston management was still not happy with his overall performance. Thinking that their so-called best player was overpaid and underachieving (especially in the playoffs, where Thornton only had 18 points in 35 games), the Bruins hierarchy believed they could improve the club with a deal after they got off to a slow start in '05–'06. The San Jose Sharks swooped in and sent three players to the Bruins (Brad Stuart, Marco Sturm, and Wayne Primeau) for Thornton and have never regretted the move. The deal was completed on November 30, 2005, under Bruins general manager Mike O'Connell. Not surprisingly, O'Connell is now in the scouting department for another team!

It was now up to Thornton to show what he could do for the Sharks and to prove to the Bruins that they had, indeed, made a big mistake. In his first game with his new team, Thornton had two assists (both on goals scored by Jonathan Cheechoo) in a 5-0 victory over the Buffalo Sabres. The win snapped San Jose's 10-game losing streak and set the team off in a new direction. "I'm a San Jose Shark now. I felt completely comfortable out there, and this feels really good," Thornton said after the game. San Jose was in Toronto the next night and came from behind to beat the Leafs 5-4. Thornton recorded two more assists. Playing so close to his hometown of London had Thornton a little nervous prior to the game, but he soon recovered. "We had a slow start (down 3-0 at one point) in the first but the boys played great in the second and third. It's another good two points for us." San Jose teammate Alyn McCauley added "With Joe, maybe there is a lot more confidence that we're going to get more than two goals. I think it took the trade to wake guys up."

If anyone was awoken by the deal, it had to be Thornton himself. He went on a season-long tear with the Sharks, who made the playoffs after a 9-12-4 start. Thornton was so good (92 points in 58 games) that he was in position to win the NHL's scoring race as the Sharks got ready to play their last three games of the regular season. Although he was tied for the points lead with New York Rangers superstar Jaromir Jagr (both had 122 points), Jagr was in a better position since he had 54 goals already and would take the Art Ross Trophy on the basis of more goals scored if they stayed tied in points. However, on April 13, Thornton pulled into a tie with

Jagr when he notched three assists in a 5-3 win over Vancouver.

The next Sharks game was against Anaheim on April 15, 2006. And Thornton was at his very best with one goal (his 29th of the season) and two assists to give him a three-point lead. His goal came after just 21 seconds of play, and his two helpers once again came on goals by Cheechoo (who would finish with a league-high 56 goals thanks mostly to the set-ups provided by Thornton). This was the 44th Sharks win of the year, and while there was still one game to play, the San Jose club had come from last place in their division before the trade was made to earning a playoff spot.

Thornton did not record a point in the last game of the year, but neither did Jagr, giving the Sharks center his first Art Ross Trophy with a total of 125 points. Not bad for a player the Boston Bruins had decided to trade away only months earlier!

Joe Thornton's great performance in 2005–06 was also recognized with the Hart Trophy, given to the most valuable player in the NHL.

LORNE "GUMP" WORSLEY
BORN: MONTREAL, QUEBEC
NHL SEASONS: 1952–53 TO 1973–74
DEFINING MOMENT: 1968 PLAYOFFS

Lorne "Gump" Worsley was pretty miserable when he was with the New York Rangers. He started out with the Blueshirts in 1952–53 and in 50 appearances, he won only 13 games while losing 28. He was named rookie of the year for his performance, but it is more likely that the writers who voted were sympathetic about him playing behind a bad team.

The Ranger teams of the 1950s had good offensive talent (players like Andy Bathgate, Dean Prentice, Larry Popein, Andy Hebenton, and Dave Creighton provided goal scoring), but were severely lacking a direct defensive game. Worsley rarely had a winning season as a Ranger and at one point was replaced by minor league goalie Johnny Bower. Worsley rarely got along with his coach (his battles with New York coach Phil Watson are the stuff of legend) and his attitude toward his team was somewhat lacking. "Don't mention back checking in here. It's a dirty word," Worsley would lament about his squad. Another time, he was asked which team gave him the most trouble. His quick witted reply was, "The Rangers!"

Even though he was on a losing team (only four trips to the playoffs and no series wins) for most of his time in New York, Worsley was regularly one of the best Ranger players year after year. However, when the 1962–63 season came to an end, the Montreal Canadiens were interested in trading away award-winning, all-star goaltender Jacques Plante. The Rangers wanted to add the six-time Stanley Cup–winning netminder and made a large deal with the Habs which saw Worsley head back to play in his hometown alongside stars like Jean Beliveau, Bernie Geoffrion, and Henri Richard. The portly netminder was less than thrilled to find out about the seven-player deal over the radio; nevertheless, he was happy to get out of New York and get a fresh start. However, Worsley got off to a bad start in 1963–64 and Montreal replaced him with Charlie Hodge. It was back to the minor leagues for Worsley, and it looked like his NHL career might be over.

However, Worsley returned to the Canadiens in the 1964–65 season and was in net the night Montreal reclaimed the Stanley

Cup in May 1965 with a 4-0 win over Chicago in the seventh game of the finals. The rejuvenated Worsley (who posted a 29-14-6 in the 1965–66 regular season) was also in net when Montreal took the Cup again in 1966.

The 1967–68 season was the first season of the great expansion and more teams were now using two goalies on a fairly regular basis. Worsley split netminding duties with Rogie Vachon, who had established himself the previous year. Worsley played in 40 games in the '67–'68 campaign, posting an impressive 19-9-8 record. His goals-against average was a spectacular 1.98 and he registered a career-best six shutouts, earning himself a place on the NHL's first all-star team. He and Vachon also shared the Vezina Trophy, capping a truly great year for a goalie many thought was over the hill at the age 38!

Worsley saved his best for the '68 playoffs when he appeared in 12 games and won 11 times. He did not lose a single contest. The Habs ripped past Boston (in four games) and Chicago (in five games) before meeting the first-year St. Louis Blues for the Stanley Cup. Montreal won the first game 3-2 and then took the second 1-0 on May 7, 1968, on the strength of a Serge Savard goal and the net-minding of Worsley. Montreal got into penalty trouble in the third, but Worsley made all the saves necessary to preserve the one-goal lead. His best save came against Dickie Moore of the Blues. Still displaying brilliant agility, he worked on his knees to block the drive. He made 19 saves in total, warning his teammates after the game: "Anybody who thinks we're going to skate away and hide on them is nuts. They (the Blues) don't give you enough free ice to get into high gear."

Montreal won the next game 4-3 with a chance to wrap up the title on home ice. It was the night of May 11. Trailing 2-1 going into the third, Montreal rallied and scored twice to win the game 3-2. It was Worsley's third Stanley Cup win and he had been in net all three nights when the Canadiens hoisted the silver trophy.

Before the final game, Worsley implored his team to win it for him because he did not want to play the fifth game of the series which would have been held on May 14, his 39th birthday! "I don't want to spend my birthday in St. Louis," he said to his teammates prior to the fourth game. Worsley made 19 saves in the last game, and while he gave up a pair in the second period, he did not let the Blues score in the second half of the contest.

Later on, Worsley would reflect on his career in Montreal. "I was now playing on a great team. The Canadiens were more conscious of what it means to win. To them, winning was the only thing. And they gave me great protection. I had fewer shots to handle than in my days with the Rangers." Worsley would never have accomplished so much in his career if the Montreal Canadiens had not made a deal for him back in the summer of 1963.

Gump Worsley was elected to the Hall of Fame in 1980.

JASON ARNOTT
BORN: COLLINGWOOD, ONTARIO
NHL SEASONS: 1993–94 TO PRESENT
DEFINING MOMENT: JUNE 10, 2000

When the Edmonton Oilers first joined the NHL, their drafting record was the envy of the league. They were allowed to hold on to Wayne Gretzky from his days in the World Hockey Association, and they were also able to add Kevin Lowe, Grant Fuhr, Paul Coffey, Jari Kurri, Mark Messier, and Glenn Anderson through the NHL Entry Draft. The team would win a total of five Stanley Cups in the process.

But the great drafting record soon turned abysmal with first-round flops between 1982 and 1992 (with the one exception of Jeff Beukeboom in 1983) becoming the norm in Edmonton. The pattern would change in 1993 when they selected a big (6'5", 220-pound), rangy center from Wasaga Beach, Ontario, named Jason Arnott.

Arnott had enjoyed a great season in Oshawa, where he had played for the Generals of the OHL, scoring 41 goals and 98 points in 56 games. He made the Oilers as a 19-year-old rookie and showed he belonged with the big club by potting 33 goals and notching 68 points as a rookie. He also showed a strong, feisty side with 104 minutes in penalties. The future looked bright for Arnott and it seemed as though the Oilers had found a new team leader.

Arnott performed well over the next two seasons, but it was clear he was still a young man who had some growing up to do. His production did not get better; in fact, his numbers started to slide (although he managed a 28-goal season in 1995–96). As a result, his popularity among Oiler fans started to wane just as quickly as it had started. Personal off-ice issues only made things worse for Arnott and soon, he was being booed by his own fans. By the time the 1997–98 season began, the hard-shooting pivot was facing the wrath of Edmonton fans on a regular basis. Edmonton coach Ron Low said, "I think it's really tough on a guy to start every shift you play getting booed before you get a chance to do anything." In early January 1998, Arnott met with Oilers general manager Glen Sather, and asked to be traded so he might get a fresh start. "It was time for both sides to move on," Arnott said after he was sent to the New Jersey Devils. "I think it's best for both teams and I'm excited to go to New Jersey. It was hard playing in a building where the people are booing but they're entitled to do that. It was a tough atmosphere to play in."

If Arnott was hoping for a strong finish in the '97–'98 season, it did not happen. He racked up just 15 points in 33 games for New Jersey, but he rebounded to score 27 goals in his first full year with the Devils. He hit the back of the net 22 times in the 1999–2000 campaign, but saved his best for the playoffs when he had 20 points in 23 post-season games. New Jersey made it all the way to the finals, beating out Florida, Toronto, and Philadelphia in the first three rounds of the playoffs. The Devils were down three games to one against the Flyers, but came back to take the series in seven games. Their next challenge was to play defending champions Dallas Stars for the Stanley Cup.

The final series was close all the way, but the Devils managed to get a 3-2 lead going into the sixth game in Dallas. It was June 10, 2000. The Devils opened the scoring in the second period on a goal by Scott Niedermayer, but the Stars tied it up shortly afterward. There was no scoring in the third period and the game went into overtime with the Cup on the line. In the first overtime period, Arnott took a foolish cross-checking penalty (a type of infraction he was prone to making, especially early in his career), but his teammates bailed him out with a strong penalty-killing effort as he watched anxiously from the box. Arnott vowed that he would do something special to thank his teammates.

As the tension increased in the second overtime period, the Devils center suddenly saw an opportunity when teammate Patrik Elias picked up the puck in the corner of the Stars end. Arnott moved smartly toward the net and quickly shot Elias's pass over goalie Ed Belfour into the Dallas net for the Stanley Cup–winning goal! "It was tough. I didn't want to be the guy to lose this for us. The guys did a great job killing the penalty, I felt I had to go out and do something after that," Arnott said after the game (a contest that saw him play 25:43, take four shots, and make four hits while winning 14 of 18 face-offs). It was the fourteenth time in league history that the Stanley Cup had been won with an overtime goal.

Arnott got the opportunity to be a hero when he decided to take a chance and ask for a trade. It could not have worked out any better for Arnott, who had a championship by the time he was just 25 years of age. Over the summer of 2000, he took the Cup back home and partied on the waters of Wasaga Beach.

Jason Arnott went on to play for the Dallas Stars and Nashville Predators (where he was named team captain) before returning to the Devils for the 2010–11 season.

TONY ESPOSITO
BORN: SAULT STE. MARIE, ONTARIO
NHL SEASONS: 1968–69 TO 1983–84
DEFINING MOMENT: 1969–70 SEASON

Goaltender Tony Esposito never really wanted to be a member of the Montreal Canadiens. After attending Michigan Tech for three years, the 23-year-old Esposito felt he should have been a free agent (he was never drafted by an NHL team) with the ability to sign with any club who might want his netminding services. However, the Canadiens had been scouting him while he was in college and put his name on their negotiation list. The young netminder found Montreal general manger Sam Pollock very difficult to deal with in contract talks, but he finally signed with the team at the end of training camp before the start of the 1967–68 season.

Esposito knew he needed professional experience, and he spent most of the '67–'68 campaign in the minors, playing 63 games for the Vancouver Canucks of the Western Hockey League. There he posted 25 wins.

The next season was split between the Houston Apollos (recording 10 wins in 19 appearances in the Central Hockey League) and the Canadiens (going 5-4-4 with the big-league team), but there were simply too many quality goalies in the Montreal system. Rogie Vachon and Gump Worsley were Stanley Cup and Vezina Trophy winners, while Phil Myre showed promise in the minors. Montreal also had the rights to a goalie named Ken Dryden who was developing his craft in U.S. college hockey. Although Esposito had performed reasonably well in Montreal during the '68–'69 campaign (including two shutouts), neither Pollock nor coach Claude Ruel were especially enthralled with his performance. "My troubles in Montreal were mainly with Sam Pollock," Esposito recounted later. "Sam is a good hockey man—one of the best in the business. He's talented and knows how to recognize talent. He didn't recognize me though and that's how I wound up with the Chicago Blackhawks."

Pollock was going to leave Esposito unprotected for the 1969 intra-league draft which was held every year in June. Minnesota held the first pick, but Pollock convinced the North Stars to take a pass on Esposito to complete an earlier deal that had seen Montreal trade Danny O'Shea to Minnesota. Pollock's maneuvering (he was very good at getting others to give him "favors" in exchange for little) left the 5'11", 185-pound Esposito for Chicago, who had the next pick. The Blackhawks had missed the playoffs in '67–'68, finishing in last place in the East Division, and were looking to add new players. In addition to Esposito, Gerry Pinder, Paul Shmyr, Terry Caffery, Jim Wiste, Keith Magnuson, and Cliff Koroll all made their debuts with Chicago in '69–'70. The Blackhawks also knew Denis DeJordy was not a top goaltender and were anxious to give "Tony O" a chance to be a number-one netminder. Esposito got off to a rocky start but felt much better when he beat the Canadiens with a 5-0 shutout (his first of the year) right in the Forum. "We had snapped the Canadiens home-unbeaten streak (24 consecutive games) and handed them their first defeat of the season," Esposito recalled about the first of many special moments in the '69-'70 season. "And after seven games, we finally had our first victory. (Chicago coach) Billy Reay complimented me on the shutout and said, 'Tony, I think we're ready to roll now.'" It had to be an extra sweet victory for Esposito, who had beaten Pollock's team right in his own building.

As the season moved along, Esposito piled up the shutouts and eventually tied the modern-day mark held by Harry Lumley with 13. On March 27, 1970, the Blackhawks travelled to Detroit for a contest against the Red Wings. Chicago's Pit Martin scored the only goal of the game in the third period, with Esposito turning back 35 shots to set a new record with his 14th shutout of the year. A save on Detroit's Frank Mahovlich was especially great as Tony dove across his crease to rob the Red Wings star of a sure goal. "Frank hesitated for just a split second," Esposito said later. "I scrambled back and when he fired I slid my leg across the goalmouth. The puck hit me on the inside of my left knee as I turned my leg sideways and bounced out." Just a few day later, Esposito shut out the Maple Leafs 4-0 for his 15th of the season—a record that has yet to be tied or surpassed.

The best night of the year for Esposito occurred in the very last game when he held the Canadiens to just two goals in a 10-2 Chicago win over his old team. The win, the 38th of the year for Esposito, secured first place for Chicago and eliminated the defending champions from post-season. Even Claude Ruel had kind words for the Blackhawks netminder. "Tony beat us. He is really something. He flops all over the ice but he always stops the puck," he said.

Esposito had not only shown he was a quality NHL goalie (he won the Vezina Trophy and made the first all-star team for his '60–'70 performance), he had also proven that moving to a new team can give players the chance they need to succeed at the highest levels.

Tony Esposito recorded 82 career shutouts (including playoffs) and was elected to the Hall of Fame in 1988.

EDDIE GIACOMIN
BORN: SUDBURY, ONTARIO
NHL SEASONS: 1965–66 TO 1977–78
DEFINING MOMENTS: OCTOBER 23, 1966 & MAY 4, 1972

Most deals involving minor-league players are usually overlooked, and for good reason—they rarely amount to anything significant. There are, however, exceptions to the rule. Consider the New York Rangers who had just enough patience to see the acquisition of goalie Eddie Giacomin turn into one of the greatest steals of all-time!

When Giacomin was 15 years old, he was invited to a Detroit Red Wings tryout camp. He had played in net for local teams around Sudbury, and since Detroit had the rights to players in the area, it meant he had to travel to Michigan to attend the camp in the fall of 1954. It was there that he met Detroit legends like Terry Sawchuk and Gordie Howe. But it didn't work out and one of the

Red Wing officials told young Eddie to go home and forget about playing in net.

Eddie returned to Sudbury and went to school while working as a mechanic's assistant in a plant. His father urged him to forget about hockey, but the youthful netminder would not give up the dream just yet. He was asked to try out for the Detroit-sponsored junior team in Hamilton, but just like before, he was told to go home and forget about being a goalie. The words stung as he watched other goalies who would never make the NHL propel ahead of him.

Dejected and unhappy, Giacomin nearly gave it all up, but a phone call changed everything. It seemed the team from Washington of the Eastern Hockey League needed a goaltender during the 1958–59 season. They called Giacomin's brother, Rolle, who was also a goalie, to come down and help out for a while. Rolle could not leave his job, but insisted that Eddie take the assignment. The scared and frightened 19-year-old reluctantly agreed and won all four games he started for the team. He was also noticed by some American Hockey League scouts and eventually offered a tryout with the Providence Reds of the AHL for the next year. Incredibly, Giacomin nearly did not make it to the tryout because of severe burns (first degree to his left leg, hip, buttocks, and second degree burns to his right ankle) suffered in a home fire during the off-season. After a stay in hospital, he was finally able to go to Providence—beginning a climb that would take him to heights he never would have imagined. The Reds did not have an immediate spot available for Giacomin and sent him to the New York Rovers of the EHL. He played in 51 games for the Rovers in 1959–60 and gave up a significant number of goals, but he was improving and happy to be finally getting a chance to play pro hockey.

Giacomin split the 1960–61 campaign between the Reds and the Rovers (posting a combined 19-34 record), and Providence management thought they had a good young netminder on their hands. He became a regular member of the Reds the next year with a winning record of 20-19-1. Giacomin stayed in Providence for the next three full seasons (that included a 30-win campaign in 1963–64), but then the New York Rangers, Detroit Red Wings, and Toronto Maple Leafs began to show interest. The Rangers were keenest because New York general manager Emile Francis thought he had uncovered a gem. During the Sixties, NHL teams could make trades with AHL teams, so the Rangers sent four players to the Reds to put the Giacomin, then 26, on Broadway. "It always takes a goalkeeper longer to develop than it does a forward or a defenseman," said Francis. "We've taken a big step in the right direction toward improving the Rangers and making the club a playoff contender by getting Eddie Giacomin."

However, it did not go well for Giacomin early on in New York. He played in 35 games in 1965–66 and won just eight times. He was sent back to the AHL for seven games, but Francis was a stronger believer in Giacomin's abilities. The Rangers were not a very good team, and Giacomin wanted to live up to the four-player deal that got him into the NHL. Fortunately, things got better starting with the 1966–67 season. On October 23, 1966, the Rangers geared up for their first home game of the season against the Leafs. The teams were scoreless going into the third period, thanks largely to Giacomin's 16-save effort in the second period. New York finally scored at the 7:15 mark of the third and Giacomin stopped the Leafs the rest of the way, turning back 29 shots in total to earn a sparkling 1-0 shutout.

It was a sweet victory for Giacomin, who remembered Toronto coach and general manager Punch Imlach saying he would never become an NHL goalie. "Anytime I play Punch Imlach's team, I try that much harder," Giacomin said while he held a souvenir puck of his shutout. "Anytime it's against him, I want to win that much more. Anytime I can beat his team, I get much more satisfaction." Giacomin would shut the Leafs out three times in '66–'67, forcing

Imlach to admit that the Ranger netminder was a much improved player. In 68 games played, Giacomin posted a neat 30-27-11 record to go with a league-leading nine shutouts. He was also named to the NHL's first all-star team.

Over a number of seasons with New York, Giacomin won an amazing 30 or more games five times and never posted a losing record during the regular season until his final year as a Ranger (1975–76). He was a league all-star five times and won the Vezina Trophy during the 1970–71 season.

The Rangers were always in contention but could never get beyond the first two rounds of the playoffs until the 1972 post-season when they got past Montreal and Chicago to face Boston in the finals. However, New York fell behind Boston 2-0 in games and returned home for the third contest on May 4, 1972. New York came out firing, scoring the first three goals of the game to defeat the Bruins 5-2 and get back into the series. Ranger captain Vic Hadfield paid a high compliment to Giacomin after the game. "Ed Giacomin gave us tremendous goalkeeping when we needed it. He robbed them a few times when they had their power play out there." It was Giacomin's only win in the finals as the Bruins won the Stanley Cup in six games.

Giacomin never returned to the finals and the Rangers lost his rights (and upset many of their fans) when the Red Wings picked up the very popular goaltender on waivers early in the '75-'76 season. He finished his career with 289 wins and 54 shutouts in 609 appearances, proving that the Rangers had made a great trade to acquire his rights in May 1965.

Eddie Giacomin was elected to the Hall of Fame in 1987.

REGGIE LEACH

BORN: RIVERTON, MANITOBA

NHL SEASONS: 1970–71 TO 1982–83

DEFINING MOMENT: MAY 6, 1976

Reggie Leach got used to being traded away very early in life. Before he was even born, his father decided to go to work in the mines, leaving behind any thoughts of nurturing a family. His mother decided she would have a better life if she left her son with his father's grandparents and moved to Edmonton.

Leach was part of a family that already had 12 other children. It was a life that featured little discipline—especially when it came to alcohol. There was little by way of money, although his grandmother did take work when she could find it. But there was nothing left over for hockey skates, so Reggie learned to borrow and make the most of whatever he could find. The inventive youngster also took the time to create an ice rink (hauling buckets of water in the process); it was there that Leach found some refuge—and honed his hockey skills.

He was very good at skating and shooting the puck—and he was not the most interested student at school. At a certain point, he was spotted by scouts when he played locally and was invited to play for the Flin Flon, Manitoba junior team known as the Bombers (MJHL). In 1966–67, he scored 67 goals in just 45 games. He was only 16 years old. It was while with the Bombers that Leach struck up a friendship with Bobby Clarke (a junior teammate for three seasons) who was soon to be a major force in the NHL with Philadelphia. Leach then played for the Bombers in the major junior league (WCJHL) and potted 188 goals in just 138 games. Leach had become a legitimate major league prospect.

The Boston Bruins held the third selection of the 1970 NHL draft and chose Leach with the pick. He spent the 1970–71 season playing in the minors (24 goals in 41 games in Oklahoma City) but was traded away to the California Seals in a 1972 deal. Leach scored over 20 goals twice for the Seals, but they were a terrible hockey team for the most part, and Leach begged to be rescued. Clarke was now captain of the Flyers and strongly suggested to Philadelphia management that they try to acquire the hard-shooting, 6', 180-pound right winger. The Flyers listened to Clarke and sent two players and a number-one draft choice to California to complete the deal. Leach would thrive once he reunited with Clarke. He scored 45 times in 1974–75 and totaled 78 points in 80 games. He added eight more goals in the post-season as the Flyers won their second consecutive Stanley Cup. But Leach was even better the next year.

The 1975–76 campaign saw Leach score an unheard-of 61 times (by way of comparison, Montreal superstar Guy Lafleur scored 60 in his best year) to lead the entire NHL. He was even hotter in the playoffs, scoring 19 times and helping the Flyers get to the Stanley Cup finals for the third straight season.

His best game of the post-season came on the night of May 6, 1976, when he tied an NHL playoff record with five goals in one contest. This great performance came on home ice as the Flyers were ready to eliminate Leach's former team, the Boston Bruins, in the semi-finals. The Flyers had dropped the first game of the series but had taken the next three when they returned to Philadelphia for the fifth game.

Leach opened the scoring at 5:45 of the first period after he beat Bruins defenseman Brad Park to a loose puck and put a shot into the Bruins net. That goal gave Leach a marker in nine consecutive playoff games. The Bruins tied in the second period but

Leach made it 2-1 when he took a pass from Clarke and drilled a 15-foot shot past Boston goalie Gilles Gilbert. His third goal came on a backhand drive with a Boston defender draped all over him. His next goal came off a drop pass from Clarke, giving the Flyers a 4-1 lead going into the third. Boston narrowed the gap to 4-2 on a goal by Don Marcotte, but Leach got that one back with his fifth of the night (on only seven shots). The Flyers would add one more to make the final 6-2.

"It was one of those nights that I caught the corner every time," a modest Leach said after the game. "I felt sharp and hot. It was the biggest thrill of my life. Five goals in the playoffs, that's like the Rocket," Leach continued as he compared his performance to that of Maurice Richard, the first man to score five times in one playoff game. Leach also added that he did not consider himself a super-star despite all his goal-scoring feats. "I just do my job," he said.

Leach would score four times in the finals against Montreal, but the Flyers were wiped out by the mighty Habs, a team that featured Hall of Fame forwards such as Guy Lafleur, Steve Shutt, and Jacques Lemaire. The Conn Smythe Trophy, however, went to Leach—in one of the very few times the coveted award went to a player on a losing team. He also played for Team Canada during the first Canada Cup Tournament later that year.

Leach struggled with his discipline off ice, but still managed to score 32, 24, and 34 goals over the next three seasons. In 1979–80, while playing under new Flyers coach Pat Quinn, he scored 50 times to help the team make it back to the finals (before losing to the New York Islanders). After two more good years (totaling 60 goals) in Philadelphia, Leach—known as "the Rifle"—finished his career with one last year in Detroit. He sought help with his drinking addiction and developed a lawn service business after his playing days were over.

"I was one of the best at getting into scoring position and I knew I could score from anywhere," Leach reflected on his career.

"I worked hard on my shot. I would take 200 after practice. Sometimes I could hit the crossbar ten times in a row from 30 feet out. I averaged 32 goals and I don't think that's bad. I accomplished everything I wanted in the NHL."

Reggie Leach overcame great adversity in his life with a memorable NHL career sparked by a great trade to a great team.

Reggie Leach scored 381 goals in 934 career games and made the NHL's second all-star team in 1975–76.

RAY BOURQUE
BORN: MONTREAL, QUEBEC
NHL SEASONS: 1979–80 TO 2000–01
DEFINING MOMENT: 2001 STANLEY CUP FINALS

The city of Boston has been very fortunate to have had some of the greatest players in professional sports play. Many have thrived and won championships in Beantown, like Bill Russell, John Havlicek, Larry Bird, Manny Ramirez, Tom Brady, and the greatest of them all, Bobby Orr. Others have provided great service but never tasted ultimate victory (like Carl Yazstremski, Steve Grogan, and Cam Neely). After 21 seasons as a Boston Bruin, it appeared defenseman Ray Bourque was going to end up in the latter group of outstanding Boston athletes.

Bourque was very reluctant to leave the city that had become his home since he was drafted eighth overall back in 1979. During his time in Boston, he won the Calder Trophy (best rookie), played in 18 all-star games, took home the Norris Trophy (best defenseman) five times, and scored 395 goals to go along with 1,111 assists in 1,518 games as a Bruin. He also appeared in the Stanley Cup finals on two occasions (1988 and 1991), but the Bruins lost each time. He was easily the second most popular Bruin of all-time next to Bobby Orr. However, Boston struggled mightily in the 1999–2000 season, and the 39-year-old Bourque finally decided it was time for a change and for another shot at the Stanley Cup.

On March 6, 2000, the Bruins sent Bourque and winger Dave Andreychuk to the Colorado Avalanche in exchange for three players and a first-round draft choice. "We limited ourselves to teams where Raymond Bourque would have a chance to win the Stanley Cup," Boston general manager Harry Sinden said about the deal he made. "It may not be his (Bourque's) first choice. It may be. I'm not sure." It was speculated over a period of time that Bourque was not at all interested in leaving Boston and if he was, it was said that Philadelphia was his preferred destination. "I worried about this but finally agreed to it," Bourque said. "Everything came apart this year in Boston. I'm very satisfied here. The Bruins have treated me well. This is my home. But I would like a shot at a ring so I finally agreed." It could not have been an easy decision, but Bourque was comfortable that he had made the right choice.

Bourque posted 14 points in 14 games to close out the '99–'00 season, but the playoffs did not go as planned for the Avalanche. They did knock off the Phoenix Coyotes and the Detroit Red Wings in the first two rounds, but the Dallas Stars eked out a Game 7 win to keep Bourque from the Stanley Cup. It was a tremendous disappointment, but Bourque decided to give it one more season. Colorado won 52 games the next season and recorded 118 points, with Bourque chipping in with 7 goals and 59 points in 80 games. But the regular campaign was not as important as the playoffs, and everyone knew this was Bourque's last chance to get his name on the big silver trophy.

Colorado swept aside the Vancouver Canucks in the first round (in four straight games) before subduing the Los Angeles Kings in seven games. The third round proved to be no contest as they easily beat St. Louis in five, setting up a final-round meeting with defending champions New Jersey Devils. Colorado won the first game 5-0 on home ice but lost the next 2-1 as the Devils evened the series. The third game was set for New Jersey on the night of May 31, 2001. The Avalanche won the game 3-1, and it was Bourque's power-play goal that provided the winning margin for his team and gave them back the series lead. "I know we are two games away but we've taken one step closer," Bourque said. "We'll have to work like we did tonight to give ourselves a chance. It was probably the biggest goal I have ever scored. " Bourque's goal came from about 40 feet out as the defenseman blasted a shot just under the crossbar, even though Devils goalie Martin Brodeur had a clear view of the drive. In addition to his goal, Bourque blocked three shots and played 26:23 of the contest.

The Devils, however, won the next two games to take a 3-2 series lead. The sixth game was set for New Jersey but the Avalanche did not panic and came back with a shocking 4-0 victory to even the series. Bourque had rallied his team with a speech which his teammates took to heart. The Devils stood no chance in the seventh game played back in Colorado. They scored the first three goals and only gave back one for a 3-1 win. A Stanley Cup for Bourque was finally a reality.

It seemed everyone in the hockey world (outside of the Devils, of course) was hoping to see Bourque lift the Cup and, with tears in his eyes most of the contest, the superb defender did not disappoint, playing over 29 minutes of the last game. Colorado captain Joe Sakic took the Cup first as is the tradition but gave it to Bourque next as a sign of respect for the longtime veteran. Raising the Cup above his head, Bourque smiled and cried at the same time. Colorado goaltender Patrick Roy pointed out, "A name was missing from that thing (the Stanley Cup). And today it is back to normal. It was so special seeing Ray raise that Cup, seeing his eyes, seeing how excited he was." Bourque also received a congratulatory phone call from Canadian Prime Minister Jean Chretien, to which he simply replied *"Oui, Monsieur Chretien."*

Bourque shared in all the love shown to him and wisely retired, deciding not to return for another season after ending on such a high note. Of course, it might not have happened if he had not said yes to a trade that will go down as having one of the best endings in NHL history.

Ray Bourque played in 1,612 NHL games, recording 1,579 points (410G, 1,169A). He was elected to the Hall of Fame in 2004.

BIBLIOGRAPHY AND SOURCES

BOOKS

Batten, Jack. *Hockey Dynasty*. Toronto: Pagurian Press, 1969.

———. *The Leafs in Autumn: Meeting the Maple Leaf Heroes of the Forties*. Toronto: MacMillan of Canada, 1975.

Baun, Bob. *Lowering the Boom: The Bobby Baun Story*. Toronto: Stoddart Publishing, 2000.

Bower, Johnny and Bob Duff. *The China Wall: The Timeless Legend of Johnny Bower*. Toronto: Fenn Publishing, 2008.

Brodeur, Martin and Damien Cox. *Brodeur: Beyond the Crease*. Mississauga: Wiley and Sons, 2006.

Bucyk, Johnny and Russ Conway. *Hockey in My Blood*. Toronto: McGraw-Hill Ryerson, 1972.

Carpiniello, Rick. Messier: Steel On Ice. Toronto: Stoddart Publishing, 1999.

Carrier, Roch. *Our Life with the Rocket: The Maurice Richard Story*. Toronto: Penguin Canada, 2001.

Chadwick, Bill and Hal Bock. *The Big Whistle*. New York: Hawthorn Books, 1974.

Cohen, Russ, John Halligan and Adam Raider. *100 Ranger Greats: Superstars, Unsung Heroes and Colorful Characters.* Mississauga: Wiley and Sons, 2009.

Cohen, Tom. *Daredevil Goalie: The Roger Crozier Story.* Toronto: Nelson and Sons, 1967.

Cox, Damien and Gare Joyce. *The Ovechkin Project*: A Behind-the-Scenes Look at Hockey's Most Dangerous Player. Mississauga: Wiley and Sons, 2010.

Delano, Hugh. *Eddie: A Goalie's Story.* New York: Atheneum Books, 1976.

Dionne, Marcel and Ted Mahovlich. *Triple Crown: The Marcel Dionne Story.* Toronto: HarperCollins, 2004.

Dryden, Murray and Jim Hunt. *Playing the Shots at Both Ends: The story of Ken and Dave Dryden.* Toronto: McGraw-Hill Ryerson, 1972.

Duplacey, James and Eric Zweig. *Official Guide to the Players of the Hockey Hall of Fame.* Richmond Hill: Firefly Books, 2010.

Esposito, Phil and Peter Golenbock. *Thunder and Lightning: A No-B.S. Hockey Memoir.* Toronto: McClelland and Stewart, 2003.

Esposito, Tony, Phil Esposito and Tim Moriarty. *The Brothers Esposito.* New York: Hawthorn Books, 1971.

Fischler, Stan. *Bobby Orr and the Big, Bad Bruins.* New York: Dodd, Mead and Company, 1969.

———. *Heroes of Pro Hockey*. New York: Random House, 1971.

———. *Hockey Stars of 1970*. New York: Pyramid Books, 1969.

———. *Stan Mikita*. Chicago: Cowles Book Company, 1969.

Fitkin, Ed. *Come On Teeder!: The Story of Ted Kennedy*. Toronto: Baxter Publishing Company, 1950.

Gadsby, Bill and Allen Kevin. *The Grateful Gadsby*. Wayne, Michigan: Immortal Investments Publishing, 2003.

Geoffrion, Bernie and Fischler, Stan. *Boom-Boom: The Life and Times of Bernard Geoffrion*. Toronto: McGraw-Hill Ryerson, 1997.

Germain, Georges-Herbert. *Overtime: The Legend of Guy Lafleur*. Toronto: Penguin Books, 1991.

Gilbert, Rod. *GOAL! My Life on Ice*. New York: Hawthorn Books, 1968.

Greenberg, Jay. *Full Spectrum: The Complete History of the Philadelphia Flyers Hockey Club*. Chicago: Triumph Books, 1996.

Green, Ted and Al Hirshberg. *High Stick. New York:* Dodd, Mead and Company, 1971.

Harris, Cecil. *Breaking the Ice: The Black Experience in Professional Hockey*. Toronto: Insomniac Press, 2003.

Henderson, Paul and Mike Leonetti. *Shooting for Glory: The Paul Henderson Story*. Toronto: Stoddart Publishing, 1992.

Hewitt, Foster. *Hockey Night in Canada: The Story of the Toronto Maple Leafs*. Toronto: Ryerson Press, 1962.

Hiam, Michael. *Eddie Shore and that Old Time Hockey*. Toronto: McClelland and Stewart, 2010.

Hodge, Charlie. *Golly Gee, It's Me: The Howie Meeker Story*. Toron to: Stoddart Publishing, 1996.

Howe, Gordie. *My Hockey Memories*. Toronto: Firefly Books, 1999.

Hull, Bobby. *Hockey is My Game*. Toronto: Longmans, 1966.

Hunter, Douglas. *Yzerman: The Making of a Champion*. Toronto: Doubleday Canada, 2004.

Hunt, Jim. *Bobby Hull*. Toronto: Ryerson Press, 1966.

——. *The Men in the Nets*. Toronto: Ryerson Press, 1967.

Irvin, Dick. *The Habs: An Oral History of the Montreal Canadiens, 1940 to 1980*. Toronto: McClelland and Stewart, 1991.

——. *In the Crease*. Toronto: McClelland and Stewart, 1995.

LaFontaine, Pat. *Companions in Courage*. New York: Warner Books, 2001.

Larionov, Igor and Jim Taylor. *Larionov*. Winnipeg: Codner Books, 1990.

Leonetti, Mike. *Canadiens Legends: Montreal's Hockey Heroes*. Vancouver: Raincoast Books, 2005.

———. *Hockey Greats*. Toronto: Scholastic Books, 2010.

———. *Hockey Now!* (4th, 5th and 6th editions). Richmond Hill: Firefly Books, 2010.

Leonetti, Mike and John Iaboni. *Maple Leafs Top 100: Toronto's Greatest Players of All Time*. Vancouver: Raincoast Books, 2007.

Libby, Bill. *Great Stanley Cup Playoffs*. New York: Random House, 1972.

———. *Rookie Goalie: Gerry Desjardins*. New York: Julian Messner Books, 1970.

Lindros, Eric and Randy Starkman. *Fire On Ice*. Toronto: Harper Collins, 1992.

Lowe, Kevin and Stan Fischler. *Champions.* Toronto: Prentice-Hall, 1988.

MacPeek, Walt. *Hot Shots of Pro Hockey*. New York: Random House, 1975.

MacSkimming, Roy. *Gordie: A Hockey Legend*. Vancouver: Greystone Books, 1994.

Maher, Peter and John Iaboni. *The Eternal Flames*. Toronto: Mc Clelland and Stewart, 1989.

Malcolm, Andrew H. *Fury: Inside the Life of Theoren Fleury.* Toronto: McClelland and Stewart, 1997.

McDonald, Lanny and Steve Simmons. *Lanny.* Toronto: McGraw-Hill Ryerson, Toronto, 1987.

McDonell, Chris. *For the Love of the Game.* Richmond Hill: Firefly Books, 2007.

———. *The Game I'll Never Forget.* Richmond Hill: Firefly Books, 2002.

Mikita, Stan. *I Play to Win.* Toronto: Longmans, 1969.

Parent, Bernie. *Bernie! Bernie! Bernie!* New Jersey: Prentice-Hall, 1975.

Potvin, Denis and Stan Fischler. *Power On Ice.* New York: Harper and Row, 1977.

Powers, John and Arthur C. Kaminsky. *One Goal: A Chronicle of the 1980 U.S. Olympic Hockey Team.* New York: Harper and Row, 1984.

Richard, Maurice and Stan Fischler. *The Flying Frenchmen.* New York: Hawthorn Books, 1971.

Roche, Bill. *The Hockey Book.* Toronto: McClelland and Stewart, 1953.

Sadowski, Rick. *Los Angeles Kings: Hockeywood.* Champaign: Sag amore Publishing, 1993.

Salming, Borje and Gerhard Karlsson. *Blood, Sweat and Hockey*. Toronto: HarperCollins, 1991.

Shea, Kevin and Paul Patskou. *Diary of a Dynasty: Toronto Maple Leafs 1957-1967*. Richmond Hill: Firefly Books, 2010.

Sittler, Darryl and Chrys Goyens. *Sittler*. Toronto: MacMillan, 1991.

Ulmer, Michael. *If the Cup Could Talk*. Chelsea: Sleeping Bear Press, 2000.

Vipond, Jim. *Gordie Howe: Number 9*. Toronto: Ryerson Press, 1968.

Worsley, Lorne and Tim Moriarty. *They Call Me Gump*. New York: Dodd, Mead and Company, 1974.

Young, Scott. *Frank Mahovlich: The Big M*. St. Paul: EMC Corporation, 1974.

GUIDES AND RECORD BOOKS

NHL Guide & Record Book (various issues)
Total Hockey (2nd edition)
Total NHL
Total Stanley Cup (Playoff Guide)

MAGAZINES

ESPN The Magazine
Hockey Digest (various issues)

Hockey Illustrated (various issues)
Hockey News, The (various issues)
Hockey Night in Toronto (various issues)
Hockey Pictorial (various issues)
Hockey Scene
Hockey World (various issues)
Inside Hockey Magazine (various issues)
Inside Sports
Sports Illustrated (various issues)

NEWSPAPERS

Globe and Mail
Kingston Whig Standard
Montreal Gazette
Toronto Star
Toronto Sun
Vancouver Province
Yukon World

RADIO

FAN590 (in Toronto)
AM640 (in Toronto)

TELEVISION

Hockey Night in Canada on CBC
That's Hockey on TSN
The NHL on TSN
Leafs TV

WEBSITES

www.boston.com
www.cbcsports.ca
www.faceoff.com
www.hhof.com
www.nhl.com
www.si.com
www.theglobeandmail.com
www.thehockeynews.com
www.wikipedia.org
www.youtube.com
www.canoe.ca/slamsports
Websites of each NHL team